THE PURSUIT
OF PERFECTION

THE PURSUIT
OF PERFECTION

A Life of Celia Franca

by CAROL BISHOP-GWYN

Cormorant Books

**Canada Council
for the Arts** **Conseil des Arts
du Canada**

 Canadian Patrimoine
Heritage canadien

The publisher gratefully acknowledges the support of the Canada Council for
the Arts and the Ontario Arts Council for its publishing program. We acknowledge the
financial support of the Government of Canada through the Canada Book Fund (CBF)
for our publishing activities, and the Government of Ontario through the
Ontario Media Development Corporation, an agency of the Ontario Ministry
of Culture, and the Ontario Book Publishing Tax Credit Program.

LIBRARY AND ARCHIVES CANADA CATALOGUING IN PUBLICATION

Bishop-Gwyn, Carol
The pursuit of perfection : a life of Celia Franca / Carol Bishop-Gwyn.

ISBN 978-1-77086-043-8

1. Franca, Celia, 1921-2007. 2. National Ballet of Canada--
History. 3. Ballet dancers--Canada--Biography. 4. Choreographers--
Canada--Biography. I. Title.

GV1785.F724B58 2011   792.8092   C2011-904036-0

Cover photograph: Celia Franca, circa 1960. Photo by Janine.
Jacket design: Angel Guerra / Archetype
Interior text design: Tannice Goddard, Soul Oasis Networking
Printer: Trigraphik LBF

Printed and bound in Canada.

FSC
C003594
This book is printed on 100% post-consumer waste recycled paper.

CORMORANT BOOKS INC.
215 SPADINA AVENUE, STUDIO 230, TORONTO, ONTARIO, CANADA M5T 2C7
www.cormorantbooks.com

To Richard
My *Danseur Noble*

Contents

Introduction

O N AND OFF STAGE, Celia Franca presented herself as exactly what she was — a ballerina, poised and unblemished. She carried herself with perfect posture; standing tall, her upper body held in a graceful *epaulement*, the better to highlight her elegant nose and her extended Nefertiti-like neck. To this she added full theatrical makeup with dark, pencilled-in eyebrows and bright red lips. Her imperious manner and clipped English accent intimidated most who met her. Her appearance and carriage and manner all sent out a clear, unmistakable message that she was someone who knew exactly what she wanted and would do just about anything to get it. And what Celia wanted at first was to be a professional *danseuse* — in fact, a classical prima ballerina. Aware that there was only so far she actually could go as a dancer, she later dreamed of forming her own ballet company that would fuse together the best technically trained dancers with the best choreography and production values to create an experience as close to perfection as possible. By circumstance, the opportunity to do this occurred in Canada. For the country, it was pure luck, and for Celia Franca, it was her destiny.

My initial introduction to Celia Franca was indirect. Like most aspiring ballet students in post–World War II Canada, I had a copy of a little book published in 1953 called *The Ballet Student's Primer: A Concentrated Guide to Beginners of All Ages*. English writer and illustrator Kay Ambrose had written the book in collaboration with her good friend, Celia Franca. Scattered through the chapters were Ambrose's line drawings of Franca in a variety of dance roles, such as in *Giselle* and *Les Sylphides*.

Realizing I would never be a ballerina, my fallback was to become enthralled with ballet and the musicals of the mid 1950s and 1960s. I have never forgotten seeing the Sadler's Wells Ballet dancers shivering on a stage built over the ice rink at Toronto's Maple Leaf Gardens. With adulthood came a shift of allegiance to modern dance, now referred to as contemporary dance. Ballet recaptured my imagination while living in Moscow in the late 1980s because the Bolshoi and Kirov (once again named the Mariinsky) were ballet meccas. Afterwards, living in London, England, the highlight of my regular visits to Covent Garden's Royal Opera House to see the Royal Ballet was the night I was standing at the bar during the interval, spying the very elderly Dame Ninette de Valois sipping on a flute of champagne just a few feet away. To give some stiffening to my dance-observing credentials, I managed along life's way to get two postgraduate degrees in dance history, one in Canada and one in England.

I met Celia Franca only a few times. I lived the next street over to her in Ottawa. Working for CBC Radio, I would pop over to her house with a tape recorder to get her reaction to events as they were unfolding in 1974 and 1975 as she lost her grip as the National Ballet of Canada's founding artistic director.

Twenty years later, in 1994, I was contacted by a publisher to assist in the completion of Franca's biography after the death of its author, Frank Rasky. He had done an immense amount of original research, including oral histories of practically all the major players in Celia Franca's life, both family and professional. For a period of time while the project was on hold, Celia and I corresponded. In one letter she complained that we all could be dead by the time the problems were ironed out. And there were problems. Rasky had completed very few chapters and, during a meeting with the new writers — including myself and the publisher — Franca made it clear that she expected to have complete control over the contents of the book. Quietly, the biography was abandoned.

While some people have suggested that Franca would not have wanted her life examined by a biographer, my guess is that this is not true. For one thing, rather than destroying her papers, she donated a vast amount of material, including some very personal and revealing items in notebooks, diaries, letters, memorabilia, and photographs, to our national repository of history, the Library and Archives Canada. For another, she had agreed to work with Frank Rasky in the early 1990s (and to take half of his publisher's advance) on her biography. Lastly, she had cooperated fully in the making of the 2006 documentary *Celia Franca: Tour de Force*.

As part of my own research, I spent weeks wearing a headset that gave me a headache by the end of every day, eavesdropping on the lengthy interviews Celia granted to Rasky. His often clumsy and downright annoying questions bemused Celia and at other times infuriated her. But the depth of Rasky's research impressed her, if it also unsettled her.

In England, Rasky had tracked down both professional colleagues, such as Dame Ninette de Valois, as well as extant family members, such as Celia's aunt Lena. Franca was particularly exasperated at Rasky's frequent references to her Jewish heritage.

In my role as interloper I was able, somewhat akin to a therapist, to discern the meanings behind both the words and the silences. Rasky, either as an interviewing technique or through disorganization, often repeated questions. Celia, taking this as a sign that he did not believe her, lashed back, "You keep checking up on me. I'm not a liar." Frequently, in that haughty voice, she would add, "Carry on, dear." During those long hours listening to Celia Franca I realized my great luck. Using some discretion, I could give readers her own words without the censorship she would have imposed on Rasky. Particularly when she lost her temper at his repetitive questions, the real Franca came through loud and clear.

As a proponent of the British "stiff upper lip" attitude, she resolutely refused to be self-reflective. She had a convenient habit of forgetting unpleasant experiences in her life and refused to discuss them, employing the dismissive "I forget." Ballet and music were the stuff of Celia's life. Outside of the dance world, she had few hobbies or interests besides her beloved cats. So it has been a struggle to discover the "inner Celia" — a psychological expression she would have detested. While she attracted a great number of people with her charismatic and dramatic personality, she had few intimate friends. She had a bad habit of dropping people if they no longer were helpful. While her rehearsal pianist, Mary Macdonald, was a stalwart friend throughout her life, for a period of time Celia even snubbed her. She told Rasky that she had trusted many people who had turned on her. "You get cautious," she said. Many people who considered themselves Celia's friends tended to be in awe of her or pander to her. And while she craved the respectability and standing of being in a marriage, she managed to lose three husbands.

One fact never changed from that day in February 1951 when she arrived in Toronto, stepping off the aircraft in her black Persian lamb coat. Celia Franca was a celebrity, one of Canada's first cultural stars (Glenn Gould and Margaret Atwood and the rest were still to come), a status of which she made adroit and conscious use in order to advance her own cause. With her perfect posture and distinctive profile, her nearly white makeup, hair pulled tightly back, Celia Franca was the embodiment of her own art form.

Franca's story falls neatly into three broad sections: her formative years in England to the age of twenty-nine, her career as the artistic director of the National Ballet of Canada, and her almost three decades post–National Ballet, some of those years being lonely ones. She died in 2007 at the age of eighty-six.

During her long life, Celia Franca was loved and loathed, a loyal friend and a dangerous enemy, arrogant and insecure, self-centred, and yet thoughtfully generous. This is the story of a woman who rarely stepped out of her role.

ONE ✑

In Step with Bow Bells

A LTHOUGH MANY PEOPLE BELIEVE the National Ballet of Canada
is Celia Franca's greatest creation and coup, this achievement
takes second place to an even more impressive accomplishment:
her creation of Celia Franca. Whether or not she was aware of
what she was doing, she manufactured a distinctive, bold, and
unforgettably dramatic personality that made her an instant celebrity when she arrived in Canada in 1951. As did the National Ballet
of Canada, its creator started out with virtually nothing.

In the making of the persona of Celia Franca, she had a great
deal of help from her family. Their project began before she was
born. At birth her last name was not Franca (her own invention),
but Franks; had she been born several years earlier it would have
been Frankelstein. According to family lore, Celia Franca came
into the world in the midst of a ferocious summer thunderstorm
on June 25, 1921, in London, England's East End.

Led by Celia's paternal grandfather, Moshe, and his wife, Rivka (Rebecca) Yenta Stall, the Frankelstein family had come to England in 1892 in a large wave of Polish immigrants, both to improve their economic prosperity and to escape anti-Semitic persecutions or pogroms. They fled the town of Konin, in central Poland. Frankelstein relatives who remained there vanished along with the town itself during the Nazi occupation. Celia's grandparents settled in London's East End, a ghetto of Jewish immigrants. Among them was Celia's father, Solomon, then aged two. His parents found comfort in the tightly knit community where Yiddish was the language predominantly used on shop signs and in newspapers and local theatres.

Solomon Franks grew up within a typically Jewish extended family. He was the middle of three sons — the eldest was Sam, the youngest Harry (known as Hashie) — and had four younger sisters. Solomon had the traumatic experience of witnessing three of his four sisters die in their teens of respiratory illnesses as a result of their unhealthy living conditions in a dank basement apartment. Only his youngest sister, Annie, survived.

Moshe Frankelstein, a cobbler, died shortly after the birth of Annie. Rebecca, his widow, took in laundry to help support her impoverished family. Celia retained strong memories of her paternal grandmother, her "Buba," as a rather severe old lady with reddish hair who lived in that dark basement apartment and who only spoke Polish and Yiddish. Celia's first cousin, Esther, however, has much fonder memories of her grandmother. Despite the bleakness and dampness of that apartment, their grandmother planted orange pips in the aerie. Celia remembered only that her grandmother gave her oranges on her reluctant visits.

Her father, Solomon, who had been a bright student in London, had English as his main language although he (and later his daughter, Celia) peppered his speech with Yiddish phrases. Solomon, known to his intimates as Solly, worked as a shoe salesman before developing skills as a tailor. At some point, he anglicized his name to Franks.

Around 1912, Solomon, then twenty-two, met seventeen-year-old Gertrude Morris. From a similar family history, she had arrived in England as a very young girl accompanying her mother, Nicha Tzvia (nee Grundlash), and father, Moshe Akiva (known to his family as Moshe'Kiva) Feigenbaum, along with five brothers — Sam, David, Joe, Benjamin, and Andre (Isaac) — from Wyrozeby, a town in Poland, about sixty miles west of Warsaw. They joined Moshe'Kiva's brother Herschel[1] in Grimsby, northern England. The family remained in Grimsby, where Moshe'Kiva worked with his brother as a tailor. Their conditions were better than those of the Franks family in East End London. Three more children — Alf, Solly, and Lena — were born. They anglicized their surname from Feigenbaum to Morris, probably as a reaction to the 1905 Aliens Act restricting immigration, itself a reaction to the large number of European Jews entering England in the 1890s.

Gertrude, known to her family as Gertie, had gone down to London after leaving school, most likely to live with one of her older brothers. It was there she met Solomon Franks. Tragedy hit the Morris family in 1914 when their mother died. Gertie returned to Grimsby to look after the children still living at home, the youngest being six-year-old Lena.

Just how the courtship between Solomon and Gertie progressed is unknown, but in February 1915 Solomon Franks travelled up to Grimsby to marry Gertrude. The entire prosperous-looking Morris family posed for a photo with the bride and groom, smartly dressed in street clothes, standing in the second row. Included in the front row were Gertie's father and the young child, Lena, understandably looking slightly worried. A formal studio portrait of just the newlyweds shows a handsome, well-dressed, and serious looking young couple, both exuding ambition and determination. The couple maintained an affectionate relationship throughout their long lives, and their mutual ambition of bettering themselves and providing greater opportunities for their children gave them a clear, shared purposefulness, of which the principle motor was Gertrude, known by her in-laws for her strong personality.

Ten months after their marriage, a son, Vincent, was born. After a relatively wide gap of six years, Celia was born in 1921. Gertie, having brought her youngest sister, Lena, with her to London, now had three children to care for.

The children were quite clearly well-loved and looked after. A snapshot shows Vincent, around age four, seated proudly on a tricycle with his aunt Lena standing protectively beside him. Both have neatly combed hair and are dressed tidily in warm coats and sturdy lace-up leather shoes. Another family photo reveals a bob-haired Celia, affectionately nicknamed Cele, around the age of three wearing a dark dress with a ruffled collar and a long strand of pearls around her neck, while an equally well-dressed Gertie stands beside her with one hand curled protectively around the little fingers of her daughter.

Celia's brother Vincent with their aunt Lena.
Courtesy of Library and Archives Canada, e008439029

Celia's first home, on Nicholas Street near the Thames docks, where she shared one gas-lit room with four other family members.
Courtesy of Library and Archives Canada, e008439026

Since Celia's brother, Vincent, was six years older and had greatly different interests, the two siblings were never close. Vincent took after his gentle father in personality while Celia inherited her mother's feisty and bossy character. Celia also inherited her exotic good looks with high cheekbones, a jutting chin, thick black hair, and a sense of style.

The first home for the Franks family was a two-storey brick house that Solomon had rented at 37 Nicholas Street, close to the Stepney Green tube station. Their surroundings were sparse and cramped. The five of them shared a single room on the second floor. Relatives, including Solomon's brother Harry (Hashie), a bachelor, lived downstairs in the same crowded conditions. As was common in East End dwellings of the day, there was no indoor toilet, so the family bathed in a public bathhouse. There was no electricity, as again was common, and every evening Celia's mother went around lighting the gas lamps.

Left to right: Vincent, Gertrude, and Solomon, with Celia in front, in a formal portrait. Photograph by Henry Shaw, courtesy of Dance Collection Danse.

As modest as their accommodation was, it was in one vital respect well-appointed. Gertrude was an immaculate house-keeper, determinedly scrubbing away the grime deposited by the smog from London's omnipresent coal fires. Freshly washed white lace curtains hung on the windows. She was an excellent cook and well known by her extended family for her almond tarts and gefilte fish. She would prepare meals for her little family on a gas range for which space was somehow found on the stair landing. Celia herself, though, had little interest in food and from an early age found her mother's traditional meatballs heavy and hard to swallow. Later she would describe herself as a natural vegetarian. Nevertheless, she recalled loving the Passover meal of fish (she specifically remembered it as being plaice) and delighting in the Shabbat ceremony begun every Friday evening by Gertrude lighting the candles. As part of the Franks family tradition, Solomon brought home treats on Friday night. Celia's particular favourite was licorice allsorts.

Back row, left to right: Grandmother Franks, Celia, Aunt Annie. Front row, left to right: Esther, Trudy, Marion. Courtesy of Esther Stern

Besides their own parents, Vincent and Celia were surrounded with both Morris and Franks uncles, aunts, and a myriad of cousins who gathered together for Jewish festivals. Solomon's younger sister, Annie, lived with her husband and three daughters — Esther, Trudy, and Marian — around the corner from her mother. Uncle Alf, one of Gertie's younger brothers, came to stay with the Franks until he got himself settled into the hairdressing business in London. He bought his own barbershop near Westminster Abbey, although still too young to be able to own property. Instead, his older brother David took the lease out in his name and the two brothers lived together in rooms above the shop. David, a ship's steward, was often absent.

Gertie frequently took her children back to Grimsby to visit their grandfather, Moshe'Kiva, and to go to the nearby seaside town of Cleethorpes for holidays. Family snapshots show Celia along with Vincent and various cousins frolicking in the sand or sitting in rented deck chairs, wrapped up against the cold winds. Celia had warm recollections of her maternal grandfather, whom she regarded as distinguished-looking and kind. When she visited him in 1926 and he did not take her for their usual walks together, she had been spared the truth that he was dying.

AN ESSENTIAL PART OF Franks family lore is that Celia first revealed her talents as a dancer at the wedding of her uncle David and aunt Bessie. A flower girl, she attracted attention when she walked up the aisle with another cousin. But it was at the party afterwards where she captivated all. As she sat on her father's knee, the music began, and Celia slipped down and waltzed around the room. Family and friends were amazed at her ability to keep time with the music. Afterwards, as Solomon recalled, "We were advised to take [Celia] for dancing lessons."

A formal wedding portrait shows Celia standing beside the bride wearing a satin and lace dress, with an elaborate fabric flower sewed onto one shoulder, fancy mid-calf white socks, and white party shoes.

While these early steps into the world of dance entertained, no one in attendance could have anticipated the ambition Celia would develop — or the unlikelihood that someone of her background could realize that ambition. Celia, a cockney from one of the poorest parts of London, would aspire to be part of the ballet world that had originated in the courts of seventeenth-century France to display royal power and aristocratic supremacy. The classical ballet codification of the twentieth century had its roots in the French Royal Academy of Dance founded by King Louis XIV.

But Celia was blissfully unaware of such obstacles. Her earliest concept of the art form to which she would dedicate her life was what she called "fairy dancing," with wings and flapping arms. She had no clue where this idea came from as she hadn't been taken to see any professional dance — the first performance she

Celia, flower girl (right side), at the wedding of her uncle David and aunt Bessie, where she made her impromptu dance debut, entertaining the guests. Courtesy of Library and Archives Canada, e008406982-v6

attended wouldn't come until she was twelve and went to see Colonel Basil's Les Ballets Russes de Monte Carlo during its four-month run at Leicester Square's Alhambra Theatre in 1933. She recalled being disappointed it was not "fairy dancing."

Celia adored being the centre of attention and had an innate sense of musicality. The question — a difficult one because it involved money the family could not spare — was how to nurture her apparent natural talent. Neighbours — musician Lionel

Bowman and his sister — suggested to Solomon that they take the talented Celia along to the Guildhall School of Music to audition for a scholarship.

Celia already had taken some rudimentary piano lessons from a neighbour trying to earn extra money to feed her brood. But the odour of urine from diaper-clad babies quickly put Celia off, and she informed Gertie that she did not want to go back. It was with a combination of *chutzpah* and trepidation that, in January 1926, Gertie took the four-and-half-year-old Celia to the imposing Guildhall School on John Carpenter Street, near the Blackfriars tube station.

The principal, Sir Landon Ronald, a renowned conductor and pianist, recognized quickly that this determined little girl had real talent and awarded her a scholarship to take piano lessons. Whether by Gertie or Celia, they discovered that the Guildhall school also taught ballet classes, and the Franks somehow found the money for the practice tunic and pink ballet shoes for Celia's ballet lessons. While her first teacher, Madam Soutten, was very fond of Celia, bouncing her on her knee, she knew precious little about dance. Many years later, Celia wryly commented, "Fortunately for me, she died." Her next teacher, Lillian Oakeshott, was considerably more accomplished.

While in no way a typical stage mother, Gertie fully supported her daughter's passions, and Celia's piano and ballet lessons became a focal point in the Franks family. The support Celia received was astounding considering that, as far as anyone knows, there had been no artists in either the Franks or Morris families for generations. A degree of creativity was expressed indirectly in Solomon's dressmaking talents and in Uncle Alf's flair as a hairdresser, and there was great respect for culture and learning throughout the European Jewish community, but high-art cultural events were far removed from life in East London. Despite the family's support of Celia, the Franks didn't have the financial means to attend performances of Diaghilev's Ballets

The Franks found the money to have professional postcard photographs taken of their young ballerina. Courtesy of Library and Archives Canada, e008439028

Russes, or of Anna Pavlova, the Russian prima ballerina who appeared at music halls and at Covent Garden. The most Gertie could manage was to take young Celia along, as an occasional treat, to the local cinema.

When Celia was about six, the Franks paid for another professional studio portrait of her, this time in a proper ballet tutu and en pointe. That a six-year-old was up on points shows the lack of knowledge of correct ballet dance training at the Guildhall School at that time.[2] Her sturdy legs were not shown to best advantage in white mid-calf socks and pointe shoes. Nevertheless, the picture shows her feet turned out in fifth position, and from a heart-shaped face framed by dark shiny hair in an exquisite bob, her eyes stare out at the viewer saying, defiantly, "I am a ballerina."

Her cousins, among them Asher Tarmon, were a passive audience watching Celia practise her ballet exercises at home, with Gertie sitting straddled in a high-back chair to provide a stable barre. They also dutifully went along to the Guildhall School of Music to watch Celia in her dance recitals, in several of which she performed solos. Already she was a cut above her numerous cousins, who reacted to her talents with admiration and puzzlement.

Not long after Celia started at the Guildhall School, the Franks family moved to 65 Globe Street, which had two rooms, a proper kitchen, and an indoor bathroom in an apartment over a shop. Vincent and his aunt Lena shared one bedroom, while Celia shared the other with her parents. Most of their time was spent in the warmth of the kitchen. Solomon, who had been working as a shoe salesman at the time of Celia's birth, was by now working in a factory making ladies' coats. It's likely that his connection to the Morris family of tailors had given him the entry into the garment industry. He often cut out patterns on the kitchen table in the evenings, no doubt moonlighting to earn extra income for Celia's lessons.

At considerable sacrifice, the Franks bought a piano for Celia, which could only be squeezed into Vincent and Lena's bedroom. Always the pragmatist, and perhaps to help pay for the instrument, Gertie decided to make use of the time she spent watching Celia taking her dance lessons at the Guildhall School. Audaciously, she gave lessons teaching the local children rudimentary ballet exercises in the tiny Globe Street apartment. Celia, by this time around ten and able to read music with comparative ease, played the piano. She now knew more than her mother, and was very aware of that fact. At one point, when Gertie was teaching a simple barre exercise, Celia stopped her playing to inform her mother that she was giving improper instruction.

England during the 1930s, while in difficult economic circumstances, did not suffer the same devastating unemployment and deep misery that the United States did during the Great Depression. The Franks family continued to improve their circumstances during this difficult decade. They moved again, and this time entirely out of the East End. Solomon rented premises at 85 Camden High Street,[3] where he established a ladies' dress shop. While presenting an elegant front, the new property had a toilet in the back garden. Celia fondly remembered her teenage brother going out to the privy in an effort to sneak a secret smoke — a plan foiled by the privy's door, which had a pattern of little holes, out of which the cigarette smoke would waft.

At 85 Camden High Street, the dress display room was on the ground floor while Solomon's alterations were done upstairs. Gertie, always impeccably groomed and dressed in the latest fashions, managed the shop itself. They worked all day and half of the night. Each lunchtime, Celia would return to the shop and practise her pirouettes in front of the large mirrors, while Gertie put on an apron and prepared for her family a midday meal in the small kitchen at the back. Hard work and self-improvement were the cornerstones in the Franks family's ethos.

To be nearer to the shop, the family moved to a rental property near Regent's Park. This dwelling proved to be uncomfortable and the Franks family moved again, but for their last time in London. Solomon bought a semi-detached house in the suburb of Golders Green. This brand-new house at 56 Golders Gardens had no fewer than three bedrooms on the second floor, a living room, dining room, and kitchen on the first floor, and an enclosed back garden where Celia would often lie and sunbathe in the summer. Several family photos show a suntanned Celia in the garden with a background of shrubbery and flowerpots.

The Franks' final London home, at 56 Golders Gardens. A brand new home in middle-class Golders Green. Courtesy of Library and Archives Canada, e008439024

These moves by the Franks were part of a mass exodus from the working class East End. Herbert Morrison had won the leadership of the London County Council in 1934 under the slogan "Up with Houses! Down with the Slum," and between 1934 and 1939 nearly twenty thousand East Enders moved into what were then London suburbs. The Golders Green area was much favoured by the Jewish community.[4]

The new house in north London was palatial compared to their previous residences. More importantly, it was not a rental; though it was heavily mortgaged, it was their house. It's possible that Uncle Alf provided some financial assistance. Alf had prospered and by this time had a hair salon on Regent Street near Aquascutum, catering to a clientele of mainly upper-class ladies. In 1931 he had also established a school called the Morris School of Hairdressing and Beauty Culture.[5] He took on his nephew Vincent as an apprentice and taught him; Vincent became an award-winning hairstylist.

Vincent began to cut his sister's black hair. Still at school, Celia wore it in a bob with straight bangs. A photo taken in the Franks' back garden shows a tall, handsome Vincent — smartly dressed in a

Celia with her handsome older brother, Vincent, in their Golders Gardens private back garden, where she enjoyed sunbathing.
Courtesy of Library and Archives Canada, e008439027

three-piece suit, one hand casually in his pocket, the other holding a drink — and a bare-legged Celia, around the age of twelve or thirteen, wearing a plain-coloured shift dress, and woollen blazer, posed beside him with one arm casually draped over his shoulder and the other possessively on his arm. One physical characteristic the siblings had in common was big ears.

DURING ALL THESE CHANGES in the family's fortunes, Celia and her brother, Vince, had been moved from school to school. Celia began her primary education in a prefabricated, tin-roofed shed aptly named the Tin School on nearby Globe Street. Her teacher, Miss Drake, taught her little songs and recitations, such as "Have you ever seen the little pink daisies?" or "I've only one word to say to you — come shake hands — how do you do," which little Celia sang to entertain her family at home. From the earliest classroom photographs, it was clear Celia was a natural subject for almost any camera. In the midst of rows of students, Celia, with her erect posture and shiny black bobbed hair, stands out. Even as a little

Class 2 of the Tin School, with Celia Franks (second row, fourth from the left) already showing her dramatic, photogenic attraction. Courtesy of Library and Archives Canada, e008406981

girl, she had pretensions of grandeur, describing herself as *raffinée*, or very refined.

While living in Primrose Hill, Celia attended the nearby Princess Road School. Strongly encouraged by her parents, Celia next tried out for and won a scholarship at the academically rigorous Camden School for Girls. Dressed in the traditional school uniform of blazer, pleated tunic, and pale green shirt with collar and long sleeves, she attended this school in 1932–33. Though obviously intelligent, Celia daydreamed during class, doodling pictures of people in costumes in the back of her exercise book. She did the least work necessary to get by. In her geography workbook, she was chastised for not dating her homework. In one assignment, she was instructed to write a letter about taking an imaginary trip from England to Winnipeg, Manitoba — a city she would later visit often. Using her natural cunningness, Celia managed to do her assignment with the minimal amount of research. Padding madly to get the prescribed number of words, she wrote of her imagined trip across the Atlantic, "At last we arrived at Quebec. Can you imagine my excitement. I took a quick glance around the harbour. This was Canada." Her teacher gave her a somewhat generous seven out of ten. The next week, Celia drew two pictures in her workbook — "A Red Indian Wigwam" and "Canoe made of birch bark." This was the extent of Celia's early knowledge of Canada.

Confident physically, Celia was very good in gym activities. She wore navy-blue wool gym bloomers that turned her body blue when she sweated and the dye came out. She played centre in netball because she could run fast. For a short period she played tennis until she realized she was developing one arm more than the other and immediately abandoned the game.

Celia coveted winning her "gym colours" — represented by a little silver shield pinned to the gym tunic. She worked very hard for this pin, always being careful to walk down the stairs and sitting in class with correct posture: "I was a good girl and I won my gym colours and I loved it."[6]

She loved dancing most of all. Her main recollections of her school years were those of exhaustion and "strap hanging" on the tube. She was laden down with a back satchel full of school books along with another bag containing her ballet practice clothes. On the ride home, Celia's body would be aching from the exercises, while her bag was full of wet, woollen, practice clothes. If she was lucky enough to get a seat, she could start her homework as she travelled up to the Golders Green tube station.

For nearly a decade the Guildhall School of Music was the centre of Celia's universe. Besides dance and piano classes, more and more of her time was taken up with rehearsals for recitals. From her first public dance performance in the July 1928 concert program, she appeared continuously until her last Guildhall appearance in July 1935. In 1932, she was awarded a medal inscribed "Celia Franks/Pianoforte/London" (which she proudly kept to the end of her life), and in October 1935 a Guildhall School of Music ten-pound Corporation Scholarship for Dancing.

She also won a scholarship for two dance classes a week with Judith Espinosa[7] to prepare for the examinations of the Association of Operatic Dance (later named the Royal Academy of Dancing or RAD). Attending these classes, wearing the required white tutu with a lace collar around the neckline, Celia sailed through her exams, receiving eighty-five percent for her grade one exams in the winter of 1930 when she was nine years old and ninety-two percent for the winter 1932 exams. As one of the Association's stellar students, she was chosen to take part in an afternoon dance reception at Claridge's Hotel in July 1934. She appeared as one of the "scholars" giving a side practice (barre) arranged by Phyllis Bedells, the English ballerina and teacher who had helped to create the Association's first syllabus.

Celia may have felt slightly more comfortable at Claridge's Hotel because of an older classmate at Guildhall who had befriended her.[8] Reminiscent of Professor Henry Higgins tutoring the cockney flower girl, Eliza Doolittle, Margery Tymms and her mother invited Celia to their home for elocution lessons. After reading from Shakespeare, Celia remembered most vividly "the fizzy lemonade and cream pastries" given as a reward for her efforts.

Celia's considerable accomplishments in ballet and music did not, however, impress the headmistress of Camden School for Girls. Accosting Celia in the hall one day, headmistress Olive Wright bluntly told her student, "With those circles under your eyes, you look like an old woman. You'll have to give up this ballet business."

Her father went to Miss Wright to ask that his daughter's homework load be reduced as she was heavily involved in music and dance lessons. Miss Wright's reply was a flat no. So Solomon applied for a grant from the Jewish Education Aid Society, an organization set up to help fund the education of children with artistic talents,[9] to send Celia to the King Alfred School in north London. The scholarship was dependent on an audition, for which Gertie made her daughter a costume consisting of translucent wings and a tutu of Prussian blues. Although the floor was dangerously slippery, Celia performed her self-choreographed dragonfly dance well and won the scholarship.

It's not clear what Celia's parents thought would be the eventual outcome of their daughter's obsession with ballet. These lessons were certainly providing her with poise and a trim figure, but in the 1930s a career as an actress or dancer was considered utterly unsuitable for a young woman. While Britain was just beginning to spawn its own ballet companies, dance tableaux and foreign ballet stars had been appearing on the English music hall stages for decades. Nineteenth-century novelist William Thackeray observed that seeing a dancer on stage in flesh-coloured tights was akin to the thrill of a public execution. Although rather overstating things, there is no doubt that, at this time, ballet's appeal to many men in the audience was the opportunity to catch sight of shapely, bare limbs. It was only after the feminist movement of the late 1960s and 1970s and the "male gaze" theory that it became politically incorrect for men to overtly ogle dancing girls in their brief costumes.[10]

The King Alfred School was refreshingly progressive. School uniforms were not required and, whenever possible, classes were held outdoors. The teachers were approachable and interested in the arts. Celia was encouraged to pursue her ballet lessons.

One spring day in 1936, fourteen-year-old Celia travelled by tube to Shaftesbury Avenue and walked on to the Saville Theatre, a new art deco building decorated on the outside by a forty-metre sculptured frieze depicting "Drama Through the Ages." She had come to audition for a dance part in the new West End musical *Spread It Abroad*.

She had gone alone and with no notion of what a professional audition entailed. One of the last to be called, she realized she had been expected to have her own sheet music as well as a prepared dance routine. To make matters worse, the roles called for tap dancing. Watching the older, experienced chorus girls perform their routines, Celia quickly invented a dance. Requesting that the pianist play the piece used by the previous auditioner, Fred Astaire's "I Won't Dance," she made up a lively number. She recalled that the choreographer, jaded at watching street-smart chorus girls with sloppy footwork, was so taken by her flair and easygoing musicality that he failed to take in that she was a gawky schoolgirl and hired her on the spot.

Spread It Abroad, a smash hit, opened on April 1, 1936, and ran for half a year, with 209 performances, often to houses of well over a thousand people. One of the six girls in the chorus line was Celia Franks. Amidst the glowing reviews, one critic took note of "a pretty chorus who might well have more to do." A magazine photo featured the dance, "Aubade," with, in descending order, the stars, Walter Gore, Maude Lloyd, Frank Staff, and then the line of chorus girls standing on a staircase silhouetted in profile. Near the end of the line, Celia, with her long neck and elongated jawline, is unmistakable."

While the Franks had supported Celia in her artistic pursuits, they failed to be as supportive of their daughter's ambition to have a professional stage career. Solomon's initial reaction was shock and strong disapproval. His temper improved only somewhat once Celia started bringing home her hard-earned three-pound weekly pay packet.

Having won a professional audition against far more experienced girls than herself, then earning good money in the midst of the glittery world of show business, there was no chance whatsoever at the end of the run that Celia could be convinced to go back to King Alfred School. Instead, she set out to educate herself about the world of professional dance.

TWO 〰

Rambert Years

IN THE WIDER WORLD, decidedly less-pleasant events were taking place in the 1930s. In the cinemas, newsreels were reporting the rise of Nazism in Germany and Crystal Night, when the windows of German Jewish homes and businesses were smashed. In the Franks home, the large influx of Jewish refugees into England, and the reason why, must have provoked intense discussions, yet Celia's recollections of these years were predominantly about dancing and choreography. She was totally focused on her art and on herself.

While the world watched events that would shape the rest of the twentieth century, Celia watched Maude Lloyd dance night after night in *Spread It Abroad*. She came to recognize that her aspiration was to become just like Lloyd. She admired the older dancer's serene beauty and her refined, fragile, yet not vulnerable style.

Originally from South Africa, Lloyd had travelled to England to become a scholarship student with dance teacher Marie Rambert in 1926. Rambert herself had studied with two seminal European teachers, Emile Jaques-Dalcroze, who created a form of rhythmic gymnastics known as Eurhythmics, and Enrico Cecchetti, who developed a method for teaching ballet that included long, complicated *enchaînements*, or sets of ballet steps. Although not a major star, Rambert had danced in the corps de ballet of Diaghilev's Ballets Russes during 1912–13. She had arrived in London in 1914, opened a ballet school and then created England's first permanent ballet company, where Lloyd quickly became a star ballerina. Nicknamed "Mim," Rambert was known for such eccentricities as turning cartwheels without warning and in the most inappropriate places.

Lloyd recognized Celia Franks' burning ambition and suggested to the teenager that she take master classes at the Marie Rambert School. Celia found it hard-going. She almost didn't make it at all. Rambert was quite a snob, despite her zaniness. When Celia applied to take classes, quite prepared to pay for them from her earnings in *Spread It Abroad*, Rambert, categorizing her as a chorus girl, turned her down. She was only accepted after Maude Lloyd vouched for Celia's talent.

Celia was assigned to the afternoon class, which proved a great benefit. She called it her "lucky day." Her teacher was Antony Tudor, widely regarded as one of Britain's leading choreographers. He responded to Celia's resilience and toughness. They got along well when Tudor recognized that she was a fast study. In class, when he tested her by setting a fiendishly difficult *enchaînement*, he discovered she could do the steps as quickly as he dictated them.

As a further connection, Celia and Tudor were both cockneys, having grown up in East End London. They could talk to each other in cockney rhyming slang, a code in which a simple word is replaced with a phrase that rhymes with the word such as using "apple and pears" to replace the word "stairs." Anyone not conver-

A publicity photo of Celia Franks, who had joined the Ballet Rambert.
Courtesy of Library and Archives Canada, PA210138

sant with this slang doesn't have a clue what is being said. Tudor could also be extremely sarcastic and harsh, but Celia could read through this code as well to appreciate his care in coaching his students. In a rare exercise in self-analysis, Celia said, "I suppose there is a bit of the masochist in all of us because we didn't even mind being beaten by him, verbally I mean."[12]

While Lloyd and Tudor helped her enormously, Celia's real driving force came from deep within herself. At this same time, but in secret, because Rambert did not like her "girls" — even her afternoon girls — taking classes outside of her own school, Celia was travelling to London's fashion district and there climbed up to Stanislas Idzikowski's bright and airy Great Portland Street ballet studio. Here Idzikowski, once a soloist with Diaghilev's Ballets Russes, put his students through their paces. Diminutive in stature (he bore a resemblance to the tiny, perfectly attired Prince of Wales), he was always impeccably dressed in a smart suit and tie with highly polished street shoes, even in his dance studio. Another of his students remarked on Idzikowski's shoes, "In spite of their robustness in shape and weight, never once could you hear him land upon the floor when demonstrating movements. His *tours* were a miracle of precision, silently executed."[13]

These clandestine sessions taught Celia other lessons. "Idzi was a sweetheart. He was strict in the classroom. Very strict. And he went through the exercises like wildfire. No matter what emergency might crop up, you were expected to know what you were doing and carry on."[14] When she once failed to grasp a series of dance movements and dissolved into tears of frustration, Idzikowski sent her out of the room. He told her to go into the dressing room and bang her head against the wall. "I did. It taught me a lesson. You're not allowed to just let go every time you feel like having a cry. It taught me discipline."[15]

He also taught her a most useful trick for dancers — how to stop panting after an extended session. Between exiting the stage and waiting for the next entrance, he told her to close her mouth, breathe slowly through her nose, and at the same time bite her tongue hard. This, Idzi explained, would stop the panting and start the saliva flowing.[16]

ᴣᴐ

CELIA'S DILIGENCE AT RAMBERT'S school and in secret simultaneously with Idzikowski paid off. Rambert slowly began to recognize her talent as a dramatic dancer. At the beginning of 1937, she invited Celia to join the company's corps de ballet. The years spent with Ballet Rambert were the bedrock of Celia's professional training. On January 3 she appeared for the first time at the Mercury Theatre as one of the Athenian women in Tudor's *Lysistrata*. She also began rehearsals for *Dark Elegies*,[7] which premiered February 19, 1937, and was the last ballet Antony Tudor choreographed for Ballet Rambert.

As a member of the corps de ballets, Celia watched the company's principal dancers (including Agnes de Mille in the only role she performed with Ballet Rambert) and Tudor himself perfecting this dramatically dark ballet to the music of Gustav Mahler's *Songs on the Death of Children*. De Mille, niece of Hollywood film mogul Cecil B. de Mille, went on to become a celebrated choreographer for American musicals, including the groundbreaking *Oklahoma*, which was the first Broadway musical to use a ballet sequence to advance the plot and develop character. Celia was not initially impressed with de Mille, finding her rather vulgar, but conceded that she went on to become a true innovator.[18]

That summer sixteen-year-old Celia accompanied the Rambert Ballet on its first European tour. Starting in Nice on July 24, the troupe toured southern French resort towns, including Vichy (where Diaghilev's Ballets Russes had given its last performance in 1929). Because Celia was still a minor, the company had to post a surety bond and were required to check in with the British Consul in each town.

The story goes that the troupe lost Marie Rambert for two days because she had been so engrossed in reading Thomas Hardy's *Tess of the d'Urbervilles* that she failed to exit the train and travelled straight on through to Paris. Perhaps Rambert's absentmindedness was deliberate and she was just tired of being den mother to a bunch of mainly teenage ballet dancers.

Solomon and Gertie Franks happened to be in the south of France at the time. Although they were doing well with the Camden Street dress shop, it was nothing close to the success Celia's paternal uncle Alf had achieved with his hair salon and hairdressing school. He had bought an apartment in Nice and could offer his relatives the luxury of a Riviera holiday. Celia joined her parents in an excursion to the Casino in Monte Carlo. Initially refused admission for being underage, Celia ducked around the corner, tied a scarf around her head, put on dark glasses, and boldly walked in.[19]

For the start of the fall season, drastic adjustments had to be made to the Rambert company. Tudor had left at the end of spring to form his own company with Agnes de Mille. He then poached from the Rambert company, taking star ballerina Peggy van Praagh and his own personal partner, Hugh Laing. Dance writer Mary Clarke, describing this crisis, said, "Rambert was not pleased. This was a mass exodus and it meant a vast amount of rehearsing for the Birmingham season. Fortunately, Frank Staff could take over nearly all Hugh's parts and there was a dark girl of striking appearance called Celia Franca in the corps de ballet. She had quality and intelligence, thought Rambert; she might replace Peggy."[20]

Plucked from the corps, Celia began the daunting task of learning major dance roles. Tudor himself taught his former student the role of The Woman in his Past in his seminal ballet, *Jardin aux Lilas*. This story of an Edwardian engagement party held in a moonlit garden filled with lilacs was Tudor at his psychological best.

The private rehearsal time with Tudor was one of most exhilarating experiences in Celia's career as a dancer, "The learning experience was fantastic," she recalled. "He'd say, 'When you make this entrance, imagine that you have just arrived at the top of the crush bar staircase at Covent Garden. Its beautiful red-carpeted foyer has a lovely balustrade leading from the dress circle down to the bar itself. And everyone's eyes are on you.' This remained in my memory when I made my first entrance across from downstage left down to downstage right. And he said, 'Use your arm as though you are using an enormous fan.' That kind of thing really excited me, and although he could be very sarcastic, he could also be very encouraging. There was a *pirouette en dedans* at one place, an inside turn that must be done on pointe. Well, I never had a very strong technique, and out of the corner of his eye he saw me trying this pirouette, and I did three of them, on perfect balance. It probably never happened again. But anyway he said, 'Did I see a triple pirouette there?' Which was very sweet. He didn't have to say it but he did."

As Celia gained confidence, her particular talent as a dramatic character dancer became steadily more evident. Her technique was never strong, and her feet, with little natural arch, were not those of the traditional classical ballerina. But she could and did steal a scene with her strong sense of drama and showmanship. Rambert cast her in several of Tudor's ballets. She was also chosen for the first cast as the Dope Fiend in Walter Gore's 1939 ballet *Paris Soir*.[21]

At this period of her career, Celia would describe herself as "addicted" to dance; it was her entire life. Each day, she took the tube from Golders Green arriving at the Mercury Theatre studios on Ladbrooke Road to start classes at ten a.m. Until the dancers warmed up, the small stove in the main studio gave off a pitiful amount of heat. As the classes and rehearsals progressed, the smell of sweat and wet wool from their practice clothes permeated the studio. If Celia was not performing in the evening, she often remained in the smaller downstairs studio either rehearsing or working on her own choreography.

The lack of space in the tiny Mercury Theatre compelled the unconventional Rambert not to occupy one of the seats herself, but rather to sit on a shooting stick in the aisle as she made correction notes for the dancers. The principal girls' dressing room was a long, narrow passage right above the stage itself with a mirror along one wall over the makeup table space, while costumes hung off hooks on the other wall. The stairway up to the dressing room was actually onstage and was often incorporated into the set design. When the lighting onstage was dim, the ballerinas would be forced to turn off the dressing room lights in order not to have a beam of light coming from under their door. They had to whisper. One of the dancers described them as sitting like chickens on a perch, "trapped until the end of each ballet unless we escaped through the window onto the fire-escape."[22]

Audiences came to recognize that a particular magic existed between Celia and Leo Kersley. The young duo were favourites in such popular one-act ballets as *Le Rugby* with Celia, as cheerleader, clad in a striped sweater, brightly coloured tutu, and beret, spurring on Leo, the football champion, or Celia as the Bird and Leo as the Wolf in *Peter and the Wolf* to Prokofiev's music, amidst a childlike setting with a tree constructed from a stepladder with branches made from long-handled mops with their ragheads painted bright green. In his 1946 book *Sixteen Years of Ballet Rambert*, Lionel Bradley noted, "Celia Franca's exotic beauty, her astonishing resilience when leaping into the air and her poetic grace of movement and Leo Kersley's strength and speed were for several years a rich asset to the company."

Off stage Celia and Leo became close friends. Leo provided Celia with a key to unlocking the mysteries of a wider cultural world. Along with dance, Leo was drawn to other art forms. The pair started going to theatre and dance performances together, queuing to get the cheapest tickets in the upper gallery, known as "The Gods." Celia liked Leo's knowledge of the arts. "He read a lot of poetry. He saw a lot of theatre. His knowledge of music and ballet was extraordinary. I was just naturally drawn to him as we grew up together at the Ballet Rambert."

Of all the art forms, dance is the most physical. Young dancers have taut and well-muscled bodies and the nature of dance creates

The ever-intense Leo Kersley reading while on holiday with Celia.
Courtesy of Library and Archives Canada, e008439018

Celia taking an uncommon jaunt into the countryside, accompanied by Leo.
Courtesy of Library and Archives Canada, e008439023

2-1B

physical intimacies. Most of them are sexually attractive — to individual admirers, to the audience in general, and to each other. When Leo first laid eyes on Celia in a class, he was struck by the fact that her ears were large and she seemed to have no eyebrows; but over time he came to recognize that this slip of a girl was a stunner with a tiny waist and pert bustline. Eventually, Leo's interest in Celia became unabashedly sexual. That attraction became mutual.

While on tour, Leo and Walter Gore,[23] the choreographer who had hired Celia for Spread It Abroad and who was also a dancer with the Rambert Ballet, figured out a devious plan to spend the night with Celia and Walter's girlfriend, Sally Gilmour. The company's stage manager was obliged to keep a list of the digs where each dancer was lodging. The two lads always made sure they and their respective dancer girlfriends were billeted at the same house. The official list then recorded as roommates Walter and Leo and Sally and Celia. What occurred after the lights went out was never discussed.

THREE

Dancing in the Dark

C ELIA WAS OUT OF work and vacationing on the beach in Brighton when war was declared on September 3, 1939. She had left the Ballet Rambert at the beginning of 1939 to return to London's West End stage as a chorus girl. She, along with the financial backers and the rest of the cast, had gambled that J.B. Priestley's new musical *Johnson over Jordan* would have a long, successful run. The impressive production team of Priestley as playwright, Benjamin Britten as composer, and Antony Tudor as choreographer made it appear a sure bet.

But audiences stayed away from this morality play, much of it taking place in a hallucinatory state between life and death. It was a challenging expressionistic play with the use of grotesque masks. Tudor ran into difficulties when the Lord Chamberlain censored a nightclub scene in which an elderly woman dances suggestively with an attractive young girl. There's no record of who this young girl was in the expurgated scene, but Celia Franks, with her dramatic flair, would have been a natural choice for the role. She definitely was part of that particular scene as her name was listed in the program in a variety of roles from stenographer in the first act to one of the people in the night club in the final act. The *Daily Telegraph*, March 4, described *Johnson over Jordan* as "the most spectacular failure in the theatre for a long time."²⁴ It closed on May 6.

Celia managed to get another job that May in a BBC Television drama called the *Insect Play* by Karel Capek, the story of a tramp who shrinks to the size of an ant. Celia performed amidst the butterflies and the moths.

AFTER THE DECLARATION OF war, all performers were out of work. The government, in anticipation of air attacks, ordered the immediate closure of London theatres. Marie Rambert moved her school to Newbury, Berkshire, while the Sadler's Wells Ballet Company evacuated further afield to Cardiff in Wales. When the bombings did not happen, Ballet Rambert returned in November and presented a West End season. The Sadler's Wells returned to its Islington theatre on Boxing Day, 1940.

No group of dancers could have been more detached from reality than Ninette de Valois and the Sadler's Wells company, who agreed to do a tour of the Netherlands in May 1940. Shortly after the company's arrival the Germans began the invasion of Holland. After a dramatic retreat, which included a bus ride and midnight walk through thick woods, the dancers were put on a cargo ship. They made it back home to London on May 14. Although there were no casualties among the dancers, the company lost all its sets, costumes, and music for six ballets.

In September 1940 when the Blitz began, the Sadler's Wells Theatre in Islington was shut down for the rest of the war and turned into a rest centre for air-raid victims. Administrator Tyrone

Guthrie (later to play a key role in establishing Ontario's Stratford Festival) made sure the ballet school remained in the building, though, as Leo Kersley remembers; "Guthrie made quite sure that us horrible whippersnappers [were] upstairs making sure that the inhabitants of Islington didn't wander out of where they should be."[25]

In the confusion of the closings and openings of the established ballet companies, several ragtag troupes were formed to provide dancers with employment and Londoners with light entertainment. Celia and Leo joined *Les Ballets Trois Arts*, which had been formed by John Regan,[26] an eccentric Irishman who pulled together a bakers' dozen dancers, young experimental designers, and a small orchestra made up of young musicians from the Royal College of Music. Regan could only pay his dancers their transportation costs, but if performances earned any profit, they were commonly split. Many of the dancers were "on the dole" and slipped out of rehearsals on the day they had to register at the Labour Exchange.

While all of England was now consumed with war, Celia remained consumed with ballet. She seized upon an opportunity to create her own choreography.[27] On December 6, 1939, Celia presented *Midas* with music composed by Elizabeth Lutyens, a daughter of the famed architect Edwin Lutyens. Toni Del Renzio, then the *enfant terrible* of the English surrealist artists, designed the sets and costumes with the dancers in blue unitards painted all over with veins. The simple set included an umbrella hanging upside down from the stage flies. Franca later admitted she had little idea why the umbrella was there. "God knows what that symbolized. I do remember that I danced the role of the Freudian subconscious of King Midas. And John Regan played King Midas sitting downstage left at a table counting all his money."

ॐ

THE NAME CELIA FRANKS did not appear on *Les Ballet Trois Arts* cast list. Sometime between appearing in *Johnson over Jordan* in 1939 and joining the new ballet company, she had gone to considerable trouble to change her name to Franca. She herself explained that she didn't like the look of her surname in print, so she had it changed to Franca at the National Registration office. With that name and her dark black hair, people thought she was Italian. It was a common practice for dancers to choose more exotic names to enhance their career prospects. Ninette de Valois had started life as Edris Stannus and Margot Fonteyn as Peggy Hookham.

The inevitable question arises whether Celia changed her name in an attempt to disguise her Jewish heritage. Official records would have quickly established her origins. Even before the threat of possible invasion by Germany, anti-Semitic events had been occurring in England. The government had limited Jewish immigration in the late 1930s until the brink of war when unaccompanied Jewish children were hurriedly brought over. British black-shirt fascists fronted by the loathsome Sir Oswald Mosley painted anti-Semitic slogans on buildings in London's East End and occasionally resorted to attacking Jews. It is certainly odd that she had not made the name change at the beginning of her professional dance career in 1937. Perhaps Celia suddenly took a look at the wider world and confronted her potential vulnerability as a Jew. Certainly, forever afterward, she downplayed her Jewish heritage in public.

HAROLD RUBIN, MANAGER OF the Arts Theatre Club in Leicester Square, realized once the Blitz began that the public craved diversion from the horrors. He launched daily ballet performances beginning with lunchtime ballets and progressing to after-lunch, tea-time ballets (3:30 to 4:30 p.m.) and then sherry-time ballets (6 to 7 p.m.), the early shows allowing people to get home before the blackout and falling bombs. These daytime ballet performances proved to be so popular that Rubin leased another theatre, the Ambassador, and produced three separate ballet companies for the two venues: Ballet Rambert, London Ballet, and the Arts Theatre Ballet. Celia, having rejoined Ballet Rambert, shared top billing along with Sally Gilmour and Lisa Serova; she danced up to four or five performances a day. Servicemen on leave, along with London office workers wanting to forget the war, flocked to the theatres to spend a carefree hour being entertained while drinking tea or sherry. The theatre became thick with cigarette smoke. At the end of the day, Celia, scurrying home under the threats of bombings was, like many others, constantly frightened. "[B]ut life goes on," she said. "You do your job."

When the Blitz began, both the Kersley and Franks families moved out of London. On nights when it was too dangerous to travel by tube or train, Leo and Celia would remain in town, staying with their friend Bill Meadmore in his Chelsea home. A popular joke at the time went, "I'm not that type of a girl; besides, where could we go?" But Leo and Celia had solved that problem.

On February 27, 1941, Leo and Celia married in a registry office in Watford, Hertfordshire, near to where their families had evacuated. She became Mrs. Celia Kersley, taking a solid Anglo-Saxon name traceable back to the thirteenth century. The Franks had been against the marriage, and Solomon refused to attend. Celia's father was still reeling from the very recent the death of his brother-in-law (Annie's husband), a victim of the bombings. This was followed a week later by the death of his mother, Rebecca. Gertrude gave in and was a witness at the registry office.

Why Leo and Celia chose that particular time to marry remains a mystery. It may have been that, once Gertie Franks realized Celia and Leo were lovers, she concluded, however reluctantly, that a daughter married to an unsuitable husband was better than the possibility of a pregnant unwed daughter. Birth control in the 1940s was still hard to come by; haphazard and unpleasant, before the pill, contraception consisted of condoms, messy contraceptive jelly, diaphragms, and douches, along with illegal abortions.

To Celia's parents, Leo Kersley was unsuitable in almost every way. He was not Jewish. He had no ambition to become upwardly mobile. He boasted of his humble roots: "I was quite a different kettle of fish to all the other middleclass people around and they treated me as such." His father, Edwin, was an adventurer who had travelled across Canada as a vagabond and briefly ran a café in Cobalt, Ontario. He had returned to London to become a dealer in antique books and art prints. His mother, Annie Ethel Hollowell, had leftist leanings. Leo grew up in a shambles of a household where his father and mother, known respectively as Puff and Muff, were a dramatic contrast to the upwardly mobile Franks.

Once married, Celia and Leo lived with his parents. Celia became fond of her unconventional raffish Kersley in-laws. "I loved Puff and Muff. They were completely honest, good, cultured, working class people. No snobbery." Puff was a gifted chatterbox while Muff tended to be quiet. Celia found their conversation and arguments stimulating.

Leo had not been Celia's only suitor. Cyril Frankel first laid eyes on Celia in October 1939 when she was appearing with the Trois Art Ballet Club at the Collins Theatre in Islington. Celia played a circus equestrian in *The Big Top* opposite Leo, who played a clown. Taken backstage by his cousin, Gerald Frankel, to meet the attractive ballerina, eighteen-year-old Cyril switched his allegiance from opera to ballet.

Cyril was not ready for marriage. In 1940 he went up to Oxford to read law. Smitten both by the ballerina, Celia, and the art form itself, he established the Oxford University Ballet Club and began to publish a dance magazine called *Arabesque*. Socially and culturally sophisticated, Frankel convinced ballet luminaries, including the two ballet doyennes, Marie Rambert and Ninette de Valois, to give talks to his Ballet Club. He also presented a series of ballet divertissements, which sometimes featured performances by Celia. During one visit to Oxford, Celia had to climb a gate to leave because it was after hours. Later, when questioned what she was doing there so late at night, Celia, gigglingly replied, "Boyfriend, of course."[28]

After leaving Oxford, Cyril trained as an officer cadet at Sandhurst and went overseas in 1943. Before leaving, he and his cousin Gerald, along with another Sandhurst officer, Michael Frostik, made up their minds to start their own ballet company once the war was over. Celia was to play a major role as both a dancer and the ballet mistress. This dream of a new ballet company would sustain all the players during the war years.

Through most of the succeeding war years, Celia and now Lieutenant Frankel of the King's Dragoon Guards, ignoring her marital status, carried on a romance mainly through letters, but sometimes with overnight trysts. Much of this story is contained in a cache of letters Frankel preserved for decades afterwards. The paper is still permeated with the smell of cigarettes smoked by Celia while writing them and Frankel while reading them.

He adored the spirited and intellectually curious Celia, sending her presents of jewellery, including a filigree butterfly brooch, European leather shoes and gloves, French silk stockings, and perfume. He sent her flowers through emissaries. In January 1944 she wrote to thank him for "the most heavenly red tulips I've ever seen."

Even more than Leo, Cyril became the person with whom Celia could discuss books and ideas. She reported gleefully in one letter that she had found in a second-hand store, a copy of William Morris's *Hopes and Fears for Art*, in which he had proposed making art available to a wider public because art was necessary for the improvement of England's industrial society. Although she left school at the age of fourteen, Franca continued her education on her own.

Celia poured out her heart to Cyril in letters she wrote faithfully each Sunday, her one day off. Sometimes she needed to use three and four aerograms to accommodate all her thoughts. For a period of time, though, her letters stopped. The reason was that she was having an affair with a mysterious serviceman, known only as Mortie. Confiding to a friend, Celia wrote, "He loves me very much and I suppose I shouldn't but I'm very glad he does. The awful thing is that I love him too. I wish I didn't." When the relationship ended, she again picked up her pen to write to Cyril. "I've had an affair with a very ordinary, polite, charming man in the Air Force and somehow I couldn't bring myself to write to you — Conscience or something. At any rate, it's out of my system now. He started hinting about careers interfering with marriage so I wrote to him and said that I wasn't having any marriage interfere with my career."

Celia simply ignored that these were adulterous affairs. In this she was no different from many people trapped in war conditions who, realizing that each day could be their last, took pleasure and solace with friendly strangers.

FOR A SHORT PERIOD in the spring of 1941, Celia and Leo, along with Moira Shearer and several other dancers, joined another new ballet company called the International Ballet. Founded by the twenty-two-year-old dancer Mona Inglesby and bankrolled by her father, she ambitiously planned to remount Russian ballets from the Mariinsky, giving herself top billing as prima ballerina. Although Celia's beloved teacher, Stanislas Idzikowski, was the ballet master, she simply could not stand the repertoire of what she considered to be "museum pieces." After only nine weeks, Celia and Leo left their good paying jobs. The fact that Inglesby gave herself all the best roles may have also factored into Celia's decision to leave the company.

Celia was once more unemployed. Leo found work with Sadler's Wells Ballet company. The scarcity of male ballet dancers had been magnified incomparably by the war and the call-up for healthy adult males. Leo declared himself a Conscientious

Objector and was twice jailed. As a settlement, he agreed to work as a hospital orderly. De Valois did not support Leo's stand and for a time let him go. In his off-hours, he picked up work with a variety of London dance companies.

The particular threat that confronted the jobless Celia was being called up for the rough and tumble work of the Auxiliary Territorial Service. To avoid that fate, she signed up for an eighteen month tour with Entertainments National Service Association (ENSA), nicknamed "Every Night Something Awful."

Luck in the form of ill-luck for two other ballerinas rescued Celia from banal high-kicking with ENSA. June Brae, one of the Sadler's Wells best dramatic dancers, had married a Cambridge man, David Breedon, who did not want his wife touring the provinces. Shortly afterwards, Pamela May seriously injured her leg. Now down two principal dancers, de Valois contacted Celia. She, though, had just signed her ENSA contract. This was a minor problem; de Valois contacted ENSA's head and promptly Celia was released.

The Sadler's Wells Ballet, originally called the Vic-Wells and today the Royal Ballet, was founded in 1931 in London by Ninette de Valois. De Valois created an English style of ballet without the flourishes and embellishments of the Russians yet incorporating the Imperial Russian ballet classics such as *Giselle* and *Swan Lake* into the repertoire. Although in competition with the Ballet Rambert, the two artistic directors — Marie Rambert and Ninette de Valois, otherwise respectively known as "Mim" and "Madam" — remained on friendly terms. In the early days the dancers and choreographers moved back and forth between the companies to scrape together a living wage.

Six decades after hiring Celia, de Valois recalled her impressions of her. "From the day she joined the company, I liked Celia. A very handsome girl she was. And had much to offer. Brainy. Dedicated. Self-disciplined. Well-balanced. Had strength of character and good taste too. She had ambitions to be a classical ballerina. But I felt that classical ballet was her second-best talent. She simply didn't have a ballerina's classical foot. It's like an aspiring opera soprano who can't reach all the high notes. You can't argue with mother nature. Either you're born with certain attributes or you're not." De Valois added, "We both excelled as character dancers. But she had a lyrical quality that I lacked. And she had a lovely jump as well."[29]

Celia's welcome to Sadler's Wells was brisk. De Valois hurriedly rehearsed her, bundled her onto a train, and then, on October 27, 1941, she glided on stage in front of an audience in Edinburgh as Myrtha, Queen of the Willis. There, she danced with Robert Helpmann as Prince Albrecht and Margot Fonteyn in the role of Giselle, despite having never rehearsed with the pair before. The new castmates were impressed with Celia both for her high jumps and her ability to rapidly learn complex choreography. "It was then that Bobby [Helpmann] realized that he could count on me to be a quick study and a reliable dancer who never let him down," Celia said.[30]

All of Celia's resilience, street smarts, and tenacity — characteristics developed in her early childhood in hardscrabble East End London — came to full use during the four wartime years that she travelled with the Sadler's Wells Ballet company. The schedule was a ten-week circuit of the provincial towns followed by a four-week stint at the New Theatre (now known as the Noel Coward Theatre) on St. Martin's Lane. There was a two-week holiday in August.

The tour schedule was exhausting, but the hardships were increased because of wartime rationing. Costumes and shoes created a special challenge for ballerinas. Their job was to be beautiful, to communicate ethereal magic created by their unearthly ability to glide across the stage en pointe. Today, it is commonplace for a ballet dancer to use two or three pairs of pointe shoes in a single performance. During wartime, dance supplies were virtually non-existent. A December 8, 1945, magazine article told that Sadler's Wells' female dancers received five pairs of silk stockings per year. Prima ballerinas such as Margot Fonteyn, Pamela May (who returned after her injury healed), and Beryl Grey got two pairs of pointe shoes a week. The soloists

This photo of Celia appeared in the April 1942 issue of *Dancing Times* to announce her joining the Sadler's Wells company. While having a high *ballon*, or elevation, she lacked the classical dancer's body and high instep.
Courtesy of Dance Collection Danse

(Celia would have been among this group) received three pairs a fortnight while the corps de ballet had to make do with one pair a week. Celia needed her pointe shoes to last for at least eighteen performances, besides using them in rehearsals. This worked to Celia's advantage because she couldn't wear shoes unless they were thoroughly broken in. The dancers would have two or three pairs of shoes going at a time so that after darning the toes with pink silk thread (itself hard to acquire), they could shellac the pair that had gone soft and dance in one of the other pairs.[31]

But despite the hardships, the Sadler's Wells Ballet dancers, like so many people who lived through the Second World War, remembered the years with great fondness. The company's war years have been well documented in Lynne Wake's film *Dancing in the Dark*.[32] Letters, photographs, and memorabilia show how the dancers' fatigue and fear of death was counterbalanced by their sense of dedication to bringing entertainment to war-weary audiences. Ballerina Beryl Grey talked about dancing through the air raids: "One got on with things and didn't stop to analyze how one felt. This was my career: I was doing what I loved, and if there were bombs going off, that was how it was." Jean Bedells, another dancer, recalled, "We were a group of friends working jolly hard but doing what we loved doing. I wouldn't have missed it for the world." Franca's memories were the same. "The war brought the dancers closer together. There was a lot of camaraderie. Nobody was stuck up. Like a family under attack, we went out of our way to help each other."[33]

Like many British people who experienced the Blitz and, later, the V-1 bombings of London, Celia lost family members. Her aunt Annie's husband was killed in January and, shortly after, their East London home was demolished. Solly Franks took in his sister and one of his nieces for the rest of the war. The other two nieces were evacuated to the countryside.

Although the Sadler's Wells company never experienced a direct hit while performing, there were plenty of near misses.

The dishevelled trio of Walter Gore, Bill Meadmore, and Celia during the blitz in Chelsea. Courtesy of Library and Archives Canada, e008439022

Once the air sirens began, a red light flashed on from the stage, stating "Air Raid in Progress." A notice in the program advised the audience that, in the case of air raids, it was permissible to leave the theatre, but to do so calmly and quietly. The dancers never left the stage.

The provincial towns did not escape bombings. An engagement in Bath had to be cancelled after the venue received a direct hit the night before the company had been scheduled to perform. Several of the company's men, including the musical director, Constant Lambert, who had bedded down in the theatre, were very lucky to remain alive. Writing at midnight on August 28, 1942, from Newcastle, Celia captured another close call.

Well, the warning went about five minutes ago when Palma [Nye] and I were in the bath. The guns are making a hell of a row and they don't sound very comforting so having donned our pyjamas ready for bed, we've undonned them and put on skirts and jumpers in case we have to run. It's a nuisance.

This week I'm really tired and want to go to bed early and there has to be a raid. We did *Lac* tonight. It was so hot. We were all dripping when we came off.

On their "free" Sunday, the dancers were busy mending tights or trying to find hot water to wash sweaty practice clothes, responding to fan mail or just catching up on sleep. Frequently, they travelled in standing-room only trains filled with servicemen, and once they arrived expected to find their own accommodations. Many of the artists' lodgings were shabby and bedbug-infested. Food, of course, was strictly rationed. This was particularly hard for Celia, who remained a vegetarian. All basic necessities, including hot water, were in short supply. Regulations dictated that bathtubs could only have five inches of water, which had to be reused by a number of dancers. By the time the last person got out of the tub, the water was black. Dancers returning to their digs in strange towns would whistle out ballet music, and those who had already arrived would respond by whistling back the same tune and so guide them through the pitch black night to their lodgings.

Occasionally they would take in a film on a rare afternoon off. In London, between the matinee and evening performances, Celia might join other dancers at a Greek café on nearby Bleecker Street. They often left their stage makeup on as they lingered over a pot of tea and a pastry. When Cyril Frankel got leave, he took Celia for cakes at the Bertaux coffee shop on Greek Street.

While touring, Celia liked to nip into junk shops looking for inexpensive Victorian jewellery. Offstage, Celia dressed up for the minor celebrity role she had created for herself. She favoured a black skirt and sweater, which she dressed up with brooches. While in York she got her ears pierced and thereafter wore earrings. She wore her shiny long black hair either loose, in pigtails, or swept up in a chignon. For an exotic, dramatic look, she applied to her face the white foundation she used on stage, with darkly pencilled-in eyebrows and a slash of dark red lipstick; this was her "face," and throughout her life Celia made sure she never appeared in public without it.

Celia was far from alone in recognizing she had a public image. English dancers — above all, prima ballerina Margot Fonteyn — acquired celebrity status. While the American troops had their pinups, such as Jane Russell or Betty Grable, the equivalents for many of the English soldiers were Moira Shearer and Margot Fonteyn. Touring throughout England, the company danced in garrison theatres and special performances for factory workers. Servicemen, English as well as Canadians and Americans, attended ballet performances in provincial towns. Even Tyrone Guthrie was surprised by the men's reaction to ballet. "*Les Sylphides*, with a young gentleman whirling around among white muslin cory-phées to waltzes and mazurkas of Chopin, proved exactly the stuff to give the troops. Indeed, what everyone wanted almost as much as food or drink during those years was to see youthful and beautiful creatures beautifully moving through ordered evolutions to a predestined and satisfactory close."[34] There were, of course, servicemen who catcalled at the sight of men in tights and for whom the sole reason for not falling asleep or stomping out was the promise of seeing the shapely legs of the ballerinas. But Guthrie had recognized an essential truth: at the very least, ballet provided the redemptive qualities of grace and beauty in contrast to the brutality and death everywhere around them. Back in London, ballet tickets became as hard to get as butter. People queued for tickets for as long as ten hours.

ALTHOUGH CELIA NEVER REACHED the prominence of Shearer or Fonteyn, she developed her own coterie of special fans, some who sent her letters and food parcels. Easily her greatest fan was Doris Margolis. Unlike the so-called "gallery girls" — young women who could only afford tickets up in the galleries and who hung around the stage door to catch a close-up glimpse of their favourite dancer — Doris, who had come to London from South Africa, was a mature woman who watched from a comfortable seat in the dress circle. She focused on Celia Franca. One connecting link likely was their Jewish heritage. Their friendship began in 1942 with Doris sending her notes and food parcels. Celia replied, addressing her first as Miss Margolis, but later "darling Dotty" or "Dotski." Whenever Celia was on tour, Doris would send welcoming telegrams and postcards to help brighten up the dancer's dressing room or digs. "I find it cheers me to look up and see something lovely when I'm not feeling good," Celia wrote back.

Celia began to stay with Doris during her four week periods in London to avoid Leo, from whom she was becoming increasingly estranged. Eventually, along with another dancer, Doris and Celia rented a flat at 37 Ascot Court, in fashionable St. John's Woods. Doris became a kind of house mother to her dancer flatmates, cooking, forever running errands, and providing some financial support. In return, this lonely spinster got a vicarious inside view of the ballet world.[35] While on tour, Celia sent her daily letters, pencilled on small notepads, detailing the minutia of the dancer's life: finding digs, the terrible food, the gossip and the personality tensions, critiques of her performances and of those of other dancers. Thus, Celia reported from Bristol,

> Everything's going wrong this week and we've just about had enough of it. Rotten *Prelude* tonight — kept forgetting *Quest* and even *Hamlet* was awful. This morning in the dressing room I stood on the dressing table to open the window and the heavy mirror fell and hit Sheila on the head — nothing serious, but it didn't do our tempers any good. At the same time I stood on my hand mirror and broke that.

The Sheila in Celia's letter was Sheila Fleming, who went by the stage name Anne Lascelles, often referred to by Celia as Annie, and who was the other dancer forming the trio at the Ascot Court flat. A member of the corps de ballets, Anne was considered high-strung — but, in one particular instance, for good reason. The company's musical director, Constant Lambert, was the Svengali-like lover of Margot Fonteyn and had been for years. If not earlier, the company learned about the affair on the night of the evacuation from Holland when someone flung open the door to warn Lambert to get dressed, only to discover Fonteyn in bed with him.[36]

Lambert's considerable appetite was not satiated by Fonteyn. Sheila Fleming/Anne Lascelles had also caught his fancy. While others had silently submitted to Lambert's advances, Lascelles' involvement became more obvious. Celia said, "Anne was not exotic but she had a physique very much like Margot's: nice legs and feet, a slim body and a pretty head. Dark brown hair. Constant had his eye on her. She would be sitting on the stage as a fairy in *The Nutcracker* and he would be conducting and looking at her the whole time. It was a little embarrassing, but it was not a long-lived affair." Acting as a go-between, Celia was invited to Fonteyn's hotel one afternoon. "We chatted about it briefly — she was very cool and dignified — it was all typically British."[37] Lascelles dropped out of the company in 1944 and left Ascot Court to move back home. There was no concept of sexual harassment in 1940s England.

THE JULY 1944 DANCE season at London's New Theatre had been a particularly harrowing experience due to the daily V-1 attacks. A majority of London theatres had decided to close. During one performance when Robert Helpmann and Margot Fonteyn were dancing the *Black Swan* pas de deux, an ominous silence occurred as a rocket's engine cut out. While the audience froze waiting to hear the explosion, the dancers continued and Fonteyn, with sang-froid, turned to the audience and gave her radiant smile.[38]

Celia became so physically and emotionally exhausted that occasionally she slept through the bombings while Doris cowered in the flat. Other times, the two of them, as Celia explained in a letter to Cyril, had to "trot down to the basement."

IN AN IDYLLIC RESPITE from the incessant bombing, Celia and Anne were invited to spend their August 1944 two-week vacation at Eversley, Hertfordshire — the country home of a new friend, Kay Ambrose. Though seven years older, Ambrose rivalled Celia for vitality and capability. They had met through their mutual friend, Cyril Frankel.

While Kay enjoyed boasting that she had been thrown out of her home by her father after he found nude sketches from her life studies class at art school, she had, in fact, received a solid middle-class upbringing as the second of three daughters of Captain Charles and Lina Ambrose. A talented illustrator, Kay had studied Fine Arts at Reading University, there meeting dance writer Arnold Haskell and collaborating with him on two books: *Ballet* (1938) and

Kay Ambrose sketching Celia at her country home in August 1944. While the war food rations had made Celia slightly plump, her golden tan and her black hair made her look luscious. Courtesy of Library and Archives Canada, e008406974

Balletomane's Sketchbook (1943). A fan of more than ballet, Ambrose later became the artistic director of Indian dancer Ram Gapal's company and accompanied them to India and North America.[39]

When Kay was not working with the RAF Benevolent Fund, she was backstage in the wings of the New Theatre sketching ballet dancers, many of her illustrations being published in the *Dancing Times*. She regarded it as her mission to educate the English public about dance and published a series of her own books. She dedicated *Ballet Lover's Companion: Aesthetic without Tears for the Ballet Lover* (1949) to Celia Franca, "Whose inspiration and beauty are equaled only by her love and understanding of the art of ballet and by her patience with her grateful friend, Kay Ambrose." Interspersed are illustrations of Celia in poses for *Les Sylphides*.

During their vacation, Kay came up with the idea for another book, this one using photos of Celia and Anne Lascelles in an outdoor setting. *Ballet Impromptu*[40] captured the two dancers in practice. Kay wrote accompanying text. The photographer shot the ballerinas putting Ambrose through a ballet exercise. The caption read, "Does that hurt, good." One compelling picture captured Celia in side-profile with that famous Nefertiti-like long neck and jutting chin with her long, tousled, dark hair swept back from her face.

Quite different versions of their vacation reached Cyril in letters. Kay reported that Celia got as brown as a berry and looked beautiful. She always illustrated her letters with charming little sketches, and this letter included a whimsical drawing of Celia and Sheila, dressed in ballet tutus while up to their knees in water, picking flowers. She explained, "Below is a sketch which is not a fantasy but (practically) the Naked Truth."

Celia also wrote Cyril about her holiday. But the tone of her letter was curiously truculent.

> Last night she [Ambrose] told me about the time when she was in Oxford and you told her to part her hair in the middle

and when she got to your room there was a photograph of me in it, so she pretended to you that she was jealous or something. Well, that's how she is all the time. She has the local air force in almost every evening but makes quite sure that they all admire her the most. For instance, one evening there was some swing music on the gramophone. Kay was busy talking with one bloke — another bloke was looking at me and we were both clapping our hands in rythum [sic] and any moment were about to break into dance. Just as he got up to move towards me, Kay sprang up and dragged him off. She's very quick — very witty — very clever — but is purely wasting her time being completely superficial. She mistrusts me slightly cos' she knows I see right through her, but we are really very good friends and she even went so far as to say that I was the only person she could be natural with. Not that she often behaves naturally to me. She'd be afraid I'd get a hold on her or something. Then she'd no longer be Queen of the May but would have a rival ... However when she forgets to act with me, I perceive a very strong sincerity and an ability to get things done if she can get a bit of glory out of it. I think we'll probably work well together afterwards.

What is especially revealing about this rambling tirade is Celia's inability to recognize her own jealousy of Kay competing for Cyril's affection and, even more startling, her own need to be centre of attention. It's possible that Kay, besides sharing intelligence and a raunchy sense of humour, was infatuated with Celia. Celia had a vitality and quick-wittedness that made people want to be with her.

Celia had permanently left Leo Kersley. After she had moved into the apartment at Ascot Court, Leo would often drop by. Celia resented him visiting her there and tried to avoid him. She began to find his behaviour disturbing. She wrote to a friend, "Have had many extraordinary letters from Leo. Am convinced he's going mad. Margot says she's had one from him that she couldn't make out at all. Have you seen him at all?"

After a tumultuous period in which they tried to get back together, Celia declared that they had nothing in common and that she was "fed up." Each of them went their separate ways. Leo had written to her near the end of 1942, "Celia, I really can't see what else love can be than what we share and I think that the same miserable results will ensue whenever you turn a friend into a lover unless he is mighty lethargic." It seems that Leo had been disappointed in his wife's lack of enthusiasm in having sex with him. Quite likely Celia feared becoming pregnant and thereby losing her career as a ballet dancer. While her physical feelings towards him cooled, she never lost her deep appreciation of the nurturing role Leo and his parents had played in her artistic development. In a letter to Doris from Newcastle, Celia said, "I stood on a bridge for hours looking at the water and twisting streets hundreds of feet below and I blessed Leo for having made me realize six years ago that eyes are meant to be seen with." But once Celia had benefited from his teaching her to open her eyes to nature and culture, she no longer had use for him.

While the two of them never lived together after 1942, Leo remained hopeful. He wrote her a note on February 27, 1947, reminding her that it was the fifth anniversary of their wedding "that we've celebrated—or passed over!—and I wonder how many more there will be." Their official divorce was the next year.[41]

THE WARTIME YEARS HAD taken Celia to some of her highest peaks as a dancer. She had joined the Sadler's Wells to take over June Brae's roles, such as the source of evil in Frederick Ashton's *Dante Sonata* or Myrtha in *Giselle*. But as ballet companies must continue to create new repertoire for their audiences, Celia Franca began to have roles created for her by some of England's greatest choreographers.

At the end of 1941, Frederick Ashton, Sadler's Wells' main choreographer, was called up to serve in the Royal Air Force. The Australian-born Robert Helpmann, a principal dancer, who was exempt from service, stepped in as a choreographer and began to create his dramatic—some may say melodramatic—ballets. In each of his wartime ballets he choreographed a role specifically for Celia, recognizing her theatricality and her talent as a dramatic dance actress. The two of them were able to play off each other on stage.

In 1942, Celia danced the role of Hamlet's mother, Gertrude, in Helpmann's interpretation of Shakespeare's tragedy as a type of Freudian nightmare with scenes flashing through Hamlet's mind as he lies dying. In this short mime drama dance, Celia, costumed in a dark turquoise and green velvet gown with gold braid, played the evil mother opposite Margot Fonteyn as the vulnerable Ophelia, in a pale green gown. Celia enjoyed the role. "I loved drinking the poison and falling down the stairs."[42]

Hamlet opened at the New Theatre on May 19, 1942. A photo of Franca, Fonteyn, and Helpmann in a scene from *Hamlet* still hangs on a staircase wall amid photos of such British theatre luminaries as Lawrence Olivier and Richard Burton.

Helpmann's choreographic notes show that he specifically had Franca in mind for the role as the Bad Woman or prostitute in his fall 1944 ballet *Miracle in the Gorbals*.[43] The role was a natural for her; with her dark, suggestive looks and willingness to take risks, Celia was ideal for wicked-women roles being cast as either a witch or a bitch.[44] Set in the slums of Glasgow, this was a morality dance using social realism to explore religiosity and violence. Celia made her first appearance on stage, a lit cigarette in hand, lurking provocatively in a doorway while three crones looked at her askance as a young man approached her. To play the part, Celia did some on-site research. She hung around West End London watching prostitutes in action to study how they walked, strutted, and leaned up against the wall in their short, tight skirts.

To look the part, Celia wore a revealing dress with a low-cut

Margot Fonteyn as Ophelia, Robert Helpmann as Hamlet, and Celia Franca as Hamlet's mother. Helpmann had commissioned artist Leslie Hurry for the magnificent backdrop. Hurry would later design for Ontario's Stratford Festival. Courtesy of Tunbridge/Tunbridge-Sedgwick Pictorial Press/Hulton Archive/Getty Images neck, shiny black patent shoes, and black silk stockings. As it was wartime, a single pair of stockings had to do for every performance. Celia made them herself from a pair of rationed black stockings, which she sewed onto black panties. When her silk stockings got a run in them, she used a black eyebrow pencil to "fill in" the holes.

In advance of its London debut on October 24,[45] *Miracle in the Gorbals* generated widespread anger in Glasgow, with the Lord Provost protesting that "The traditional razor slashers of Glasgow are pure fiction as applied to the city today."[46] This publicity naturally heightened the interest of the London audience.

The reactions of dance critics were mixed. The *Daily Express* found it "a sensational modern allegory, brilliantly executed and staged"; the *New Statesman,* though, commented, "But isn't slap-up melodrama, however well mimed and put over, a waste of this company's talent for dancing?" Celia, though, was singled out for praise in the December 1944 *Dancing Times:* "Highest praise must be given to Celia Franca as the Prostitute, who in a most exquisite piece of acting revealed all the delicate shades of emotion that this most difficult role demands from a brazen effrontery to madonna-like simplicity." Dance critic Arnold Haskell gave an intriguingly ambivalent compliment of Celia's portrayal, "Her prostitute is altogether admirable and develops as the performance proceeds, until it finds a spirituality missing in so much of her work."

Celia was not impressed with Helpmann's choreography. In a January 1945 letter to Cyril, she wrote, "As for *Gorbals,* there isn't one psychologically correctly drawn character in it. At the best it's a quick dramatic thrill because everything is vulgarly, blatantly stated."

Celia paid a personal price for her role in *Gorbals.* The role called for her to come on stage with a lit cigarette in her mouth, and this led her to become a heavy smoker. It was not the first time she had started smoking; she had, in fact, smoked when she was fourteen — likely influenced by the chorus girls she was working with in *Spread It Abroad* — but had given it up a short while later. This time, however, the habit took several decades to break.

Earlier in 1943, Frederick Ashton was given time off from the Royal Air Force to choreograph a new work. *The Quest* was a reworking of the story of St. George and the Dragon, although there was no dragon in the production. Fonteyn danced as Una, who symbolized Truth, while Celia was the false Una, a temptress who tries to seduce the saintly knight. Celia also played the Wrath, dressed in pink and orange flame colours, and carrying a dagger and blazing torch. When making the quick costume change from the false Una to the Wrath, Celia struggled to pull clinging woollen garments onto her sweating body.

During the rehearsals of this ballet, the music composer, William Walton, sent sections of the score by train. His hastily scribbled music was rhythmically difficult and Ashton, knowing that Celia read music, asked her to decipher the score. "As I worked out the number of beats in the bars, I couldn't help reading some of Walton's handwritten instructions, including 'This is where Saint George fucks Una.'"

Celia treasured for the rest of her life a letter Ashton sent her in April 1943. "It was a great pleasure for me to work with someone so musically sensitive and with such a keen dramatic sense in the best of the word. You do your small part most beautifully and I couldn't be more pleased. Love, Fred."[47]

Three weeks after the allied D-Day invasion of Normandy in June 1944, Celia found herself on the New Theatre stage hanging high off the ground perched in a huge gleaming spider's web. She was starring in Andrée Howard's *Le Festin de l'Araignée* (or *The Spiders Banquet*). In order to move as a spider, she had to imagine that she had eight limbs instead of just her legs and arms. She had taken a book out of the library to research spiders.

Moira Shearer played the role of the pretty butterfly, caught in the bottom of the web, waiting helplessly to be attacked by the spider. A stagehand, Horace, sitting up in the flies, had the job of shifting Celia up and down like a puppet. To move, she had to make jerking movements with her head, signalling when Horace should take her up or down. One performance she jerked her head down several times. Nothing happened and Shearer whispered loudly, "Come down, come get me, why aren't you here, you're late on your cue." Long past her music cue, Horace unceremoniously dropped her down. Afterwards, a furious Celia confronted Horace, demanding an explanation. His reply was, "I went out for a beer."[48]

In its July review of *Le Festin,* the *Dancing Times* again singled out Celia's performance. "The role of the Spider was brilliantly danced by Celia Franca, who gave a very clever suggestion of the movements of this unpleasant creature."[49]

Celia actually didn't think much of the choreography for *Le Festin de l'Araignée,* but she relished her success. Writing to her confidant Doris on July 24, she boasted, "Andrée Howard was very

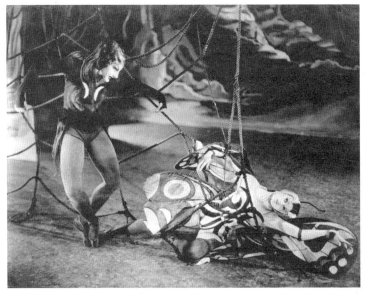

Celia as the rapacious spider attacking the beautiful butterfly, Moira Shearer, in Andrée Howard's ballet *Le Festin de l'Araignée.* Kay Ambrose suggested Celia request danger pay for dangling high up in the spider's web. Photograph by Edward Maninian, Dance Collection Danse

pleased with me and thanked me for understanding her language. I've made a small personal success out of the Spider."

While rehearsing *Le Festin de l'Araignée*, Celia played with fire by dating the twenty-three-year-old set designer, Michael Ayrton. This bad boy attracted a bohemian set to his glass-roofed studio flat in All Saints' Place. From her comments to Doris, she knew he could only be a short fling. "I've been out with him a couple of times. He seems to be very much under Constant's [Lambert's] influence and drinks too much and therefore won't last too long, but he's had an interesting life — wounded in the leg in Spain. Traveled considerably and altogether might be of use."

WHILE CELIA, AS A dramatic dancer, was certainly not a prima ballerina at the Sadler's Wells, she made many friends among the company. Although regularly cast in roles as the dark against Fonteyn's light, she admired her. "Margot knew she was the star, but she was never uppity or snobbish. I never heard her say anything nasty about anybody. She was a kind person. She was a little reserved and kept to herself. But that was understandable, because she had so much responsibility playing major roles." They called each other nicknames. Celia was "Ruby." And to Celia's last days, other elderly retired Sadler's Wells dancer friends still referred to her as such.

Celia also had her jealousies. She never liked Moira Shearer, the flame-haired, beautiful butterfly to Celia's wicked spider. Her animosity to Shearer began during her short interlude with the International Ballet when Celia had had to take over another dancer's role with no time to alter the costume, which was too big. During a pirouette, she turned but the costume did not and she was thrown off pointe. Returning to the dressing room, she heard Shearer crowing over the fact that Celia had fallen off pointe.[50]

Celia managed to have the last laugh on this famous dancer during one of their 1944 tours. Celia reported to Doris that she had become infected with scabies. Celia had been treated at the Manchester Royal Infirmary. "I laughed like hell when they stretched me out naked on the plinth and whitewashed me all over with an enormous brush. Then they left me to dry off." She was ordered not to perform for a week for fear of passing scabies along to the other dancers, but Celia wrote with glee to Doris, "If Shearer wears my Gorbal's dress, she'll catch them for sure."

In her personal life, Celia tended to forge her closest friendships with other Jews, such as her roommate, Doris Margolis, or Cyril and Gerald Frankel. They shared a common background, having grown up in households that observed the various Jewish holidays and Friday night lighting of the candles followed by the traditional meal. Until she married, Celia had lived amidst Jewish communities, first in East End London and later in Golder's Green with its nearby synagogues and kosher shops.

IN THE BITTERLY COLD late January of 1945, the Sadler's Wells Ballet crossed the Channel to entertain the troops in newly liberated France and Belgium. To Celia's astonishment, Madame de Valois whipped out a bottle of brandy. "We passed it around and we all had a little nip — most unexpected."

The Times reported on February 6 on the effect the intense cold weather was having on the dancers. Lack of coal meant the theatre had been unheated and caused a main water pipe to burst, flooding the auditorium. It had been so cold that the grease paint in their makeup boxes had frozen solid and the dancers had to breathe on them to thaw them out enough to smear on their faces. Throwing off their army coats just before going on stage, the dancers in their flimsy costumes had been covered in goosebumps. Their billeting had been only slightly better. Although they had been put up in officers' hotels with two to a room, these luxurious accommodations had been marred by the lack of heat and hot water.

After the strict rationing in England, the army food and the frequent officers' parties made it hard for Celia to refrain from gorging, especially on sardines and chocolates. Seeing herself in a photo taken on stage during this trip, she described herself as looking "positively three dimensional."

After three weeks in Belgium, the company moved on to Paris. There they were put up in a hotel that had been commandeered by the Allied Forces. Celia observed, "While being fed the best army food, you'd look out the window and see starving French men, women and children rummaging through garbage cans for scraps of food." What Margot Fonteyn recalled most vividly were the little crosses commemorating patriots who had been killed on the streets of Paris.[51]

The performers were issued khaki military uniforms, including much-needed thick overcoats. All the female dancers hated the army-issued boots. The queen's milliner styled fashionable turbans for Madame de Valois, Margot Fonteyn, and Pamela May.

Celia in her ENSA uniform in Paris, France. Courtesy of the National Ballet of Canada Archives

Fonteyn and May substituted their khaki ties with French scarves, which they had bought on the Champs-Elysées and their boots with high heels. Celia recalled, "We were just a bunch of ballet people, for goodness sake, sent out to boost morale of the troupes and civilians. And who was going to tick us off for going against army regulations. Nobody, that's who."

Attired in their uniforms, the dancers attended social events. At one such affair in the grand salon of Princess Radiziwill Tuede, Celia found herself in company with several French dance stars such as Roland Petit.

The Sadler's Wells Ballet gave eight performances at the Théâtre des Champs-Elysées with a program that included *Miracle in the Gorbals,* and also appeared at the Théâtre Marigny, where the company performed for American service personnel. Before returning to England, the company entertained troops in Ghent, Bruges, and Ostend.

On VE Day, with the company back in London at the New Theatre, the curtain went up for the first act of *Coppelia,* revealing Robert Helpmann as Dr. Coppelius perched on a ladder. He had added a Union Jack, and a V for Victory hung over his front door. The audience loved it.

Later that year, in November, the company undertook a second European tour, this time to entertain Allied troops stationed in Hanover,[52] Hamburg, and Berlin. Celia, looking out the train window at the devastation, wrote to Doris, "You can't imagine how depressing a sight it is. Miles of derelict buildings and millions of German people with bundles clinging on the running boards of trains, sitting on top freezing, crowding into cattle trucks — all miserable and sullen."

JUST BEFORE LEAVING FOR Germany, Celia read an announcement in the *Dancing Times:* "The Governors of Sadler's Wells and the Covent Garden Committee have arranged that after January 1,

1946, the Sadler's Wells Ballet Company will operate under the management of the Covent Garden Committee as the resident ballet company in the Royal Opera House, for an initial period of four years." The Sadler's Wells was to become the country's national ballet company. Key responsibility for this reconfiguration of the Sadler's Wells Ballet was none other than the influential economist Maynard Keynes.[53] Prompted by his wife, the Russian ballerina Lydia Lopokova, Keynes had become a keen fan of Ninette de Valois and her company.

Frederick Ashton convinced an initially apprehensive de Valois that the company was ready to take up residency at the Royal Opera House. Converting the Opera House from a dance hall for servicemen — a sign, "no jitterbugging," had been posted over the stage's proscenium arch — back to its red and gold gilt splendour, required a frantic scramble. Nevertheless, the curtain went up on February 20, 1946, for Sadler's Wells Ballet's first performance of *The Sleeping Beauty*.

Absent from those dancers who glided across the stage was Celia Franca.

FOUR

Adam (Zero) and Eve (of St. Agnes)

T HE EXPLANATION CELIA CONTRIVED for her absence from that first evening of *The Sleeping Beauty* by the Sadler's Wells Ballet Company at the Royal Opera House has never varied. It was that after reading the cast list and realizing that she would "simply die of boredom" dancing the same role for three months, she quit.

There might be some truth to this account; earlier, Celia had walked out of a well-paid position with the International Ballet Company rather than perform in Russian classical ballets she regarded as "museum pieces." There was also a fair amount of craftiness to her version. In the fall of 1945, Celia had begun hearing a most disturbing rumour — namely, that June Brae was ready to return to the company. Brae was the dancer who had left the Sadler's Wells early in the war at the insistence of her husband and had started a family rather than travel across the country entertaining soldiers and civilians. Celia had inherited nearly all of Brae's dramatic dance roles. Afterwards, new roles had been created specifically for Celia.

More disturbing, de Valois had planned to give Brae the role in Robert Helpmann's new ballet *Adam Zero*,[54] scheduled to be the first new piece of choreography presented by the Sadler's Wells in its new Covent Garden home. Celia, already in rehearsals with Helpmann, had been expecting to have this major role. In the final moments of the dance, as Death, dressed in a flowing red cape, she would swoop down menacingly over Adam, a broken old man.

Apparently, Helpmann had fought on Celia's behalf but could only persuade de Valois to give her second cast status. Celia poured out her heart in a letter to Doris:

> I fear that June Brae will take back all her original roles from me. Well there is one thing I refuse to do and that is to play second fiddle to her and anyone else. I explained to Mr. Webster, our new Covent Garden boss, when I had my interview with him on Friday that up until now I'd been going up steadily and that I didn't want to suffer the embarrassment of a decline that I'd seen too many dancers suffer it. He said that he quite understood but that I must speak to de Valois about it. He told me I was to get a £2 raise in salary which is as much as any girl is receiving. He actually had the cheek to deny any knowledge of June Brae. Can you believe it? Well, unless I do the first night of Bobby's new ballet. I'm leaving. I'd rather starve than be 2nd cast in a ballet which is really nice.

As she scribbled away on the train, Celia became more and more angry.

> The cheek of these bloody dancers. They desert the ballet for years on end and when it suits them they expect to come back to as high a position as they had before. Poor old Franca

has slaved her guts out to keep up the dramatic standard in a shit company and then is expected to step down to make room for a shitty dancer who doesn't love ballet at all except when she's fed up with husband and child and feels like a bit of easy money and glory. Why should she have the press notices. She's done nothing to deserve it. She deserted the ballet when it needed her. I stepped in and filled a gap — and that's the thanks I get for it — 2nd cast. I'd rather not do it at all.

Celia ended her letter, "The regular ballet goers will now think that I was only the Queen in *Hamlet* and the *Gorbals* because June Brae wasn't there. Mind you, that's just about right but I don't see why the audience should know." In the intimacy of this note, Celia acknowledged what she had known all along. She had never really belonged to the Sadler's Wells Ballet company.

Newspapers in early 1946 were full of news about the return of Brae. One photo spread featured her in rehearsals with her three-year-old daughter, Piera Sue, peeking from behind the curtain. As a last gamble, Celia confronted directly the formidable Madame de Valois. Nothing changed. She was to be the second cast in Helpmann's new ballet.

On the first day of rehearsals of *The Sleeping Beauty*, Celia made her way to Covent Garden, later telling Cyril she had "only misery poking at [her] heart." As she scanned the cast list, her premonition of "misery" proved correct. Although perceptive enough to know she would not be given a major role, she had hoped to get the part of the Countess in the hunting scene. She discovered that not only had she not been cast as the Countess, but she hadn't made second cast. De Valois had humiliated her by giving her a minor role as an attendant to the Countess. Franca wrote to Cyril, "Then I went to the dressing room feeling that the end of the world had come." She felt trapped with no way out. As she ended her letter to Frankel: "It was all too much for me. I got dressed and walked out leaving Britain's No 1 Ballet Company to get on with it. I went home and cried my eyes out because I knew I had to leave and felt I was weak for not having stuck it out."

The February 20, 1946, opening night must have been one of the worst times in Celia's life as she sat at home with Doris. She had indeed "slaved her guts out" to keep up the dramatic standard during nearly five years of continual performing. It had been grossly unfair of de Valois to humiliate Celia by demoting her to such a minor role in *The Sleeping Beauty* and relegate her to second cast in *Adam Zero*. Franca's loyalty and dedication had gone unrewarded. The harsh reality was that Celia had been the stopgap until June Brae deigned to return.

London newspapers were full of stories and photos about the Sadler's Wells Ballet debut at the Royal Opera House. One article interviewed a group of women who had queued overnight in the chilly winter weather for the chance of getting one of the available twenty standing room tickets. The morning after the performance, the newspapers featured photographs of all the important dignitaries who had attended. Jennifer Homans, in her 2010 book *Apollo's Angels: A History of Ballet*, assigned this event the highest of marks. "Indeed, the performance, attended by the royal family, Prime Minister Clement Attlee and the full cabinet, was widely seen as a metaphor for Britain's awakening after the horrors of two world wars."[55]

Helpmann's *Adam Zero*, which premiered on April 10, was a disappointment and quickly disappeared from the company's repertoire. But Celia would have been annoyed by the rave review of Brae's performance from Arnold Haskell in the first *Ballet Annual* in 1947. "[Brae] seized it to make it a true personal triumph, both on the crowded stage, no easy task, and alone with Helpmann in the beautiful dance that terminates his existence."

This break between Celia Franca and Ninette de Valois was probably inevitable and most likely would have happened earlier but for the special exigencies of the war. If Brae and May had not left the company, de Valois likely would never have hired Franca. Class differences and also a lack of ease between them were factors. In addition Celia was a Rambert-trained dancer rather than a student of the Sadler's Wells school. Most substantively, Celia wasn't the kind of ethereal, quasi-virginal dancer de Valois favoured. The "triptych" of Pamela May, June Brae, and Margot Fonteyn, joined later by Moira Shearer, were classic de Valois girls. Despite Fonteyn's indiscretions with Constant Lambert, they were all deemed nice, middle-class, white-Anglo-Saxon-Protestant girls.

Celia had not melded into the company. The *Dancing Times* alerted readers to this soon after she joined. "Celia Franca has exceptional natural gifts but does not yet belong. Too audience conscious and too exotic in makeup, especially in *Les Sylphides*. When she realizes that true personality only exists within the framework of a company she should show us something exceptionally interesting."[56] Dance critic Arnold Haskell made much the same analysis, writing that her "purely classical work or her romanticism in the production of *Les Sylphides* is marred by over-emphasis and an intrusive personality." She was too dramatic, too earthy — perhaps too Jewish.

As a further flaw, Celia was too confident, and too determined to give Madame the kind of awed deference she commanded, and received, from almost all around her.

Dame Ninette de Valois never changed her mind about Celia's performance abilities. "She had ambitions to be a classical ballerina, but as I say, one always has ambitions not for one's best thing; there's that old saying, 'you love your second best talent best.'"[57]

For her part, Celia was often critical of de Valois's dramatic dance interpretations. After watching performances of *Les Sylphides* and *Carnival*, she wrote to Cyril, "The dancers carry on in the usual cold, insensitive, unromantic Wellsian manner and still no one bothers to produce them." When cast in the corps de ballet for one production, she told Cyril, "I feel superior to the Sadler's

Wells Ballet and therefore can not be hurt by whatever they thrust upon me."

Either at Celia's own instigation or independently, a claque of balletomanes campaigned on Franca's behalf to give her the role of Giselle, made so famous by Margot Fonteyn. Even the ballet mistress Vera Volkova's suggestion of giving Celia the role in one matinee performance met with a firm "no." It's said that de Valois's response to the petition was, "Oh, nonsense, she hasn't got the legs for Giselle."

It's uncertain whether Celia Franca today would have been accepted into any ballet company. While aesthetics and technical standards have changed over the years, Franca simply did not conform to the idealized ballerina body. She was the right height at five foot, four inches, and usually at a dancing weight of around 110 pounds. (Like many of the dancers during the war, she tended to plump up with the rationed diet). She had the classical ballerina's long neck, but she had short, slightly bowed legs and almost no arch or instep in her foot. (Today, the latter issue would matter far less, as technology has fashioned a ballet pointe shoe with a greater flexibility that enhances the arch.) What Celia did have was relentless ambition, a high jump, intelligence, musicality, and sensuality.

Long after the end of her dance career, Celia acknowledged her shortcomings as a ballet dancer. "My poor feet were famous among ballet insiders." She also recognized that she overacted. "My greatest fault as an artist is being too extroverted on stage. That's my own criticism of myself. If I'm inclined to do anything wrong on stage, it's over-exaggeration."[58]

Celia had made her mark playing whores — a dope fiend in *Paris Soirs*, a prostitute in *Miracle in the Gorbals* and *Rake's Progress* — or evil characters such as Hamlet's mother, Gertrude; the false Una; the Wrath in *The Quest;* and the poisonous arachnid in *Le Festin D'Araignee.* Her showiness, sometimes criticized as a defect, was at least as often praised. An anecdote Celia loved to tell about herself was the comment from a local shopkeeper after she left the Sadler's Wells Ballet. "Oh what a pity, there will never be another prostitute like Miss Franca."

CELIA'S ABRUPT DEPARTURE DID not entirely end her relationship with de Valois. In the same long, anguished letter to Frankel, Celia recounted, "I wrote to de Valois and received a charming letter back with a couple of backhanders thrown in." Evidently, Celia, in her resignation letter, had disclosed that she was turning her attention to choreography. Whether or not by design, she had presented de Valois with an opportunity to put right her unjust demotion of Franca from the main company. At the time of the transfer to the Royal Opera House, de Valois had negotiated for a second company, the Sadler's Wells Theatre Ballet, to remain headquartered at the old Sadler's Wells Theatre. She envisioned it as a type of incubator company to enable young choreographers to experiment using senior students from the school as well as established dancers from the parent ballet company. De Valois quickly offered Franca the opportunity to mount a piece on this junior company as she had been impressed with a small piece, *Cancion*, that Franca had choreographed and performed for the Ballet Guild in July 1942. (*Cancion* had been a family affair with her father-in-law Edwin "Puff" Kersley designing her costume.)

Celia jumped at the opportunity. She already had the germ of an idea using Sibelius's *Night Music*. She told Cyril, "Well, to cut a long story short with Gerald's [Frankel's] help I got the scenario fixed up. Then when Gerald left I spent a couple of days locked up at home and got the choreography worked out..... Now I shall write to de Valois and suggest it. She will refuse and that will be that."

In fact, de Valois's gesture in inviting Celia to come up with choreographic suggestions had not been a placatory gesture. She had identified early on Celia's aptitude for creating ballets as well as for dancing dramatic roles. Celia was shrewd enough and ambitious enough to realize this and to act on it.

The plot of *Khadra* was transparently autobiographical. The heroine, Khadra, is a young girl who watches life going on around her. She sees lovers whose solitude is disturbed by the crowd. Alone and detached she joins with the crowd, and at nightfall sees the pictures of their mingling shadows. Celia's estranged husband Leo said, "Khadra, to whom it all happened, was really the Choreographer when Young, for as a child, Franca used to sit on the kerbstone, apart in her own world, watching the other children playing in London's somewhat Oriental east end."[59]

Celia explained the plot to Cyril in a letter. "I think it's alright. I explained the whole thing — demonstrated, played the record and brought the books of Persian Art for Honor and she was most enthusiastic. She strikes me as the sort of person who wouldn't hesitate to say if she thought it was tripe."

The "Honor" Celia refers to in her letter was Honor Frost, an archaeologist and curator at the Tate Gallery who Celia had asked to design the sets. She was another intelligent, strong-willed woman friend of Cyril Frankel. Celia liked her from the beginning. "Honor Frost is everything Kay Ambrose isn't," Celia told Cyril. "She's sincere, genuine, intelligent, attractive, natural and has the goods necessary for what we want. I like her designs and drawings immensely." For her part, Honor vividly remembered going to Celia's St. John's Wood flat to hear about *Khadra* "During that first evening she told me the scenario, she played the records of *Belshazzar's Feast* on a deplorable portable gramophone, danced all the principal roles, breathlessly explained the positions of the imaginary *Corps de Ballet*. I questioned her, we went over certain passages again, and, thanks to her efforts, I left with the whole shape of the ballet clearly in my mind."[60]

Their encounter quickly developed into a true partnership with Frost designing the elaborate costumes and set designs. In order not to waste time, Celia moved into Frost's flat near Baker

Street for close to three months, working from early morning until past midnight. Along with rehearsing the dancers, Celia sewed costumes with Honor in the evenings.

Rationing was still in effect and Celia had to calculate the number of coupons necessary for costume yardage. She reckoned that for forty yards of wool stockinette, one hundred and eighty coupons were needed. She begged and borrowed coupons from whomever was around.[61] These costumes were a labour of love, all made from clinging white wool stockinette bought in bulk and dyed an array of rich, bold colours. The cut of the costumes was simple, with long-waisted, tight-fitting jumpers with straight split skirts for the girls and shorter belted tunics for the men.

At Frost's direction, over one hundred colour blocks were printed on costumes by hand by a newly demobilized craftsman who had returned to the theatre from fighting in Burma. Again because of a scarcity of materials, headdresses were improvised out of plastic-wire straw, cellophane straw, and horsehair. The brightly coloured decor featured a pink background, split by a bright blue balustrade and dark green dado covered with stylized yellow, green, and purple flowers.

The two women — Celia dark-haired and glamorous, Honor blond and usually dressed in trousers — attracted a good deal of publicity. An article in the London *Star* on April 26, 1946, accompanied by a photo of the two of them, told readers that the young women were working sixteen hours a day, sewing costumes until one a.m. with only time to grab a sandwich. Celia was quoted as saying she hardly had the time for her "all-the-year round cold bath."

Celia worked with a tiny maroon notebook in which she made notes about *Khadra*. She had the cast list with their phone numbers to call up for rehearsals and costume fittings. She reported to Cyril,

The first 2 scenes are not bad at all. Ninette has seen them — thinks they are excellent and has not asked for alterations, but as you may remember the centre of interest lies on the

Celia and Honor Frost in front of the Sadler's Wells Theatre to publicize *Khadra*.
© Roger Wood Photographic Collection, Royal Opera House Collections

principals. I've started on the 3rd scene & am hampered by
the inefficiency of the corps de ballet. I spent 20 minutes
teaching one girl one step. After the rehearsal she came
up to me & said "Oh Celia, I do like your ballet. You know
although your steps are difficult and stylized I find them
much easier to learn than Andrée Howard's because you
teach so well." I nearly hit her.

Celia had cast Leo Kersley as the passionate Persian lover, opposite the fifteen-year-old Anne Heaton. He recalls that Celia sat at the beginning of each rehearsal with a tin of one hundred Players cigarettes and that by the end her chair would be ringed with cigarette butts.

Celia backstage with Ninette de Valois after a performance of *Khadra*, a ballet in which Celia copied poses from Persian paintings and pushed the conventions of classical ballet style. © Roger Wood Photographic Collection, Royal Opera House Collections

On May 27, 1946, the curtain at the Sadler's Wells Theatre rose for the premier of *Khadra*. After a three-minute musical overture, the curtains parted to reveal a set replicating a Persian painting with exotic birds and lush plants against an ornate background featuring shades of pinks and golds.[62] The production put the knowledgeable audience members in mind of Diaghilev's Ballets Russes dances such as *Schéhérazade*: the sets and costumes evoked Oriental atmosphere and exotica, and the choreography sometimes put the dancers into positions where shoulders were turned at right angles to hips, while knees, elbows, and wrists bent sharply, rather than in traditional, graceful, rounded positions..

The audience reaction was ecstatic. Celia boasted to Cyril,

> It was so exciting and I think the reception was really genuine. What was so nice was that people realized that it was a real collaboration of music, décor and choreography. Honor did a really fine job and deservedly got much praise from critics and audience. Beaumont [Cyril Beaumont was one of the most influential British dance critics of the twentieth century] liked it but made a few criticisms when I went to see him, only one of which I agreed with.

Celia was clear-sighted enough to add,

> Now I see the ballet from the front I hate it and want to get on with another. I see so many things wrong with the choreography. Rambert liked it but criticized the choreography of *Khadra*'s dance which is shortsighted of her. You see the child couldn't do the dance my way and sometimes it looks as if the choreography is too sharp for the music, but as she at least does it another way and makes a good performance of it, I'm not grumbling at her. She's only 15 and one can't achieve more than a certain amount at that age.[63]

One particularly enthusiastic response came from none other than Celia's father, Solomon Franks. He had reluctantly attended the opening and, when Celia took her curtain call as the choreographer, he nudged the person next to him to announce she was his daughter. This was uncharacteristic for Solomon, who had never felt comfortable with his daughter on the stage. Perhaps he felt a choreographer was a more respectable occupation. When Celia told the story years later, there was a tone of bitterness as she said, "Finally he was proud of me."[64]

There were other reasons for Celia's pride. She told Cyril,

> Ninette nearly clapped her hands off I'm told. She's offered
> me a job to run her new school which she's opening in
> Baron's Court. She realizes that I produce well and doesn't
> want to lose me. She particularly wanted me to take "dance
> classes" that is to teach students the classical repertoire. She
> also wants me as a guest artist to both companies and to
> do another ballet for her next year. Of course I refused the
> school offer but will certainly do another ballet for her.

This ballet, *Bailemos*, proved to be far less successful. Celia
again collaborated with Frost to create a dance based on Massenet's
Le Cid, featuring groups of Spanish peasants and nobles. Celia
cast herself as one of the peasants while a young John Cranko
appeared as a nobleman. But when the dance debuted in February 1947, Frost's sombre black costumes did little to warm up an
audience experiencing the coldest winter in living memory. Later,
Celia candidly admitted she had not put enough creativity into
Bailemos and so it had deserved to be a flop. She added, "Once
you have a flop, the critics tend to forget you had a success the
year before."[65]

NO LONGER ASSURED A weekly salary as a company dancer, Celia
was constantly on the lookout for work. She wrote to Cyril with
hastily concocted ideas such as starting her own dance school by
borrowing two hundred pounds from Doris Margolis's uncle,
who, in fact, could ill-afford such a loan. She also considered
an offer from Australia to go there for nine months to deal with
"a lot of fat would-be ballerinas to knock into shape." Unlike
thousands of British people fed up with the bitterly cold weather
compounded by postwar fuel and food shortages, Celia did not
take up the offer to emigrate. Instead, she guest-performed with

the Ballet Rambert and agreed to teach a week of special classes at the Royal Academy of Dance. It paid her the substantial fee of twenty-five pounds.

Having turned down job security with a fifteen-pounds-a-week salary at the Sadler's Wells Theatre Ballet company, Celia took a three-month contract with Ballet Jooss at the much lower salary of five pounds a week. True to form, Celia was here making an artistic, rather than a financial, choice. Kurt Jooss, who brought his modern European dance company to England in 1936, was another one of Cyril Frankel's friends. He had had to flee Germany after Hitler's ascension to power having presented in 1932 a scathing antiwar-themed dance, *The Green Table*.

Celia agreed to give traditional ballet classes to the Jooss dancers as it would give her the opportunity to study European modern-dance technique. The latter was a bold departure for Celia, and demonstrates her desire to broaden her experiences. Much of modern dance, as espoused by pioneers such as the American Isadora Duncan or the German Mary Wigman, condemned what they saw as the artificiality of ballet. Jooss's combining of classical ballet with European modern dance meant his style was still within Celia's comfort zone. In 1947 Jooss remounted in London another of his major dances, *Big City*, dealing with the issue of urban isolation. Celia performed in it at the King's Theatre in Hammersmith, dancing the role of a flapper girl with David Walker.[66]

IN THE SUMMER OF 1947, Celia's gamble in quitting the Sadler's Wells Ballet Company appeared to have paid off when she was offered a position as a principal ballerina with the new Metropolitan Ballet, started the year before by Cecilia Blatch. She got along well with Blatch, comparing her to Maude Lloyd, observing that both were well-bred, upper-class ladies, but not snobbish.

Celia once again was touring. The Metropolitan Ballet visited the main cities throughout the British Isles, as well as Scandinavia and Switzerland. A highlight was the July 1948 performance of Vaughan Williams' *Pilgrim's Progress* at the Royal Opera House. Celia performed with two rising male dancers, David Adams[67] and Erik Bruhn, whose paths would cross with hers again.

Celia and dancers from the Metropolitan Ballet in a publicity photo outside the stage door of the Royal Opera House, where they were rehearsing for Vaughan Williams' *The Pilgrim's Progress*. Note the bemused David Adams leaning against the archway. Courtesy of Dance Collection Danse

The New Statesman and Nation reported, "The young company known as the Metropolitan Ballet has an artistic standard which is in some way beyond its present powers of realization. But it is a great thing to a have a standard. Expressively Celia Franca is easily the best dancer." *Illustrated*[68] ran a two-page spread on the Metropolitan Ballet's production of *Pleasuredome*, in which Celia, in her role of Flo the prostitute, was seen lolling suggestively on a pinball table. Although the *Dancing Times* was dubious about the overall production, the reviewer noted, "Celia Franca conveyed something of the soft-hearted floosie's feelings, but was handicapped by inappropriate choreography."[69]

During Celia's second year with the Metropolitan, she took on the added task of ballet mistress, giving the daily class as well as supervising rehearsals. In this capacity, she managed to get an extra dollop of publicity. A photo in Edinburgh's *Evening Dispatch* on October 30, 1948, featured Celia conducting a class for her company with a group of local students. The accompanying article explained that Celia had come up with the idea of

Metropolitan Ballet sylphs Svetlana Beriosova, Delysia Blake, Sonia Arova, and Celia Franca in Sweden. Courtesy of Library and Archives Canada, PA-210140

inviting advanced ballet students to attend classes in each town the company visited.

For two and a half years, Blatch and the Metropolitan Ballet struggled against half-empty provincial theatres as audiences were drawn away by less demanding musical comedies. The dancers, including Celia, slipped in and out of employment. One Christmas she reported sadly to a friend that she had no money to spend on presents and turkey and "all the nice things that nice people have at Christmas time" — a somewhat odd comment since Celia's traditions did not include Christmas celebrations. Ill-luck even followed the Metropolitan Ballet abroad; the company arrived in Holland just as clothing rationing was ended, with the result that potential theatre-goers were hurriedly buying new clothes, leaving them with no money for ballet tickets.

Adding to Celia's frustrations, the Sadler's Wells Ballet company was becoming tremendously popular. In 1948, Moira Shearer had starred in *The Red Shoes*, one of Britain's top ten films that year. The Sadler's Wells Ballet's first tour of the United States in 1949 made British newspaper headlines and earned Margot Fonteyn the cover of *Time* magazine.

But ballet itself was gaining popularity, and Celia, as one of the lead dancers of the Metropolitan Ballet, was featured twice on the cover of the *Dancing Times* magazine.[70]

CELIA'S MOMENTS OF GLORY were short-lived. No doubt she had to have seen the writing on the wall. The company had few theatrical engagements in 1949, with the exception of the Metropolitan Ballet participating in a Festival of Ballet in July, at Earls Court's Empress Hall with the headliners being the somewhat antiquated Russian dancers Alexandra Danilova and Leonide Massine.

Looking around for new opportunities for herself, Celia approached the BBC proposing that she choreograph a ballet specifically for television. "It seems to me," she wrote to BBC producer

Celia with the Danish dancer Poul Gnatt in *Bluebird*. During its short existence, the Metropolitan Ballet showed how Danish-trained dancers such as Gnatt and Erik Bruhn could fit into a British-style company. Courtesy of Dance Collection Danse

Christian Simpson "that television will sooner or later have to produce ballets specially written for the medium as they are doing now for plays." She had recognized that what worked on the proscenium stage, with the audience able to take in the full panorama, didn't work for two-dimensional, black-and-white television. With most of the cameras in pre-set locations, whenever a camera zoomed out, a group of dancers appeared as little matchstick figures. Television called for a new way of choreographing that would use close-ups to focus on facial expressions and hand gestures to evoke emotion.

It is likely Celia had been coached by Cyril Frankel about this idea. Television was a great interest of Cyril's, and he would eventually enter the British television field in 1953, going on to direct dozens of television series, documentaries, and feature films. Frankel was the first to create a ballet film shot and edited to choreography.

Celia already had experience in this new medium. In the late 1930s, she and her patron, Walter Gore, had performed some live dances, principally tap dance, for the then highly experimental television system. Apparently, Gore's blond hair and Celia's jet-black hair made the perfect combination for the primitive black-and-white screens. And the Metropolitan Ballet had performed on television several times.

The BBC producer, Simpson, hired Celia Franca to create the first dance drama for British television — *The Dance of Salome*. Airing December 9 and repeated on December 14, 1949, this live-to-air dance was described in the *Radio Times* as "A Dance Drama devised for television based on the play by Oscar Wilde. Choreographed by Celia Franca." The *Dancing Times*, January 1950, hailed it as "first class television." As Salome, Franca was at her dramatic best and, after her veil dance, she succumbed as four guards bore down on her and thrust swords into her body. Celia made her last image a camera shot of her fluttering hand slowly convulsing into stillness.

Following another live BBC television appearance by the Metropolitan Ballet on December 19 performing *Coppelia* and *Pleasuredome*, artistic director Cecilia Blatch announced that the company of thirty dancers and twenty musicians was folding. Apparently, the newly established Arts Council refused to provide grant money to the Metropolitan Ballet.

Celia continued to pursue her career as a television dance choreographer with *The Eve of St. Agnes*, televised on May 1, 1950. Based on a Keats poem, inspired by the legend of St. Agnes, Celia's story centred on virgins going supperless to bed and, following certain rituals, dreaming about the men they would marry. Audiences and critics greatly enjoyed this romantic tale.

With her limitless energy, Celia promoted her own television shows. She sent out a media release for *The Eve of St. Agnes* including her phone number at Ascot Court. To stir the interest of editors, she explained that the special problem of televised ballet was that the dancers were entirely unfamiliar with the camera

Before coming to Canada, Celia gained experience whipping dancers into shape as the ballet mistress of the Metropolitan Ballet. She was credited with achieving a high standard for the corps de ballet. Courtesy of Dance Collection Danse

requirements. Celia's pioneering spirit emerged before she made the move to Canada.

In response to some criticism, Celia scribbled copious pencilled notes ending with, "Much more could be said, but perhaps it will be sufficient to recall how many decades of experience have been needed for stage ballet to present its present high standard. It would be unrealistic to expect TV ballet to do the same in so short a time."

CELIA HAD BEEN MOVING at a frenzied pace since the beginning of the Second World War. She had danced (frequently more than once a day) for fifty weeks of the year for nearly five years. She had witnessed death and destruction in England and Europe. She had performed in half a dozen ballet companies. She had choreographed four dances for stage and two for television. She had written a book, *Ballerina*, warning readers that the dancer's life is one of constant work, strong discipline, and little reward.[71] She had been married and divorced and had had several affairs.

Brief entries in her diary from the summer of 1950 reveal that Celia had become utterly incapacitated with what she described as nausea, pains, and a total lack of appetite. Gertie had to take time off from the dress shop to come every day to Ascot Court to look after her daughter, who was unable to get out of bed. Celia jotted one entry "electrical treatment," which was used in those days to treat a variety of ailments. It's possible that Celia had become pregnant. In those days before reliable birth-control, ballerinas were as likely as other women to become pregnant. Margot Fonteyn had at least two abortions.[72] It's more likely that Celia's body and/or mind had said "enough" to her punishing work ethic. She did manage to pull herself together in late July to try out for a dramatic role at the Mercury Theatre. By August, she had fully recovered and recorded in her diary a trip to Edinburgh, likely to the Edinburgh Festival, with a group of male friends, among them Leo Kersley, who still cared deeply for her.

Returning from Scotland, Celia found a letter from a stranger in the pile of mail at her Ascot Court apartment. A Canadian, Stewart James, had written to Celia asking if she would meet with him on a business matter. By now fully recovered, Celia had won her audition and was about to start rehearsals, so she was squeezed for time.[73] Nevertheless, she agreed to meet James outside a stage-makeup store on Compton Street.

FIVE

Three Ladies Plus One Ballerina

T HE CIRCUMSTANCES THAT HAD brought Celia Franca and Stewart James together had been unfolding for about two and a half years, some three thousand miles away in a country and a city to which Celia had given little thought.

Not long after the Second World War, Toronto began to become an actual city rather than an overgrown town. While still overshadowed by Montreal, comparably more sophisticated, Toronto from the late 1940s onwards grew rapidly in size and wealth. One major reason was the return home of the soldiers, many with a new air of confidence and worldliness. A more important factor was immigration, with a flood of newcomers — most particularly Jews, Italians, and Greeks — arriving from war-torn Europe. In some of the poorer downtown neighbourhoods, lush tomatoes and exotic deep-purple eggplants began to appear in front gardens waiting to be harvested by old grandmothers dressed entirely in black who spoke not a word of English. As well, Toronto got a full share of Canada's postwar economic boom, one unmatched anywhere except next door in the United States. House construction took off and work began on Canada's first-ever urban subway system, running underneath Yonge Street.

The description of Toronto as a "sanctimonious icebox" by Modernist painter Wyndham Lewis, who lived in the city from 1940 to 1943, was still just about right. Men-only pubs and taverns were intentionally grungy, although after 1947, cocktail lounges, allowing women and men to comingle, were legalized. Fine dining was rare and mainly dry; no wine or spirits were served on Sundays. Chinese takeaway and restaurant chains such as Fran's, Diana Sweets, and the Honey Dew were one step up from corner diners.

Attitudes were changing. The pervasive Orange influence from the Protestant fraternal organization, which had originated in Ireland and embedded itself in Toronto, had begun to weaken. Whereas before the Second World War the annual July 12 Orange Day Parade attracted huge crowds along the Yonge Street route, new Canadians ignored it. After a consistent string of Orange mayors, Torontonians elected their first Jewish mayor, Nathan Phillips, in 1954. Immigrants began to soften the edges of dour Anglo-Saxon culture and the first sidewalk cafés appeared. People were seen walking around with a slice of pizza instead of fish and chips wrapped in newspaper.

The arts, though, lagged behind. Toronto did have an excellent university, a good orchestra, a museum with totem poles and dinosaurs, and a public art gallery. A standing joke among the intelligentsia of the 1940s was that while Japanese critics could at least discuss the merits of both kabuki and Noh theatre, there was *no* theatre, to speak of, in Canada. Theatre meant either Hart House or touring companies at the Royal Alexandra or Winter Garden theatres, usually starring some well-known actor on his or her way to overdue retirement. Far more popular were the movies, shown either in independent neighbourhood movie theatres known as "nabes" or in the rival large American chains such as Famous Players or Loew's, which offered live entertainment during intermissions.

Ballet, while trailing behind the other performing arts, had gained at least a slight foothold. Prewar Torontonians had had the opportunity to see the Ballet Russe de Monte Carlo, the Jooss Ballet (which Franca had danced with briefly), and the Trudi Schoop Comic Ballet (Schoop was called the female Charlie Chaplin). After the war, the American impresario, Sol Hurok, began to bring a few international troupes north of the border. The most popular, by far, was the Sadler's Wells Ballet. Later in the 1950s, Russian companies, particularly the Bolshoi, began to come to North America to earn hard currency.

In Toronto before the war, Rosedale mothers anxious for their daughters to acquire poise and grace sent them to ballet school. The most popular teacher was the charismatic Russian, Boris Volkoff, who had arrived in 1929 at the age of thirty. He had studied dance in Baku during the First World War and then went on to the Moscow State Youth Ballet. While on a tour of China in 1924, Volkoff slipped away, eventually finding work as a dancer and choreographer in Shanghai. After all kinds of self-revealed dramatic adventures — a fair share of which might actually have happened — he landed in Chicago where he got work through a fellow Russian, Adolph Bolm, a one-time partner of Anna Pavlova. When Volkoff's American visa ran out, Bolm told him about a vacancy for a dancer to perform during intermissions at Toronto's Loew's Uptown Theatre. The theatre's previous dancer, Leon Leonidoff— another exiled Russian — had moved on to New York City, where he would go on to create hundreds of dance extravaganzas for the Radio City Music Hall.

In 1931 Volkoff opened a ballet school in Toronto; soon many of the city's elite were sending their little girls to classes in tutus and pink ballet shoes. There was also a boy's class; one of those attending was the future novelist, Timothy Findley. Volkoff broadened his scope, choreographing dances for the annual carnival of the upper-crust Toronto Skating Club, one of the highlights of the city's social agenda. Volkoff's full-scale productions of *Prince Igor* and *Swan Lake*, along with his choreographed solos, took the Toronto Skating Club's show to higher levels of performance. He turned down a chance to go to New York to work for professional ice shows.

When the Promenade Concerts at Toronto's Varsity Stadium began in 1934, the highlight of the first season was an October appearance of Volkoff and his dancers. A crowd of 7,580 packed the stadium, which officially seated 4,800.

By 1936 Volkoff was sufficiently established to be invited by P.J. Mulqueen, president of the Canadian Olympic Team, to send a troupe of his dancers to the Internationale Tanswettspiele, a cultural show attached to the Berlin Olympics. In contrast, several countries, including England, France, Sweden, the United States, and Russia, boycotted the cultural festival in protest of the Nazis' ban on Jewish participants. Modern dancer Martha Graham was especially outspoken in her refusal to attend. Torontonians, though, proudly welcomed back Volkoff, who bragged that although his amateur dance troupe had competed with professionals such as the German Expressionist dancer Mary Wigman, his original choreography celebrating Canadian themes had won one of five honourable mentions.[74]

Raising Volkoff's standing in Toronto even further was his marriage to one of his students. Janet Baldwin was the great-granddaughter of nineteenth-century Premier Robert Baldwin and thus a direct descendent of one of the leading families in the province.[75] She had attended private school in Toronto, followed by Miss Penrose's Finishing School for Girls in Florence, Italy, and then toured Europe chaperoned by her mother. The appeal to him of the twenty-four-year-old, blue-eyed blonde was clear enough. The appeal to her of the thirty-six-year-old, stocky Volkoff, with his stubby nose and receding, rather greasy-looking hair was less evident. He was exotic. As had been the case with Celia and Leo Kersley, Volkoff's core appeal to Janet Baldwin was very probably that he was utterly unlike her and an affront to her family. Janet, a recent debutante, had searched the Toronto telephone directory for a dance studio. Finding the Volkoff studio, she enrolled at the age of twenty-two, impossibly old to begin a career as a professional dancer. Volkoff took Janet to California in 1935 to study with Adolph Bolm,[76] though if he had had ulterior motives, they were thwarted by Janet's mother accompanying her.

With Janet's help, Volkoff was able to create the Volkoff Ballet in 1938. This amateur company (the dancers were not paid) soon played an important role in the city's cultural life, appearing with the Toronto Opera Company as well as continuing at the annual Promenade Concerts.

Across the country, other fledgling dance initiatives also existed at this time, even if hard-hit by the Depression. In the late 1930s two intrepid English women, Gweneth Lloyd and Betty Farrally, came to Winnipeg, opened a ballet school, and in 1939 created the Winnipeg Ballet, now touted as the second oldest ballet company in North America after the San Francisco Ballet Company. In Vancouver, teachers such as June Roper turned out dancers good enough to win jobs with the later Ballets Russes companies. On the east coast, Latvian dance couple Jury Gotschalks and Irene Apiné set up the Halifax Ballet in the late 1940s.

All these small regional ballet companies, and Volkoff's, were, at best, only semi-professional. To achieve a full-time professional career, dancers had to emigrate, as did Volkoff-trained Melissa Hayden, who went to the United States to join the New York City Ballet as a soloist, and Winnipegger David Adams, who joined London's Metropolitan Ballet, where one of his co-dancers was Celia Franca.

With the war ended, a spirit of ambition began to stir among the still very small number of ballet professionals and balletomanes spread out across the country. One sign of change was the establishment of the Canadian Ballet Festival Association, which from 1948 to 1954 staged an annual festival of dance. Spearheading this development were Janet Baldwin and Winnipeg's David Yeddeau. The two had met when some Winnipeg dancers came to Toronto in 1947 to appear in a ballet sequence for a trade show. They soon realized that joining forces would further their mission of introducing ballet to a wider audience.

The first Canadian Ballet Festival, held in Winnipeg in spring 1948, almost didn't happen due to flooding from the Red River. The festival was, however, a great success, with dignitaries such as the Governor General, Viscount Alexander of Tunis, attending performances of the three finest dance companies in Canada: the Winnipeg Ballet, the Volkoff Canadian Ballet, and Ruth Sorel's modern dance troupe from Montreal.

The next year, ten companies took part in the second festival at Toronto's Royal Alexandra Theatre. In *Maclean's* magazine, rising journalist June Callwood alerted her readers to the idea that the ballet boom underway in the United States was creeping across the borders into Canada. Callwood wrote,

> Toronto before the war was a three-night stand for the Ballet Russe de Monte Carlo [sic], and the house was never full. The Ballet Russe now stays two weeks giving 12 night shows and two matinees without an empty seat in the house.

This advance came at a price. Callwood described how Canadian dancers were unpaid, the ballerinas being daytime stenographers, housewives, and shop girls, while the male dancers were everything from mechanics to factory workers. She recounted the experience of Volkoff dancer Natalia Butko, who worked for an insurance company for three years then asked for time off for an orchestra rehearsal, was refused, went anyway, and was fired. The newspapers exposed the story and the insurance company hastily backed down. Butko quit anyway and went to work for a biscuit company.

This interest and excitement about ballet would have gone on gradually building, but an event in late 1949 sent it leaping ahead when the Sadler's Wells Company made its first ever North American tour with *The Sleeping Beauty*, performing in Toronto in late November.

All the prominent Torontonians attending the Saturday, November 26 performance received an invitation from Mr. and Mrs. Boris Volkoff to meet the Sadler's Wells dancers at a post-performance studio reception. The guests were offered a lavish buffet of assorted foods, some prepared by Canada's own culinary star and cookbook author Kate Aitkin, along with a selection of hard liquors, soft drinks, and cigarettes. One delicacy that must have puzzled the British visitors was the plate of sandwiches made from the three pounds of peanut butter donated by the Red Spot Nut Company. With the English dancers and, above all, Fonteyn herself attending this reception, ballet suddenly became a must-be-seen-at social event. A noticeable absentee was Ninette de Valois, who had written to let Stewart James know that she had been called back to London, but that choreographer Frederick Ashton would be there in her place.

One aspect of the social success of this occasion deserves to be noted. Besides the glamour appeal of Fonteyn and the sumptuous production values of *The Sleeping Beauty,* the Sadler's Wells Company came from London, England. To culture-starved, postwar English Canada, Toronto most especially, English culture meant not just refinement, but real, guaranteed-authentic "high culture." As a significant bonus, it was not American culture, and so deemed not to be "popular culture." By no coincidence the Royal Commission on National Development in the Arts, Letters, and Sciences (known as the Massey Commission) established in 1949 to provide recommendations for the development of arts in Canada, was headed by Vincent Massey, an avowed anglophile and unapologetic elitist, as well as a patron of the arts.

Supply and demand were coming into alignment. England had what English Canada wanted. No less so, Canada had what England needed. Exhausted and near-bankrupt as a result of the war, the Mother Country needed Canada's money and employment opportunities. Historian Paul Rutherford has written of how, in early postwar Canada, "a small coterie of visitors and immigrants, employed and assisted by moneyed or powerful Canadians, worked to 'civilize' a country seemingly so incomplete."[77] Some had arrived even before the war, such as John Grierson, a noted British film documentarian who came to take charge of the newly formed National Film Board in 1939. In Winnipeg the philanthropic Richardson family supported the two English dance teachers, Lloyd and Farrally.

By early 1950 the pace of progress in creating a professional ballet company in Toronto had begun to quicken, although it consisted of mostly talk and wishful thinking. Janet Baldwin Volkoff was one of its leading proponents. Another advocate began to emerge: Stewart James, who, most oddly, had changed his name

When Stewart James returned home from active duty in Burma in World War II, he discovered the delights of ballet after his doctor suggested he take lessons from Boris Volkoff to regain his strength.
Courtesy of Dance Collection Danse

from his original James Bolsby. During the war, Major Bolsby had been wounded in western Burma and, after demobilization, took up dancing on his doctor's advice as a way to regain his strength and stamina. The studio he chose was Volkoff's. He became a ballet enthusiast and, because he had the use of the family car, an indispensable volunteer for the Volkoff Ballet. James researched and wrote a paper, "The Case for Ballet in Canada," that advocated a professional dance company of up to sixteen dancers who would receive salaries for a forty-week season. For the key post of artistic director, James's recommendation was, naturally, Boris Volkoff, "whose reputation removed any doubt as to his claim for this position."

For her part, Janet took on an active role in furthering her husband's career. She cajoled her uncle, Harry Baldwin, private secretary to Prime Minister Mackenzie King, to arrange for the Volkoff Canadian Ballet to perform at Ottawa's Little Theatre under the patronage of the governor general; the company repeated its Olympic program.[78]

On February 8, 1950, Stewart James wrote to one of the key Canadian Ballet Festival Association committee members, Aileen Woods: "We feel the time has come when Toronto needs, wants and is willing to support a company." That spring Woods, James, and Janet Baldwin Volkoff held a series of meetings with interested and influential friends such as Hugh Lawson, Bob Lash (a cousin of Janet's), Sydney Mulqueen, and Pearl Whitehead.

Although the two groups — the Volkoff group and the Toronto establishment group — were in agreement about their mission (namely, to create a national ballet), they had substantially different ideas about the actual character of the company. The Volkoff group took it for granted that the company would be comprised of mainly Volkoff's dancers, who he had trained in the Russian style. The second group, though, had in mind a Canadian copy of England's Sadler's Wells Ballet with its tidy and dainty "Wellsian" style. As the months went by, this schism widened.

ℬↄ

COLLECTIVELY, SYDNEY MULQUEEN, AILEEN Woods, and Pearl Whitehead were known as the Three Ladies and epitomized Toronto's Protestant cultural establishment. This was still a time when women, always referred to by their husband's name, upheld their spouse's economic and professional status through their social activities. Great attention was paid to wearing the correct clothes, namely British conservative outfits, to luncheons, afternoon teas, and cocktail parties. These women were equally at home with that distinctive Canadian activity of cottage life with its boating and water sports. Sydney Mulqueen and Aileen Woods had gone to private school together; Pearl Whitehead was a neighbour to the Woods. As the wives of wealthy and powerful men, they had accumulated years of volunteer experience in amateur cultural endeavours.

The Three Ladies: Aileen (lower left), Sydney Mulqueen (lower right), and Pearl Whitehead (upper right). Courtesy of the National Ballet of Canada Archives.

Pearl, the wife of R.B. Whitehead, a lawyer in the upper echelons of the Ontario Civil Service, had focused her volunteer work mainly in the musical sphere, including a stint as the president of the Symphony Women's Committee and as president of the Women's Musical Club of Toronto. In 1952 she stood up for six musicians of the Toronto Symphony Orchestra whose contracts had not been renewed on suspicion that they had communist sympathies. Protesting this blatant McCarthyism — the board's explanation was that it was feared the "symphony six" would be refused visas to tour in the United States — Pearl resigned from the board and cancelled her subscription.

Sydney, or Syd, was mainly interested in amateur sports and it had been her husband, P.J. Mulqueen, (nicknamed Timber because he had a wooden leg), who, as president of the Canadian Olympic Committee, had sent Volkoff and his dancers to the 1936 Berlin Olympics.

Aileen Woods, the most socially prominent of the women, had first become a committee member of the 1949 Toronto Ballet Festival because of her connection to Janet Baldwin. Her husband's company, York Knitting Mills, already sponsored a national radio voice competition called "Singing Stars of Tomorrow." Douglas and Aileen Woods were members of the tony Rosedale Golf Club and the Toronto Skating Club. They would have often seen Boris Volkoff's productions for the annual Skating Club shows.

Aileen Woods came up with the idea of creating a Ballet Guild of Canada as a network of committees across the country to raise funds from corporate and personal contacts and eventually also to give the dancers a "soft landing" by looking after them when they came to town on tour. The committee was enthusiastic and well-connected, but it was also amateurish. In keeping with the times, none of these women had ever held a professional job or met a payroll or hired and fired anyone other than perhaps a cook or gardener.

In the summer of 1950, Stewart James travelled to England at his own expense to study the organization of the Sadler's Wells Ballet. He had sent ahead a list of questions including the role and function of a ballet mistress. He thought that he was scouting for a ballet mistress to assist Boris Volkoff in his role as artistic director.

Looking back on what happened, dance writer Max Wyman would call Volkoff "the right man at the wrong time." Passionate and fiery, Volkoff was well-respected for his artistic capabilities, if also regarded warily for his temper, his love of liquor, and his rumoured infidelities.

By early 1950 Volkoff's marriage to Janet was coming apart. She believed, quite correctly, that her husband was having an affair with one of his dancers, Mary McMillan. In September 1951, after he had threatened her physically, Janet left him for good. Her society friends gathered protectively around; Boris went on to have a short-lived marriage to Frieda Ogrodnick, thirty years his junior. As for Janet, she set up her own dance studio (switching to the Royal Academy of Dance system). It did not take long before Volkoff realized that his rampaging libido had effectively disqualified him from the artistic director position. Baldwin retained a fondness for her ex-husband and assisted him in his waning years. Volkoff continued to teach ballet at his Yorkville studio until 1973 when it burnt down. He died the next year.

As a further complication, Gweneth Lloyd, co-founder of the Winnipeg Ballet, moved to Toronto early in 1950, ostensibly to open a second branch of her Canadian School of Ballet. As a consequence, surely intended, Lloyd immediately became a potential candidate for the position of artistic director of the planned national ballet company. Lloyd always denied this ambition; she may simply have been escaping a fractious board in Winnipeg.

In fact both Volkoff's and Lloyd's candidacies were hindered by the fact that, as owners of ballet schools, they would have a conflict of interest in hiring the dancers.

The result was that there was no longer an overwhelming favourite among the possible contenders residing in Canada. Add to this the spectacular impact of the 1949 visit of the Sadler's Wells Company and suddenly the National Ballet Guild committee members were no longer certain who they should be looking for, or where.

AT THE TIME HE met Celia Franca on London's Compton Street, Stewart James was unaware of the Guild's uncertainty. He still assumed he was looking for a ballet mistress for the artistic director, most probably Volkoff. Then, as he later described it, "A tiny little thing in a grey flannel suit and black bangs, popped out of a store where she was buying some make-up. She was playing at the Mercury Theatre in a Victorian play, hence the bangs. She looked a picture!"[79] Celia confirmed to dance writer James Neufeld that, when Stewart James made his first overture to her, he thought Volkoff would be the artistic director.[80]

Reporting to the committee after his return to Toronto, James set out his negotiations, during which it was clear Celia had bargained hard and well on the financial terms: "Approx. Sept 20th I wrote to Miss Franca confirming my talks in London: sixty dollars per week per session of one year plus an option of second and third seasons. Return fare London/Toronto/London to be Ballet Mistress and assistant to Artistic Director position — She would like to know exact relation to Director and to dancers." James had done his job ... or so he thought.

Only a month later, on October 27, the expanded National Ballet Guild committee held a meeting, to which James was not invited, and made a series of radical decisions. David Yeddeau, from the Winnipeg Ballet, would be appointed stage director and company manager. Janet Baldwin would act as wardrobe mistress and be responsible for public relations. Stewart James was to be offered the job of business manager and advance booking agent. James was the only one of that group actually offered an administrative position.

All of this was really just housekeeping. The key decision, as recorded in the committee's notes, was that an offer should be made to Celia Franca to become ballet mistress and also what they called, for lack of knowing the correct term, "producer-director." Moreover, this ad-hoc committee, with no idea of protocol, had already made this offer. A week earlier, Aileen Woods had written to Celia, "We feel very strongly that this Professional Ballet Company would benefit greatly by having someone of your reputation and qualifications as its Producer and Director as well as being its Ballet Mistress. Can you possibly accept this further responsibility?" Aileen Woods had tried even earlier to contact Celia by phone, but failed to reach her due to poor reception. In the early 1950s overseas business negotiations still had to be made by post, telegrams, or unreliable telephone connections.

The Three Ladies had very little idea of what they were doing. None knew much about ballet itself, let alone about how to run a national ballet company. Social connections — and, by extension, financial connections — were their strengths. Yet the two key decisions they had made could not have been made any better by the most rigorous search committee process, or by the most expensive management consultants. One was to invite a neutral ballet professional from Britain. The second was to identify, among all the contenders on the other side of the Atlantic, a person with the widest scope of experience — from dancer, choreographer, ballet mistress, dramatic actress, television dance producer, and teacher — coupled with intelligence, musicality, drive, energy, confidence, and an utter dedication to the art of ballet.

The committee made a third critical decision. It decided to seek the opinion of the person best equipped, by far, to offer such advice. Ninette de Valois recommended Celia Franca highly and instructed the committee not to tie her hands artistically, allowing her to choose the company dancers herself. The Mother Country was speaking to its former colony, and the professional was speaking to a bunch of amateurs.

What de Valois had to say — it's a considerable tribute to the savvy of James and the committee that they should have sought her out and agreed to her recommendation — settled the matter. Her response to the list of possible contenders James presented to her in London is part of the National Ballet of Canada's mythology. Scanning the list, de Valois is purported to have said, "Celia Franca, if you can get her."

Several theories have been put forth about why de Valois chose Celia. The most prevalent one is that de Valois saw Franca as a potential threat and therefore manoeuvred her over to the other side of the Atlantic. This is, in fact, improbable since Celia was no longer associated with the Sadler's Wells Ballet and, while she had gone on to several successes, including soloist with another ballet company and pioneer in creating television dance drama, she was no threat to de Valois.

Far more probable is that de Valois recognized that Franca could serve as an emissary to extend British-style ballet to the Dominion of Canada. De Valois had a template for creating a ballet company. The foundation of its style and repertory had to be the classics such as *The Sleeping Beauty* and *Swan Lake*. The company had to also establish its own school to create its own stable of dancers trained in the Cecchetti style. By ensuring that one of her own would be in charge of the National Ballet of Canada, de Valois was creating a North American outpost of her own ballet empire. Already de Valois had gone to Turkey in 1947 to establish a ballet school in Ankara and had sent out two Sadler's Wells dancers as teachers. Later a ballet school was established in Tehran, where several Sadler's Wells dancers had been dispatched to serve as instructors. In the early 1960s, Peggy van Praagh would found the Australian Ballet, modelled on the Sadler's Wells Ballet company. Celia's move to Canada can be seen as part of this cultural colonization.

While de Valois had not appreciated Celia as a classical dancer, she certainly had a high opinion of her intellect. When de Valois, at the age of ninety-one, was questioned about Celia Franca, she said her protegé had dedication, a disciplined mind, good taste, an intelligent outlook, and was extremely well balanced.[81]

There was one dimension to de Valois's recommendation of which the Canadians could not have been aware. She owed Franca a favour for having replaced her at the Sadler's Wells Ballet with June Brae. Now she was recommending Franca as founder and artistic director of an independent ballet company. Celia, herself, never had a doubt about the importance of the role de Valois had played. During her first visit to Canada, she wrote back to Doris Margolis that de Valois "has sung my praises everywhere so all is well."

THAT CELIA WOULD ACCEPT so attractive and challenging an offer was now a virtual certainty, but one difficulty remained: the Guild had failed to raise the necessary private money to form a ballet company. No alternative to private funding existed at this time. The Canada Council, the main recommendation of the Massey Commission, would not come into being until 1957.

The committee members, however, displayed inventiveness. The third annual Canadian Ballet Festival was to take place in mid-November 1950 in Montreal. The committee convinced the T. Eaton Company to provide the funds to cover Celia's travel and expenses to attend. The festival would give Celia Franca an overview of what Canada had to offer in the way of trained ballet dancers and the chance to assess whether there was enough available talent to start a national company.

Aileen Woods lived up to her pledge to "do our utmost to make sure your time in Canada is as happy and congenial as you could possibly wish." Celia was treated royally. On Tuesday, November 14, she flew from London to Toronto by Trans-Canada Air Lines. As she had quipped in a letter to James, "Is air travel safe in winter? I don't want to die yet." Of ten passengers, she was the only female. She spent the long flight either writing to Doris on the airline stationery or stretched out across two seats trying unsuccessfully to sleep.

The welcoming party saw a stylish and poised twenty-nine-year-old woman dressed in a full-length black Persian lamb coat, high-quality leather shoes and handbag, a sheer silk scarf artfully knotted around her neck and held with a large brooch, large matching earrings, her hair swept back, and the ever-present cigarette held casually in one hand. The entire Franks clan had helped Celia pull together this look with a fashionable dress from her parents' shop and her aunt Ethel's fur coat. She made her entrance down the stairs from the airplane with elegant precision.

From the airport, she was taken to the Rosedale home of Aileen and Douglas Woods. Celia wrote to Doris,

> My room is about the size of our flat at Ascot [Court] but very cosy, very warm. Writing desk, thousands of ashtrays and cigarettes and stamps and paper and rosebuds on every dressing table (there are two dressing tables) two built-in cupboards for clothes, two beautiful beds of some antique wood, wonderful crystal candlesticks etc. etc. Breakfast was brought to me in bed by one of the maids and I have my own bathroom.

Although outwardly calm, Celia was stressed by lack of sleep, the strangeness of the fast Canadian speech, and, far from least, her realization that she was always in the spotlight. She wrote to Doris, "The social strain is terrific and I definitely have not enough diamonds with me. They were flashing like mad over the dinner table. Today is going to be one round of engagements so I must get ready. There is a cocktail party for me tonight for me to meet the ballet people here." On the Saturday before leaving for Montreal, Stewart James took Celia to one of Toronto's quintessential cultural events — the T. Eaton Company's annual Santa Claus Parade.

The following day Celia was driven to Montreal. She settled into the Ritz-Carlton where, for her breakfast in bed, she was served freshly squeezed orange juice in a silver bowl with ice in the bottom. "I hated it," Celia reported back across the Atlantic. "Cold. Freezing cold!"

Celia spent the week of November 20 to 25 in a constant round of attending dance performances at His Majesty's Theatre, going to cocktail parties, and indulging in delicious food and much too much whisky. The rich food and free-flowing alcohol made her face break out in spots.

Many she met were excited that her very presence meant a national ballet company might actually happen. Bernadette Carpenter, the major Canadian retailer of dance supplies at the time, recalled the welcome Franca received after the opening evening performance.

> Our room was a hive of activity, each and every "drop in" came with the hope we could interest Celia enough to stay to form a National Company. On into the early morning, a few die-hards lingered on, Anatole Chujoy, Mildred Wickson, Gweneth Lloyd, Janet Baldwin, and my husband, Don — each one of us hoping we were on the brink of a better future for young Canadian dancers.[82]

Celia averaged four hours of sleep a night.

One talent Celia displayed was that of courting publicity and giving journalists the kind of quotes they were looking for. Speaking to *The Globe and Mail* on November 22, Celia said, "Great choreographic wealth is scattered through the width and length of Canada." In an interview she gave to the Canadian Press she expanded on her observations about the dancers she had seen. "In each of the companies in the Festival, I saw one or two dancers who are ready to turn professional. They are at the age when they should be dancing or training every day, however. They cannot be expected to improve unless they are given the opportunity."

She skilfully played to the hometown audiences. "Ballet in Canada will disintegrate and die and Canada will lose this splendid talent unless something is done. Those with ability and courage will go to England or the United States for the opportunities lacking here." She also showed an edge. "The dancers here have tremendous vitality; they are perhaps a shade too athletic. I have found the poetic element so essential in ballet, almost completely lacking. I missed this lyric quality." What Celia was really saying was that the Canadian dancers did not have British training.

Discussing the choreography, Celia suggested that some of the work suffered from being too ambitious or failing to develop the storyline properly and therefore lost the audience. She countered this by saying that some of the ballets were of professional calibre. She concluded, "It remains now to be seen if the dancers and choreographers are given the opportunity they deserve." In a later brief report that Celia submitted to England's *Royal Academy of Dancing Gazette*,[83] she repeated her concerns about the Canadian dancers' vulnerabilities as a result of poor teaching.

Taking advantage of being in North America, Celia took one quick side trip to New York City. During the festival she had met Anatole Chujoy, editor of New York's *Dancing News*, who had come to Montreal to review for *The Globe and Mail*. Chujoy helped her get tickets to the New York City Ballet and Radio City and gave her the use of his office to make her phone calls.

Upon her return to Toronto, she pushed back her flight departure date for days to continue to make contacts. She met twice with Boris Volkoff, who, realizing his chance of being the artistic director was gone, still hoped to play an essential role in the new ballet company. If Celia witnessed a class at Volkoff's Yonge Street studio, it would have only confirmed her disapproval of his dramatic Russian-style technique, which allowed his dancers to project their own personal style. The English style called for strict uniformity. Janet Baldwin remembered how deeply wounded Volkoff was by Franca's attitude. "Boris was hurt to the quick. Even if she had said, I admire you for what you have done in the past — she didn't say a decent word about him. She just walked all over him."[84]

FROM THE BEGINNING, CELIA recognized the challenge of enticing promising young Canadian dancers away from their local teachers to come to Toronto. Her sharpest observations were the private ones she made in letters to Doris.

> One of my difficulties will be getting around the dancing teachers. The festival showed some good talent among the dancers, but to gather them from the various groups which are scattered all over Canada will be hell's own job. You see the directors of each group don't want to part with their best dancers and the dancers trust their teachers because they don't know anyone else. What I ought to do is make a coast to coast tour and get friendly.

She also had grasped the political dynamics involved in trying to form the national ballet company. Celia summarized it neatly in a letter to Doris explaining that there were many warring factions with agreement on only one point: everyone wanted Celia Franca to be the artistic director. Therefore, they were all trying to find the ways and means to raise enough money in order for Celia to stay in Canada.

In a foreshadowing of how Celia would treat her board at the National Ballet of Canada, she told Doris, "I have already announced that when I get there, I give the orders and no-one else. I've told them that they know nothing about the business and that I was going home unless everything was left to me." While this was undoubtedly braggadocio to impress Doris, in essence, she planned to treat the Canadians as she had been treated by Ninette de Valois — autocratically.

Celia couldn't resist regaling Doris with flippant barbs about the Three Ladies, including her hostess, Aileen Woods. "The three witches as I call them, have buggered things up between them and seen O.D. Vaughan, Vice-President of Eaton's. As they didn't even know the difference between gross and net, Vaughan more or less told them to go to hell and shut the door — slam. So it is my pleasure and privilege to open it again."

Luckily, Vaughan and his wife, Nora, were a progressive, cultured couple with a great interest in Modernism. Nora, a graduate of the University of Toronto, was active with both the Royal Ontario Museum and the Ontario College of Art; Orval (always referred to as O.D.) Vaughan, was a member of the board of the University of Toronto and had delighted in importing European art wares to Eaton's between the two wars to educate Canadian tastes.[85] It would be to the embryonic ballet company's great benefit for the Vaughans to host fundraising events at their Rosedale mansion, easily able to host 150 guests amidst their collection of sculptures and paintings, which included works by Picasso and Braque.

Recognizing the awed deference which had been paid to her at the Ballet Festival and the possibility of having full control of her own ballet company, Celia considered ditching everything and everybody in England and simply staying in Toronto. She had been prepared to drop all commitments, including dancing in a live broadcast of *Giselle* for BBC Television on December 18 and collaborating with Honor Frost to present a dance at Rambert's Mercury Theatre on January 14, 1951. She mused to Doris about what she should do with Aunt Ethel's borrowed Persian lamb coat if she didn't go back home. The committee, however, was not yet ready to offer her a salary. After nearly a month in North America, Celia returned to Doris and Ascot Court.

Her parting words to the National Ballet Guild committee were, "I think you need me."

Grand Jeté to Canada

CELIA FRANCA'S MOVE TO Canada ran as a front page story in London's tabloid newspapers on February 16, 1951. Several press photographers took pictures of her getting on the boat train at Waterloo Station. A photo of Celia with her ballerina friend, Svetlana Beriosova, hugging a bottle of champagne, offered a glimpse of the going-away party held the night before. The *Daily Mirror* quoted her as saying, "If I can find thirty-five good dancers, Canada will have a National Ballet Company."

It was not quite as simple as finding thirty-five good dancers. The provisional board of directors of the ballet company, still without a name, had yet to find the start-up money. Celia had been hired to come to Canada to undertake an eight-month study to assess whether a national ballet company was a viable proposition. She had already been convinced by attending the November dance festival that there was enough raw dance talent.

But what she did not know was whether there was enough of an infrastructure to support the venture, such as a theatrical circuit across Canada, adequate facilities for ballet rehearsal halls and administrative offices in Toronto, experienced costume and wig makers, set designers, rehearsal pianists, musicians, and, most importantly, an audience with an appetite for ballet.

Although there were many practical concerns, the desire for a national ballet company was ardent. In January, the Sadler's Wells Ballet had returned to Toronto for five days of performances, which whetted balletomanes' desires even more for their own company. This time the English dancers were entertained in a much grander fashion at Lady Kemp's "At Home" held in her gracious Rosedale home, Castle Frank, which overlooked the Don Valley. Tea and dainty sandwiches would have replaced the peanut butter, hard liquor, and cigarettes offered at Volkoff's 1949 reception in his Yonge Street dance studio.

Celia's sponsors had booked her first class on the French liner, the S.S. *Liberty*. She was in her element, dining nightly amidst men in tuxedos with their wives in full evening wear. One photo shows Celia — in a long satin skirt with a dark velvet top and the ubiquitous cigarette held elegantly between her fingers — at a table with three admiring gentlemen. Her choice for dinner on February 20 included caviar, consomme, asperges with a Mikado sauce, foie gras, sole, chicken, salad, poached pears, and an extensive selection of cheeses. Reminiscent of her earliest performance at her aunt and uncle's wedding, Celia entertained the dinner guests, performing a Spanish-style dance complete with flowers in her hair, and her skirt whipping around her legs.

First landing in New York, Celia reached wintry Toronto on Friday, February 23. She was taken to the comfortable Forest Hill home of the Whiteheads. But the Whiteheads' home was not her final destination. Prior to moving from England, Celia had asked Stewart James to scout out a furnished apartment for her. James had written back, "Mrs. Woods and I are determined you have a bathroom and kitchen to yourself. It makes heavy hunting." Eventually, he found an apartment at 202 Glen Road in Rosedale.

After a night at the Whiteheads', Celia found herself alone in an apartment with no Pearl Whitehead or Gertie Franks or Doris Margolis to serve as support. What had seemed like a good idea while in London appeared less than ideal in Toronto.

Besides being in a strange city, out of reach of close friends and family, Celia had very little money. She had been tough in her salary negotiations, having rejected the initial offer of sixty dollars per week, saying it wasn't enough to keep her in vegetables and salads — she still was a vegetarian — but more importantly, it wasn't sufficient to keep up her addiction to cigarettes. She also had a variety of financial commitments in London, including an insurance policy and professional memberships. In fact, she left London in debt to Doris and was anxious to get it paid off. She accepted the offer of seventy dollars a week and the board gave her an initial advance of $160, of which seventy-five was immediately paid out as rent.

A demure publicity, photo taken soon after Celia arrived in Canada, plays down her exotic appearance. Courtesy of Library and Archives Canada, PA153945

Celia was determined to set up her apartment so that it reflected her position as the artistic director of a new ballet company. She ordered a telephone; then, seeing an advertisement in the *Toronto Star* for W.H. Smith's personalized stationery, she ordered some with her phone number and address. She had brought her books, records, and artwork, including paintings by Clifford Hall, a friend who painted dancers at London's Lyric Theatre. A pastel sketch he had done of her always had a place of honour in her home.[86]

Missing her London friends, Celia wrote them letters. She told Doris, "My apartment is very warm and would be very nice if you were here to get it straight. I decided against a boarding house because my hours are so irregular and it would drive me mad to have to tell them whether and when I was going to be in for meals." She wrote to Cyril that, on first seeing her apartment, she felt utterly lonely and depressed, but expected to feel better once she had her own pictures up on the wall.

TO PAY CELIA, THE board, still without any real funds, had concocted an innovative solution. The board would pay her twenty dollars a week, this being all they could afford at the time. The fifty dollars outstanding would be paid to her by the T. Eaton Company, which would, technically, employ her. This inventive scheme had been devised by Stewart James after a discussion with his friend, Jack Brockie, then manager of the merchandise display department that also organized the Santa Claus Parade. As Celia told Cyril, "Tomorrow I go to see Brockie at Eaton's and I'm hoping that he will set me to work straightaway so I can get some money. I haven't a bean in the world right now, and need to buy essentials for the apartment and cigarettes."

Her first encounter with Brockie went less than smoothly — he may well have been unnerved by the petite, dark-haired woman with dramatic stark-white makeup, pencilled eyebrows, and dark red lips who strode into his office. In the midst of their meeting,

Celia found the manager's centrally heated office so stiflingly hot that she asked if she could stick her head out of his window. Brockie complied by opening the window and Celia poked her head out to get a good breath of fresh air.

As part of the arrangement, Celia was given a desk in the offices of the Eaton Auditorium, a theatre seating just over a thousand on the seventh floor of the company's art-deco–inspired department store at the intersection of College and Yonge Street. Arriving for her first day, she rode up the elevator and emerged into a long spacious hall that reminded her of the elegant reception room of a luxury ocean liner. With a pale colour palette of silvery shades of beige and grey with black, the space exuded style and elegance. In addition to the auditorium, the seventh floor featured two restaurants — the Clipper and the Round Room — that offered fine dining for businessmen and lady shoppers. The auditorium was the heart of Toronto's cultural life; it was here that a wide variety of entertainers, from Billie Holiday and Frank Sinatra to the Eaton Operatic Society, performed.

Celia had been given a desk in the office of the box office staff. Her fellow office workers knew that while she shared the office with them, she would be doing her own work. While welcoming Celia, they left her to her own devices. It took her a few days to understand the Canadian accent, which she described to Doris as "filthy." In turn, the Canadians teased Celia by calling her "Merrie England" because of her tone of voice.

After the drab austerity of England, Celia found her surroundings in Toronto, in general, and Eaton's College department store, specifically, to be clean and elegant. The dining rooms and the staff cafeteria featured salad plates loaded with a variety of fruits and vegetables, all magic to the eyes of the vegetarian Celia. If she was being taken out for lunch by a board member in the nearby Round Room, she could have a salad with fourteen to seventeen ingredients including lettuce, cantaloupe balls, slices of apple, grapefruit, watermelon, pineapple, green grapes, and avocado, garnished with toasted almonds and an orange twist. The on-site bakery used cream and butter in its breads and cakes. Her friends back in London were still enthralled by the sight of a single banana.

From the six Eaton's floors, all crammed with merchandise, Celia was able to buy whatever clothes she could afford instead of single items with her ration coupons. She spruced up her office wardrobe with brown high-heeled shoes, a black crepe skirt, and, best of all, a petticoat and two blouses made from the new miracle fabric nylon. In itemizing her purchases, she explained to Doris that, although the cost of living was high, "at least you get something for your money."

Besides updating her worn-out English wardrobe, Celia took advantage of Ontario's excellent doctors and dentists to make up for the wartime years of medical neglect. Recognizing that it was unacceptable in North America to have bad teeth, she set up a series of dental appointments. She also began to see Dr. Douglas Firth, an osteopathic doctor, for treatment. Firth would be appointed the ballet company's official doctor.

Nominally, her hours of employment were 8:50 a.m. to 5 p.m., but no one objected when Celia showed up late or left early on ballet business. She did a little filing, and although she always maintained that she never learned how to work the switchboard, she became proficient enough to write Doris a letter at the same time as working the board when the regular operator was away sick.

After settling in, Celia began to tackle her real job. One of her first tasks was damage control. Different factions had either been trying to take credit for the new company or to inveigle their way into it. The intrigues of the various players were relatively transparent. Within a couple of weeks of Celia's arrival, Gweneth Lloyd delivered a talk on the development of ballet in Canada to the Heliconian Club, an exclusive club involved in cultural activities. Conspicuous by her absence was Celia Franca, who either had not been invited or had declined to attend. A couple of days later, the *Toronto Star*'s cultural columnist, Augustus Bridle, reported that Boris Volkoff had himself chosen Celia Franca to be the artistic director of his national Canadian ballet company. Bridle added that Franca would be introduced to the public on the occasion of a special fundraiser screening of the film *The Red Shoes*.

Describing Volkoff and Lloyd, along with others, as "intriguers and gossipers," Celia complained to Doris that "they are making my work very difficult, but I am determined to squash them." Years later, Celia bluntly told Rasky, "The real problem was the Volkoffs, the Gweneth Lloyds and all those people … whatever was going to be happening, they wanted in on it — and I didn't want to have people hampering me. You can not have a ballet company run by three people — three artistic directors — I had a vision of what I wanted to do and I didn't want any outside influences." That, in a nutshell, was Celia's modus operandi during her entire tenure as the National Ballet's artistic director. She had a vision and she would not accept any interference from board directors, dancers, choreographers, dance critics, or even audiences.

Stewart James figured Celia out almost from the start. He made an insightful observation about her objective, stating that Celia was building a national ballet company for Canada, a goal that stood in contrast to what Volkoff had wanted to do: build a Canadian ballet company. Celia's vision was to create a ballet company patterned on the unembellished English style of dance with herself in complete control. She was determined that no other style of ballet — certainly not Volkoff's Russian technique — would contaminate her company. She might permit some of her boys to take a few classes with Volkoff, but that would be the extent of his influence. In fact, on more than one occasion Celia told people that de Valois had described Volkoff as "just a Russian drunk." By contrast, Lloyd, academically well educated, had studied folk dance, social dance, and revived Greek dance during her English childhood. Taking up ballet studies as an adult, she had never performed or worked in any capacity in a professional ballet company before co-founding the Winnipeg Ballet company. Lloyd had made her career as a dance teacher and eventually a choreographer.[87] During the 1940s and early 1950s she had choreographed nearly forty original works, including her 1952 *Shadow on the Prairie*, with its distinct Canadian theme. Lloyd, for all her limitations, had a far broader view of ballet and how to educate Canadian audiences to enjoy this art form than did Celia.

Despite her reservations about Volkoff, Franca did agree to give Sunday master classes in his studio. Besides giving her the chance to assess potential dancers for her company, these classes gave her much-needed cash. One of those students, a young teenager named Myrna Aaron, remembers seeing Celia Franca for the first time. Celia was dressed in a grey, pleated skirt and blue, long-sleeve top with pink ballet shoes, her jet-black hair hanging loose to her waist, eyes heavily made up. Aaron thought Celia looked like a creature from another planet. "I had never seen a human being who looked that exotic," said Aaron.[88]

Celia was soon paid a visit at her Eaton Auditorium office by a representative of the Canadian Dance Teachers' Association (CDTA)[89] to raise concerns about these master classes. Celia had been unaware that Volkoff, who was not a member of the CDTA, discouraged other teachers' students from attending his Sunday sessions.

The association representative who paid Celia the visit was Betty Oliphant. She and Celia connected almost immediately; one trait common to both was their sheer professionalism. Oliphant quickly became an ally, convincing other teachers not to consider Celia Franca a threat. More importantly, the CDTA committed itself to helping fund Celia's upcoming cross-Canada audition tour.

FRANCA AND OLIPHANT HAD taken lessons at the Marie Rambert ballet school at the same time, although their paths had never crossed: Betty attended Rambert's morning session and Celia attended the afternoon class with Antony Tudor. When Oliphant grew too tall to become a ballet dancer, she opened the Betty Oliphant School of Stage Dancing and Dramatic Arts over the Twinings Tea Emporium on Wigmore Street, using money from a trust fund set up after her father died when she was six weeks old. She was a certified teacher of the Cecchetti method of ballet. Oliphant became world-renowned for turning out dancers schooled by this strict classical ballet training system in which every day has its own, unalterable set of exercises that must be followed. By stressing that the feet, legs, arms, and head are not separate parts but in relation to the whole body, the student develops an unmistakable purity of movement.[90]

Oliphant came to Toronto as a war bride in 1947 with her Canadian husband, Frank Grover, and their two young daughters, Gail and Carol. A cousin, the dean of Divinity at the University of Toronto's Trinity College, helped her to get established. To earn her living, Oliphant began teaching ballet in 1948. She first attracted public attention when she began to choreograph for the Christmas pantomimes at the Royal Alexandra Theatre.

In the meantime, her marriage ended when she discovered her husband was having an affair. Before leaving her, Grover cleared out their joint account and took the bonds set aside for their daughter Carol's medical expenses, who suffered from tuberculosis of the spine.

From this low point, Oliphant now began to rise, because of her own talents and character and because of her association with Celia. They started out as a potent team. Eventually, Betty Oliphant and Celia Franca would realize there was only room for one of them at the top. But at the beginning, and for a long time afterwards, Oliphant was absolutely dazzled by Celia. "Firstly her standards of excellence were wonderful. Secondly I really think I almost had a crush on her. I was so respectful of her talents."[91]

Celia also remembered her first impressions of Oliphant.

Celia and Betty on Bloor Street, across from the University Cinema, wearing the popular 1950s cotton shirt-maker dress with cinched-in waists. Even Celia appears conventional in this outfit. Courtesy of Dance Collection Danse

"I liked her very much. We had a lot in common, came from a similar training background."

One unspoken point of friction between the pair was that they did not come from the same social background. Oliphant was from England's confident upper middle class. Franca was from the scrappy immigrant lower class. Many years later, Oliphant put it more patronizingly. "She had a lot of chips on her shoulder, coming from a very poor family."

HERBERT RICHARD ANDERSON'S NAME first popped up in a letter Celia wrote to Doris just weeks after she started at Eaton Auditorium.

"Did I tell you about a ginger headed man in the box office staff. His name is Bert Anderson and he's very ugly, has a hard exterior, a heart of gold and lots of Jewish friends. He loves company and constantly invites people round to his cottage at the edge of the lake."

Their courtship began during break times in their office routine. "He would come into the hallway and look at me at my desk and he would make the shape of a T which meant tea break and then we'd go into the Round Room and have tea or coffee. It was very nice," Celia said. Bert invited her out for dinner and they began to dine out at the Little Denmark restaurant on Bay Street. They shared a sense of humour. He was impressed with her intelligence. "She knew one of the arts better than anybody I ever met, namely ballet, and we shared a love for music."[92]

From a respectable, but very ordinary, Scottish Presbyterian family, Bert's father, James, had owned a hardware store at the corner of Broadview and Danforth Avenue. This provided a comfortable home for his family of six children. Bert had graduated from Danforth Technical School's arts program. He took up his job in 1945 as the manager of the Eaton Auditorium box office, a position well-suited to his love of classical music. Until he rented the Port Union cottage, he had lived at home with his mother and older sister.

Bert played the church organ on Sundays at St. Andrew's Presbyterian Church in downtown Toronto. Sometimes Celia would attend the service. Once the weather warmed up, the couple would take off for Bert's cottage on the shore of Lake Ontario after the Sunday service, staying overnight and driving back into the city on Monday morning.

AS THE COLD WEATHER gave way to Celia's first spring in Toronto, she hardly had a moment to enjoy the budding of the trees in the Rosedale Valley Ravine and the calls of the bright red cardinal birds. Along with her day job at Eaton Auditorium, she had a full after-hours schedule of classes, meetings, and networking.

Celia was her own best publicist. After having her photo in all the London tabloids at the time of her departure, she posed on the day of her arrival in Toronto for a *Toronto Star* photographer. She continued to hustle for coverage both in newspapers and on radio. Television was not an option, as Canada would not have its own until 1952. She rarely turned down a request to give a lecture or dance demonstration. She had a new set of publicity photos taken within weeks of arriving, which she felt had turned out well. Whether it was at this session or later, she sat for the well-known photographer Donald McKaque in a glamorous pose wearing a dark velvet dress with stripped satin collar, holding her ubiquitous long cigarette with smoke curling upward.

Part of Celia's game plan was a summer school. Writing to Doris at the beginning of April, Celia observed, "This school should be a good way of seeing the talent and preparing the best of the little bastards for professional work."

At the end of April, newspaper ads appeared across the country announcing a ballet summer school. According to Celia's media release, "For possibly the first time in Canada, an internationally-known English ballet star — at the height of her fame and talent — with a faculty of English-trained ballet teachers will be in Canada this summer to provide training for Canadian dancers wishing to study in this country." To drive home the point further, Celia quoted herself: "I shall have teachers trained in England, where, it is generally considered, some of the world's best ballet is being presented."

The only confirmed teacher, English or otherwise, was Celia herself. When Betty Oliphant pointed out that the proposed school would be in competition with her own annual summer school, Celia suggested that they join forces. Oliphant agreed. They opted to use the Cecchetti syllabus, one of several methods for the systematic teaching of ballet. Dance historian James Neufeld has perceptively suggested that Franca's emphasis on teaching the Cecchetti style was "an astute tactical move" as Franca and Oliphant were, at that time, the only two in Canada trained in this style, although Celia had not yet taken her accreditation exams.[93]

Before summer school began, Celia accepted an invitation to perform at the Promenade Concert series at Toronto's Varsity Arena in mid-June. Using mainly Volkoff dancers to accompany her, Celia staged act two of *Coppelia* with herself in the lead role. The group rehearsed during their lunch hours and in the evenings. Celia paid for the rehearsal pianist and the dressmaker from her own meagre earnings. Realistically, she expected to lose money; but, as she told Doris, it was worth it for the "wonderful publicity." She repeated this performance in Montreal in August and returned again to Varsity Arena in September.[94]

The company's Toronto rehearsal space was in the historic St. Lawrence Hall. The City of Toronto had agreed to give Celia the Hall first for her summer school and then for the fledgling

Performing a scene from *Coppelia* at Toronto's Varsity Arena. Left to right: Joyce Hill, Sandra Francis, Celia Franca, Colleen Kenny, and Myrna Aaron.
Courtesy of Library and Archives Canada, e008439033

ballet company. It was the National Ballet's first home. Located on King Street and originally attached to the city's north food market, the building, with its Corinthian pillars and ornate cupola, reminded Celia of the Royal Opera House in London's Covent Gardens. As she explained to a *Toronto Star* reporter, she felt right at home. "On this side of the water you're so used to bright, shining chrome-plated dance studios. At home, we're just as used to working in dismal, dungeon-y sort of places. Can't you feel the atmosphere in this hall?"

The Hall had been rented for minimal cost with the proviso that, during the winter months, it would revert to a shelter for indigent men. Room had to be found for the tables, chairs, and mattresses left behind by the hostel. Celia remembered that, at times, one of the winter tenants would forget about the change of occupancy and turn up during rehearsals looking for a place to crash.

The dancers and homeless men shared, in turn, the same washing facilities — primitive toilets, showers with rusted gratings and tepid water dribbling from the showerhead, a rusty metal wash trough in the girls' dressing room. Dancers were subjected to the occasional pigeon swooping down during a rehearsal. When the heating system worked, the radiators clanked, but never in unison with the music. Nevertheless, it was a large space with a wooden, unwaxed floor. Eaton's loaned a large rectangular mirror that had to be leaned on its long side against a stage at the end of the room.[95]

Along with sounds of the rehearsal piano and Celia barking instructions, there was also the constant clicking of knitting needles. In their spare moments, the dancers, both men and women, busily knit themselves sets of woollen legwarmers. A commercial pair cost three times the price of a homemade pair. One of the best knitters was Grant Strate who created the mottled tights for Celia's *Apres-midi d'un faune* and the diamond patterned tights for Harlequin in Fokine's *Carnaval*.

Summer school ran from July 2 to August 4 at the St. Lawrence Hall. Celia reached an agreement with the National Ballet Guild that the school would be under its sponsorship and she was advanced four hundred dollars for setup costs. If it proved unsuccessful, Celia would take the loss herself. Any profits would go towards the costs of the upcoming audition tour. Moreover, Celia had taken the added risk of resigning from her job at Eaton Auditorium. At this point Celia took a gamble — it was all or nothing.

Applicants came from coast to coast in Canada as well as several from the United States. Some of the company's charter dancers attended that first summer school at great financial sacrifice. Celia paid David Adams' one-way ticket from Winnipeg, where he had left his new wife, Lois Smith, and their one-month-old baby. Irene Apiné and Jury Gotshalks gave up the income from their own summer school in Halifax to attend Celia's five-week course. Natalia Butko threw over her bookkeeping job with Barker's Bakery when she was refused time off to attend the school. Celia's gamble paid off and the summer school venture was a huge success, bringing in a profit of one thousand dollars.

ON FRIDAY, AUGUST 3, Celia ducked out from the last full day of summer school. She hurried over to Toronto's City Hall. There she married thirty-five-year-old Bert Anderson. Celia's marriage took almost everyone by surprise. The courtship had been a scant five months.

Celia had broken the startling news to Doris that she was going to marry "ugly, ginger headed" Bert Anderson.

We are very much in love and can't bear to be away from each other for very long which is unfortunate as I am going to be on tour such a lot. We have not announced anything yet because I've been pulling off very big things with Eatons and the Board and I didn't want to give the impression that I had just come to Canada for a good time. Strangely enough the work has never gone better and of course Bertie helps me tremendously.

Celia had also written to her first husband, Leo Kersley, to ask him to send over their marriage and divorce documents. She warned him not to mention her impending marriage to her family, fearing that if Gertie found out, she would come right over to stop her marrying another Gentile.

"We plan to marry on August 6th" (this proved to be a holiday and hence the change to August 3) Celia explained to Doris, "which is two days after my summer school. I shall then take a week's holiday at the cottage before going on the audition tour … I shan't see very much of my husband except for the week after we are married but fortunately he is crazy about my work which I sometimes think means more to him than to me."

They kept their plans secret until the board had secured the start-up money for the ballet company. "He wouldn't let me tell the board about us. The go ahead signal for the company should be in two weeks as the bulk of our $65,000 budget will be in the bank by then. We shall announce our engagement then." They did confide in one board member. "I forgot to say that we talked it over with Pearl Whitehead who is delighted, feels that we match each other perfectly & that it couldn't possibly do any harm to the ballet. She says that already nobody doubts my artistic integrity. Everything has happened so suddenly and I'm terribly happy." After the civil ceremony, Pearl Whitehead held a small wedding reception. Official news of their marriage appeared on Aug 8 in Herbert Whittaker's *Show Business* column.

It is clear that Bert was utterly smitten with Celia. Writing on Eaton Auditorium stationery shortly after the wedding, he tried to express his feelings to Doris Margolis. "As you can deduct (from the time it took me to pop the big question) she is one of the sweetest, sincere, intelligent women I have met, believe you me it was with fear and trembling I thought of matrimony and in such a short time, I didn't give myself a chance. However, as you now know, I made the grade and am so happy and proud with my wonderful wife."

That Bert Anderson had wanted to marry the glamorous and famous English ballerina is readily understandable. Celia's impulses are much harder to read. It may have been just as she reported to Doris — that she fell in love with Bert and couldn't bear to be apart from him. She confided to Doris that she hadn't slept with him straight away. Her observation that he had several Jewish friends and loved to entertain at his cottage suggests that Bert was a refreshing contrast to the less gregarious, more provincially minded, mainly WASP board members.

There were several advantages to Celia marrying Bert. She became Mrs. Herbert Anderson, a "good Anglo-Saxon" name. She believed she would be economically secure, as Anderson was making an annual salary of forty-five hundred dollars. Since the average income for a Canadian family in 1951 was approximately $2,250, Celia was quite correct in telling Doris, "Bertie is not rich but will always be able to support me if I'm not working which I know you feel is important. Our standard of living will be extremely comfortable." Bert was domestic, while Celia, most definitely, was not. "We shall get along well because he cooks and I don't, and in any case he doesn't expect me to be a housewife although he says that he'd like a child in a couple of years' time if, I have the time." She double-underlined "if." Celia added, "Bertie is wonderful around the house & likes to be busy — he is an excellent interior designer by the way." She had a suitable consort, one with a car, for her social engagements. A newspaper photo in January 1952 of the married couple was captioned, "Celia Franca and her husband Mr. Herbert R. Anderson entertain at a supper for the cast of the Canadian National Ballet company following their opening in Toronto January 30."

Bert's expectation of a week's honeymoon at the cottage was cut drastically short. He had just one weekend with his wife, who recorded in her diary that she had "the curse." Monday found him driving Celia to Montreal to perform at *Ballet Under the Stars*. Bert vividly remembered one incident on that trip. Driving along the highway, he suddenly smelled smoke and pulled over to see if the brakes were burning. All seemed right, but back on the road, the odour became stronger. Pulling over again, he inspected the car. To his horror, he realized Celia's long dresses, which had been laid out on the back seat to avoid being crushed, had caught on fire from a cigarette flung out the front window by one of them.

CELIA'S BOAST THAT BERT was "crazy about my work" was put to the test immediately upon their return from Montreal. Although Bert's mother had just died, Celia went off on August 19 to begin her Western Canadian audition tour, arranged by Stewart James. With military precision, it began in Vancouver, progressed to Victoria, moved on to Edmonton, Calgary, Saskatoon, Regina, and, finally, Winnipeg on August 31.

She took every opportunity to promote the importance of creating Canada's first national ballet company. Always perfectly dressed — either in a dark suit accenting her tiny waist or a crisp flowery dress, high-heeled shoes, her hair pulled back in a ballerina's bun, and full makeup — she chatted up the press.

This western audition tour was a formidable challenge. In less than two weeks, Celia had to meet, observe, assess, and make decisions about the bulk of the twenty-eight dancers she would need to form a company. Some of these dancers she had seen at the Canadian Ballet Festival in Montreal the year before, but many would be new to her. She had to keep in mind the different types of dancers she would need, making balanced judgments between those who were inexperienced-but-promising and those

Even after Celia and Bert were no longer living together, the company would have summer parties at Bert's Port Union cottage on Lake Ontario. From the Myrna Aaron photo album, courtesy of Dance Collection Danse

with more training but who might balk at adapting to Franca's dance style. She had to remember their shapes and sizes and how they might be blended together.

While almost every aspiring ballet dancer in Canada wanted to be selected for this exciting new company, this was by no means the attitude of their teachers. Across the west, James had pre-arranged with dance teachers to use their studios and they, in turn, had lined up the aspirants. One sticking point was the long-established Winnipeg Ballet company. Co-artistic director Gweneth Lloyd's abrupt departure from Winnipeg to Toronto had suggested the company was in difficulty. In response to James's request to use the Winnipeg Ballet company's studio for three days of auditions, Betty Farrally wired back, stating that she doubted very much that Celia would need such a long period of time as most of the dancers were already employed. When asked by the *Winnipeg Free Press* if she would audition Winnipeg Ballet company dancers, Celia turned the table: "I hope they will have the decency not to come. I have no time for dancers who are disloyal to their company." She had already snagged Winnipeg's star male dancer, David Adams along with his wife, Lois Smith. In truth, she had a poor opinion of the company. After reading Winnipeg Ballet program notes, she confessed, "The text was so awful and so below my standards, I could not make any kind of liaison with those people except to try and be polite and not rude."[96]

Celia hired another married couple, Irene Apiné and Jury Gotshalks, Latvian immigrants who were dancing in Halifax. Similar to resentments felt by the Winnipeg Ballet, Halifax objected to the couple being lured away.

Celia's task of forming a national ballet company was not unlike that of a Canadian prime minister assembling a cabinet; it was imperative it have regional representation in order not to offend any portion of the country. From the Vancouver area, she chose Fergus Hunter, a nightclub artist, and Mary Toochina; from Edmonton, Grant Strate, oddly enough a recently qualified lawyer with negligible dance training. From the eastern regions she added Brian Macdonald, a reporter from the *Montreal Herald*, along with fellow Quebecers Howard Meadows, André Dufresne, and Robert Ito.[97] The majority of the twenty-eight selected were from Ontario; among them were London's Earl Kraul and several dancers poached from Volkoff, including Judie Colpman and Natalia Butko.

Provincial representation was important, but not, as far as

Celia was concerned, decisive. Just as important was eye appeal. In one case, it backfired. Howard Meadows, who would eventually become the National Ballet's wardrobe master, had not proven to be a very good dancer in the auditions. Betty Oliphant had been curious about Celia's choice.

> Later when I asked Celia why on earth she had taken him, she explained that she had to have someone who would look good when stripped to the waist for the Danse Arabe in *The Nutcracker*. But it wasn't that easy; she hadn't realized that his chest was covered with a mass of curly black hair. Added to the aesthetic problem was the fact that he would have to wear brown body make-up. He was not willing to shave his chest. They compromised. He agreed to trim the hair and all was well."[98]

Celia herself was the twenty-ninth dancer.[99] Without doubt, she knew that coming to Canada would allow her to extend her own performance life. She maintained that she was forced to cast herself because of the lack of dancers of sufficient proficiency, but the fact remained that she was able to choose her own roles. She cast herself in several principal ballerina roles including *Giselle*, which had been denied her by de Valois. Although these roles were important to her, so was the well-being of her new company. She had no qualms in filling in for an injured dancer in the ranks of the corps.

All the dancers she had chosen paid their own way to Toronto and received a wage of twenty-five dollars for rehearsal periods with an extra ten dollars added for performance time. Six of the male out-of-towners lived together in the west end of Toronto.[100] Brian Macdonald recounted that they were paid in cash on Fridays and by the following Thursday, his money had invariably run out. Several of the Toronto girls adopted one of the male dancers and took him to their family for a home-cooked meal as well as bringing snacks to class. Yves Cousineau boarded at Betty Oliphant's house and studio at 444 Sherbourne for a couple of years and remembers that when he had acquired enough stamps to claim unemployment insurance, he was told that UIC didn't have a classification in their books for dancers. The girls were expected to pay for their own pointe shoes while the boys' slippers were given to them. Many of the out-of-town dancers made considerable personal sacrifices. David Adams and Lois Smith left their baby daughter, Janine, behind to be raised by Adams' family.

Rehearsals began on September 17, 1951. One of those National Ballet pioneers, André Dufresne, still remembers that first day. "Celia was simply full of joy. A great voice. Encouraging, pleasant and showing much care. Special words for each and everyone."

Celia had fewer than three months to whip into shape twenty-eight dancers who were all at differing levels of proficiency. Some were polished professionals, such as David Adams, Irene Apiné, and Jury Gotshalk; Angela Leigh had studied ballet in England and Vera Keiss had studied at the National Opera Ballet School in Latvia. Others had seriously weak technique. Days began with Celia giving an hour and a half class, followed by rehearsals. Some of the dancers went off to take extra classes — the girls with Betty Oliphant at her school, the boys with Boris Volkoff. Later on, Celia banned her dancers from taking class with Volkoff, although several continued to sneak off to his Yonge Street studio.

When dancers were unable to manage the choreography, Celia adjusted it to their capability. She described it as a "veneer of professionalism" to disguise the dancers' lack of physical technique. Betty Oliphant greatly admired the results. "Celia was brilliant at never giving away the limitation of the dancers ... The very, very first performance I ever saw of the company, I couldn't believe that out of what I knew were very different styles, and, by and large, not very well trained dancers (although some were good) she had managed to produce this effect."[101] As a starting

Charter members (clockwise from front left) Irene Apiné, Earl Kraul, Natalia Butko, Myrna Aaron, Walter Foster, Robert Ito, Celia Franca, and, behind Celia, Angela Leigh. Though having a light moment in this photo, the young dancers were terrified of "Miss Franca." From the Lois Smith photo album, courtesy of Dance Collection Danse

point, Celia chose *Les Sylphides* to train the corps de ballets to get a feeling for a uniform style.

Two days before the company's first performance, the dancers had to vacate their rehearsal space at St. Lawrence Hall.

The arrival of cold weather in early November meant it was time for St. Lawrence Hall to revert to being a shelter for the homeless. Board member Eddie Goodman scouted alternative rehearsal spaces, including a gymnasium on Yonge Street, a church hall basement, and the Strathcona Roller Skating Rink. The generosity of members of the Canadian Dance Teachers Association saved the situation. The dancers moved to Bettina Byer's dance studio while the company office relocated to Mildred Wickson's studio.

On November 12, 1951, an early freeze-up trapped 26 hunters in northern Ontario. Princess Elizabeth, leaving Canada, after a five-week tour, said, if she was happy to be going home, she was also leaving a country that had become a second home in every sense. Newly elected Prime Minister Winston Churchill, speaking in Guildhall, further astonished us by revealing that the deposed socialist government had left a mess at home and abroad. Judy Garland suffered a collapse backstage at the Palace Theatre in New York. The University of Toronto Blues defeated the McGill Redmen, 11–7, to capture college football laurels. And that night, at 8:30 p.m., in the Eaton Auditorium, the National Ballet of Canada presented the premier performance of The Dance of Salome *choreographed and performed by a Miss. Celia Franca, former leading dramatic dancer at the Sadler's Wells.*

Thus did writer Mordecai Richler set the scene for the debut of the National Ballet of Canada.[102]

By a stroke of bad luck or of poor planning, the company's performance dates at Eaton Auditorium coincided with the most ferocious competitions at the city's other theatrical venues. At the Royal Alexandra Theatre, New York's Metropolitan Opera opened Strauss's *Die Fledermaus* with dancer Tatiana Gratzeva in the cast. At Massey Hall, Shaw's *Don Juan in Hell* starred Charles Boyer, Charles Laughton, Sir Cedric Hardwicke, and Agnes Moorhead. The Ice Capades were performing from Monday to Friday at Maple Leaf Gardens with a show featuring a romantic version of the fairytale *Cinderella*. Dance fans could catch Gene Kelly and ingénue ballerina Leslie Caron in *An American in Paris* at Loew's movie theatre at prices ranging from five cents for a morning show to ninety cents for an evening show. The fact that people queued at

Balletomanes buying tickets at the Eaton Auditorium box office. As seen on the poster, the original name of the company was the Canadian National Ballet Company, or CNBC. Sounding too similar to Canada's major railways (Canadian National and Canadian Pacific), the name was quickly changed to the National Ballet of Canada. Courtesy of Dance Collection Danse

the Eaton Auditorium box office for ballet tickets, despite these rival events, attests to the hunger that existed for Canada to have its own national ballet company.

The embryonic company did not disappoint its eager audience. Celia's years of experience in England had taught her how to put together crowd-pleasing entertainment. At that sold-out opening night, with the audience in full evening clothes, the curtain at Eaton Auditorium opened to a traditional "white ballet": the second dance from *Les Sylphides*, with David Adams and a chorus of beautiful muses. Eddie Goodman, in his memoirs, described that moment as heralding the beginning of a new institution. "I closed my eyes and gave a quiet *shechianu* as the corps de ballet started to dance the Nocturne *of Les Sylphides*. It was not the best dancing the world had seen, but for me that night was the most memorable of the hundreds I have spent at the theatre."[103]

Next came Celia's dramatic interpretation of *Salome*. She used two of her strongest dancers, David Adams and Lois Smith, to perform a pas de deux from *Giselle*. Aiming to counter any complaints about a lack of Canadian content, Celia then programmed the lyrical *Étude* by the Vancouver choreographer Kay Armstrong.[104] The audience was sent back into the rain at the end of the evening after a rousing rendition of the Polovetsian dances from the ballet *Prince Igor* featuring Irene Apiné and Jury Gots-chalks. Before leaving, the audience demanded ten curtain calls.

On the day of the debut, *The Globe and Mail* ran a full spread of photos under the headline, "Talent Recruited from Coast to Coast for Ballet Opening." The next morning, *The Globe*'s Herbert Whittaker, a champion of the company, gave an enthusiastic review: "A rousing, stamping performance of Fokine's *Prince Igor* brought to a conclusion the first full-fledged performance of the Canadian National Ballet and one left Eaton Auditorium last night with a happy feeling that Celia Franca had got her dancers off to a strong start."

The spectators, though, had no idea of the pandemonium going on behind the curtain that night. Unaware that lighting was an integral part of Celia's staging, the lighting technician had been replaced at the last moment, and he had no idea of the decisions made in rehearsals. Set designer James Pape had designed the *Les Sylphides* backdrop to represent moonlit ruins, but the scene painters, in an attempt to help, added snow to make it more Canadian. The dancers had never rehearsed with the orchestra.

Of that night, Celia recalled, "[It was] hectic, organized, exciting. Those are the words that best express our first performance. There was an unexpressed, but emphatic feeling between us all that we were embarking on something extremely important."[105]

In one of her rare instances of introspection, Celia wrote to Doris in early January 1952, "The amount of money being spent on the ballet is so enormous that I live in constant terror lest the directors decided to stop functioning. That first season produced a deficit of $24.18. One thing is definite. They didn't know what they were in for when they started." She added, "Neither did I."

SEVEN

Supporting Cast

DESPITE CELIA'S INDEFATIGABLE ENERGY, she could not have pulled off creating a ballet company from scratch without the total commitment of the dancers and the selfless help of many others. Throughout her life, Celia Franca had the ability to attract people prepared to dedicate themselves to her. In England, Doris Margolis, Kay Ambrose, and Honor Frost had all gladly made sacrifices and contributed many long hours of unpaid work. It was the same in Canada. Besides Bert Anderson, several others impressed with Celia's bravery, and likely touched by her vulnerability, stepped in to give unstinting help.

Stewart James and his family were exceptionally generous. After teaching two Sunday dance classes in early April, Celia went to the James home, where she slept for the afternoon and stayed for a dinner of roast beef, vegetables, salad, lemon pie, cake, and coffee. "Delicious," she wrote Doris, adding that she was putting

Myrna Aaron snapped this photo of the two friends, Celia Franca and Kay Ambrose. From the Myrna Aaron photograph album, courtesy of Dance Collection Danse

on weight but didn't look fat — yet. Presumably the sight of a prime rib of beef with all the trimmings seduced her temporarily to forgo her vegetarianism.

James was available to give Celia any help she required. By May he was volunteering full-time for her. "Stewart James' work is invaluable and I give him a few dollars a week for his streetcar fares," Celia wrote. Once the charter dancers began to arrive in September, several were billeted in James's grandmother's large home in Mimico, a village to the west of Toronto.

In those early days, Celia had nothing but praise for the man who had met her in London and offered her the job. They travelled together on the cross-country audition. He became the company's first general manager. Mysteriously, though, James fell out of favour and resigned in spring 1952 rather than be fired. No official reason was ever given for his fall from grace. Board minutes indicate a belief that he was under-functioning. In fact, once the professional arts manager, Walter Homburger, agreed to work for the company a couple of days a week, James was no longer needed.[106] Understandably bitter, James told Lawrence Adams in an interview in the 1990s, "I made things work and when they were working I was taken out."[107] He was the first of many National Ballet of Canada administrators who would fall out of favour with Celia Franca.[108]

Celia demonstrated this kind of ruthlessness throughout her life. If a person was no longer useful, she moved on. Some people, such as Cyril Frankel or Doris Margolis, accepted it and were satisfied with the occasional letter or visit when Celia hit town. And while husbands Leo Kersley and, later, Bert Anderson were deeply wounded by her rejection, both kept an affection for this extraordinary woman. It seemed that living in the reflective glory of Celia's glamour, boldness, energy, and ambition was worth the eventual abandonment.

There was a core group of indispensable colleagues. Without Betty Oliphant, it's unlikely Celia could have made a success of it on her own during those first years. They worked as a team with the common goal of creating the very best company and dancers. Celia knew how to put together a ballet company, and Betty knew how to train ballet dancers. There was trust between them, and during the years Celia was still dancing, Betty would give her a private twenty minute warm-up. She was the only person who could give Celia corrections after a performance.

In those first months in Canada, Betty Oliphant was Celia's only friend who shared her British ballet background. After a hard day of teaching, they would kick off their shoes and have a drink or two. After all, they had bonded over "cold tea." Both women enjoyed recounting the story of the time Celia invited Betty to nip into the ladies room to have a sip from her flask of refreshing "cold tea" — that is to say, of straight Scotch. During the first summer school, in the hiatus between the day and evening classes, the two of them would sometimes duck out to Letros Tavern on King Street to relax by drinking potent Manhattans. "One particularly hot and humid evening, Betty and I floated back to the school, where it was my turn to teach the 'babies' class under the eyes of their parents. Betty tried to stifle her giggles as I staggered to place the portable barres in the middle of the classroom and she continued laughing as I taught, as I could, the most complicated polka step imaginable!"[109]

Once the company had been formed, Betty agreed to become its ballet mistress; she was able to maintain her own dance school as well. Celia became auntie to Betty's girls, Carol and Gail. Carol described her first memory of meeting Celia when she was around six. "She had really strange eyebrows and I asked her about them — she had shaved her eyebrows off as a young girl for some performance thinking that they would grow back and they didn't. She totally penciled them on." Celia often shared meals with Betty and her girls at 444 Sherbourne Street. "She talked to us very easily once we got to know her," Carol remembered. For several years, Betty, her girls, and Celia would spend their brief vacation after summer school together attending the Stratford Festival and travelling to Pinelands Lodge in Muskoka.

Carol had been under the impression her mother was Celia's boss. When Celia began discussing retirement, fourteen-year-old Carol told Aunt Celia, "If you quit, Mom will fire you." Celia put her straight that she, in fact, was the boss.

The affable and talented George Crum, hired as the company's first music director, became a good friend to Celia. Aileen Woods facilitated Crum's employment by inviting the twenty-four-year-old conductor of the Royal Conservatory Opera to lunch. He recalled his first impression of Celia: "She had very black hair and she fitted my stereotype image of what a ballerina should look like. Her hair was swept back in a severe bun. She had an ascetic look ... her looks were set in this expression, 'This is the way things are going to be.'"[110] Their shared extensive knowledge of music made them kindred spirits. Celia had several nicknames for the pudgy Crum including Georgie, Pogo, and Fairy Crumpletoes. He always had a joke for her, saying, "Cel, I've got one for you." In the early years they spent a great deal of time together, and Crum remembered that they could easily kill half a bottle of Scotch in an evening.[III]

Another young man, David Haber, also became a long-time friend and helpmate to Celia. They met in the summer of 1951 when Celia went to Ottawa to see a rehearsal of the Canadian Repertory Theatre where the twenty-four-year-old Haber was employed as the stage manager. He was impressed with her commitment: "She struck me as perfectly focused."[II2] Impressed in turn with his competency, Celia offered him a job. He was put in charge of transporting equipment and sets for the first tours in Canada and the United States. The challenges were often insurmountable. In Red Deer, the stage was simply a platform with a twelve-foot ceiling. "There was nothing we could do to mount the scenery. In Regina, the venue was coincidentally called Darke Hall, when the lights were rigged, all the fuses in the building blew. One time in the second act of *Coppelia* when Celia opened the curtain expecting to reveal the doll, she discovered Haber sitting in the trunk waving a hairy leg with a pointe shoe hanging off his foot and whispering to Celia, 'hello, darling.'" Colleen Kenney, one of the teenage dancers, remembered that Celia simply could not keep a straight face and infected all the others.

UNQUESTIONABLY, CELIA'S GREATEST HELP came from Kay Ambrose, her English friend. After the war, Ambrose became totally immersed in authentic classical Indian dance. She joined forces with Ram Gapal, an exotic, physically striking male Indian classical dancer, described as the Nijinsky of India. Ambrose became a part of his company, acting as art director, lecturer, and Gapal's personal confidante, touring with him in the United States and

India. The year before coming to Canada, she had written and illustrated a widely admired book called *Classical Dances and Costumes of India*. Kay came to Toronto just days before the company's debut, expecting to be there for six weeks to finish a book she was co-writing with Celia. She ended up staying for over a decade. She reported to Doris, in a letter, written the day before the debut at Eaton Auditorium, that Celia was exhausted. "Celia and Bert met me at the air office in Toronto in their car and I must say, Celia looked a bit like the giant Panda — the bear with the black circles under his eyes!"

Kay went on to describe the situation. "Without a moment to breathe, we went head-first into Celia's preparations, and these were all I thought they would be in every way. That is to say, the dress rehearsal was well under control, no temperaments, and smooth and stimulating, but, the costumes are not half ready ... It is more than obvious why she wanted her own people from England, stage-manager and dress-maker. It isn't that these people just don't know Celia's way, they don't know anything at all."

Kay acknowledged that Bert had been indispensable during those start-up months: "I really cannot see how Celia would have survived without him up to the present — anyone can see that things would have been far too much for her.... I think Bert must have saved her from much harm, apart from his personal care of her."

Kay joined Celia and Bert at the Port Union cottage where the newly married couple had decided to stay over the winter. That hadn't been their original idea. They had planned to rent an apartment in the city and sell Bert's car. With the returning servicemen and the flood of new immigrants to Toronto, there was zero occupancy rate for rentals. Many had to settle for make-shift arrangements. So, they were forced to remain many miles out of the city and bought a new beige and green Hillman-Minx, which they nicknamed "Two-Tone-Tessie."

Kay, in one of her evocative letters, set the scene for Doris.

"The cottage has one large living room with a big, black stove which keeps the place warm, and only certain bedrooms can be used, the others are shut up till next Spring.... The water-supply has had to be shut off during the Big Freeze of the winter and a large pan of water is kept in an enclosed veranda with a big pot of it always warm on the stove." Not used to central heating, and having survived war conditions, these two English women found it all rather a lark at first.

In January 1952 Celia sent Doris her own cottage scene-setter letter. "Bertie has been dancing up and down to the radio with nothing on but a thin dressing gown which keeps opening down the front. He also tried cooking some chocolate biscuits today. We both sat looking at our watches for 15 mins while they were in the oven. When we opened the oven door, clouds of smoke came out. We were in hysterics." Celia did not mention where Kay had been when Bert was parading around with his gaping dressing-gown, no doubt the paisley-silk one which the Franks family had sent to their new son-in-law as a Christmas present.

At the beginning, this ménage a trois worked well. Bert, in a later interview, said that Kay had a wonderful wit and was totally cat-crazy, always pretending to be a cat and stroking her pretend whiskers. The decision to remain at the Port Union cottage over the winter of 1951–52, however, would prove to be a mistake. The inconvenience of its distance, coupled with Celia's long and unpredictable rehearsal hours, meant Bert had to quit his secure job at Eaton Auditorium to become, as Celia put it, the "chauffeur come everything-else." She told Doris, "The amount of unpaid work he has put into the ballet is inestimable." This meant, though, that one of Bert's charms, his ability to support her financially, had vanished.

What initially seemed romantic began to lose its appeal. The rustic living conditions, the inconvenience of the distance, and Celia's refusal to learn how to drive a car — compounded by the intrusion of Kay Ambrose — put strains on the marriage. The

A publicity shot of Celia relaxing at home with the cat that lived at the apartment she shared on Tyndall Avenue with Kay and Doris. Photograph by Ken Bell, courtesy of the National Ballet of Canada Archives

greatest tension was Celia's singular focus on creating a national ballet company. She had neither energy nor time for any other person or activity. Celia was aware of the problem, but not of the consequences. "I adore him except that he wants me to visit his friends too often," Celia wrote to Doris. "He is quite right, but you know me! He spends all the week doing what I want and at the weekends I refuse to go out with him. I usually go in the end, but under protest. However we love each other very much and everything is fine."

But it was not fine. Celia and Kay moved together into a large west-end Toronto apartment on Tyndall Avenue, leaving Bert behind at the cottage. The relationship remained somewhat tenuous, with Celia occasionally having dinner with her estranged husband or taking the dancers for a party at the Port Union cottage. After that first winter in Port Union, Bert and Celia did not live together again.

Even though separated, Celia perpetuated her status of being a wife and in a sense depended on that title. In several newspaper articles after their actual separation, she took care to work in references to her husband. In January 1954, she told a Montreal *Gazette* reporter that, in private life, she was Mrs. H.R. Anderson, her husband being in the publishing business. By that time he had a position at Maclean-Hunter. She added, "But he happens to be very interested in the company and dancing and that makes things much easier." In this article, she advised young ballerinas either not to marry or to marry a fellow dancer. "Otherwise the poor little husband is left behind while his wife rehearses and goes off on tour." She was describing what had happened to Bert Anderson.

The following month, the *Detroit Times* captioned her photo, "Franca, married to businessman H.R. Anderson who shares his wife's love for music and the dance." As late as 1958, she was still maintaining the pretense. The *Peterborough Examiner* featured Bert and Celia with the caption, "Bert Anderson, Peterborough and his wife, choreographer Celia Franca enjoy a brief reunion before the performance. Mr. Anderson's work as Peterborough representative of the National Film Board and Miss Franca's work with the ballet company make visits infrequent." This would not be the last time Celia persisted in the charade of being happily married.

Kay Ambrose had become Celia's indispensable right-hand woman. Exceptionally capable, she took on any job needed, from chief set and costume designer to publicist to advance person. She was also Celia's speech and annual report writer. She was able to create sets and costumes on the most miniscule budget. Most of the textiles for her costumes came from the fabric department of the T. Eaton Company, which catered to everyday wear rather than ballet costumes. Kay was able to browse the rows of fabric bolts and envision how to turn a humdrum material into a dramatic costume. In those years, T. Eaton Company was underwriting most of the costume expenses. Kay signed for the textiles and an invoice was never forwarded to the company. She did have to pay cash at Dressmaker's Supplies for materials, such as the netting for tutus, which were not stocked at Eaton's. After the years of rationing and short supplies in England, sourcing for such accessories as bridal-store tiaras (which substituted for headdresses), came as second nature to the resourceful Ambrose.

Cynthia MacLennan, hired by Kay in 1956, called her boss "a one-woman force." "Kay had to make do. It was extraordinary how she coped." MacLennan, a graduate of the Macdonald Institute (now part of the University of Guelph), where she had learned dressmaking in the Domestic Science program as there were no post-secondary theatre training programs in Canada (the National Theatre School of Canada located in Montreal opened in 1960), had worked for six weeks in wardrobe at the new Stratford Festival. She never forgot her mid-afternoon job interview at the Tyndall Street apartment. As she was showing Ambrose her portfolio, a door suddenly opened and out came Celia Franca in a white nightgown with her black hair hanging loose down her back. "I had no idea that Celia lived there. I had no idea they lived together. I was just beside myself."[113]

Most of all, Kay Ambrose anchored Celia. Kay was a part of her past and they could talk about mutual friends, such as Cyril Frankel and the ballet days of wartime England. Celia relied heavily on Kay, who shared the same quick-wittedness and outlook on life. Kay had a variety of pet names for Celia, including Poos and Pussis. The two of them, wickedly, had their private nickname for Betty Oliphant based on her initials — B.O. — and called the Royal Winnipeg Ballet "Winnipiggers." They were a formidable partnership with their unbounded energy and self-assurance. Kay and Celia were prepared to dedicate every waking hour to creating a ballet company for Canadians.

By necessity, both women were experts at cadging favours for the ballet company. No one was immune from their opportunism. When an English dancer, Paula "Topsy" Dunn — who had been in the chorus of the film *The Red Shoes* — turned up on her doorstep in April 1951, having come to Canada to join her fiancé, Celia commandeered the beau into helping her. "I managed to get 2,000 envelopes 'for free' out of her fiancé," Celia boasted in a letter to Doris. "The envelopes are for my summer school circulars."[114]

Empathetic and nurturing, Kay created a home life complete with a menagerie of cats. She provided Celia with companionship while making few demands. Celia found sanctuary in her tiny bedroom, which had been painted a restful green. In her infrequent idle moments, she would go to this room to read detective novels for relaxation.

At some point, it's not clear exactly when, Doris Margolis came to Toronto to join Celia and Kay.

While Celia had encouraged Doris to come over to look after the domestic details of her life, she also had a premonition that Doris would not adapt to Toronto life. She warned her, "Life over here is so different from life in England. I can tell you now that it took me quite a while to get used to a different set of values. Even now I find I cannot accept certain things about Canada and the way people live (including Bert) but the point is that we are the 'foreigners' and must comply to their rules or not be accepted." Celia had picked up quickly on the fact that many Canadians had

Celia, Doris Margolis, Katharine Stewart, Kay Ambrose, and (seated) Oldyna Dynowska with the Tyndall cat. Celia seems to be miles away, dreaming.
Courtesy of Library and Archives Canada, e008406978

chips on their shoulders about English professionals arriving to run the new cultural institutions. She recognized that some of her fellow countrymen appeared arrogant and patronizing. In those early days she herself experienced some of the Canadian animosity she found hurtful, but tried to ignore. She failed to recognize that her imperious manner and insistence on the superiority of British-style ballet made her appear arrogant and patronizing.

Doris did not adjust to Canadian life. With Kay and Celia away all day or on tour, she was isolated and lonely in the apartment on the western outskirts of Toronto. The experiment failed and Eddie Goodman paid Doris's airfare back to London. Celia and Doris kept in touch, exchanging birthday cards and infrequent letters. Celia sporadically sent her money.[115]

On Sunday, February 21, 1954, while Celia and Kay were on tour in Milwaukee, fire broke out in their Tyndall Avenue apartment, gutting their kitchen, bathroom, and one of the bedrooms. The next day the *Toronto Star* reported, "One of the heaviest losers, firemen said, was Miss Celia Franca, artistic director of the Canadian Ballet Company, now on a U.S. tour."

The triumvirate of artistic director Celia Franca, stage manager David Haber, and ballet mistress Betty Oliphant watching a rehearsal in St. Lawrence Hall sometime in 1953. They would soon have to vacate the facility to make way for its use as a winter shelter for homeless men. Courtesy of the National Ballet of Canada Archives

After repairs, they continued to live at the apartment until 1958. The four-bedroom unit was a busy place. Frequently, dancers with no other place to go were billeted with them. For a time, they shared the rent with the young stage manager, David Haber, and one of the dancers, Maria Dynowska (Oldyna). Charter member Colleen Kenney recalled an episode when Celia and Kay took her to the Tyndall apartment for a week after her roommate had had a nervous breakdown. In the midst of this continuous commotion, Celia still did all her nightly paperwork.

IN THOSE FORMATIVE YEARS of the ballet company, Celia considered her dancers as family. Some of the original members, such as Connie Campbell, Mary Toochina,[116] and Brian Macdonald, quickly left, while others, such as Yves Cousineau, were added. In her memoirs, Celia wrote, "Most of those dancers during that first season were amateurs, being paid starvation wages and being forced by me to behave, and to *want* to behave, as professionals. That, at least, is what many of them now tell me."[117]

During that first decade Celia performed a juggling act, as the authoritative artistic director and fellow dancer. In rehearsals when she wore her hair in two long braids, she looked like one of the kids. The dancers, awed by the clipped assertive instructions barked out by Franca, began to mimic her diction. The company's first rehearsal pianist, Margaret Clemens, recalled the dancers began to adopt English accents and mannerisms. While sometimes amusing, Clemens more often thought it sad that these youngsters felt it necessary to reject their own culture."[118]

Celia had to stand somewhat aloof to maintain the discipline she needed to cajole and bully those young people into becoming technically excellent ballet dancers. Colleen Kenney, a naive seventeen-year-old when she first joined the company, remembers the total focus Celia gave in those first rehearsals. "As far as we were concerned, this was the only thing she had to do, rehearse us, at that particular time. She could see everybody." Kenney was impressed with Celia's ability to compartmentalize. "At a party, she could talk to you as if you were the only person in the room. Our dear Betty was totally different, she'd be talking to you but never, ever looking at you whereas with Celia you were the only person in the room. And when she rehearsed you, it was the same thing, her focus was right there."[119]

While strict, Celia often showed her wry sense of humour. During a month-long run at the Royal Alexandra in January 1958, teenager Lorna Geddes, not yet a full member of the company, danced in the corps in *Swan Lake*. Disappointed in the corps' performance one night, Celia gathered them together, still in costume, to give corrections. Coming to Geddes, she said, "You, you looked like the Hunchback of Notre Dame." Geddes recalls, "I'm sure I was round-shouldered and I barely knew what I was doing." Returning to high school, Geddes won the crown for posture queen. "I don't know how I had the nerve at fifteen and not even a member of the company, but I knocked on her door, it was just too ironic, and I said, 'Miss Franca, I just wanted to show you what the Hunchback of Notre Dame just got, and she nearly exploded ... she just loved it.'"

Geddes, always a madcap, still a principal character artist with the company,[120] remembers another time when she misbehaved. During a performance of Cranko's *Pineapple Poll* she and her partner, Donald Mahler switched roles with Lorna picking him up. Celia, who never missed anything, took Geddes aside right after the performance and said, "Oh darling, that was so funny, I almost wet my panties." After a pause, she continued, "But don't do it again."[121]

Another story in the company folklore involves Myrna Aaron. During a performance of *Giselle* at the Royal Alexandra Theatre, Myrna and two other corps dancers had to exit the downstage wing, race around to the upstage wing, and re-enter the stage immediately. Rather short-sighted and in a rush, she tripped, fell, and found herself being picked up. "I hope Franca didn't see that," Myrna said. Franca, having got the dancer back on her feet, replied, "It's all right dear, she didn't."[122]

Celia had her favourites as well as those she didn't particularly warm to. Her distaste for the Russian ballet style influenced her opinion of Jury Gotshalks, Irene Apiné, and Volkoff-trained Natalia Butko. On the other hand, she found Angela Leigh and David Adams, both of whom had English ballet training, quite pleasing. Although relatively untrained in ballet, Celia recognized Lois Smith's potential. Smith was startled on first meeting Franca. "She had white make-up on, it was ghost white and the penciled eyebrows. I think that was the style she came from. But we had never seen it before. She had a dramatic face to start with."[123]

AMONG THOSE IN THE first years who provided critical support for the National Ballet were, besides the original Three Ladies, several other board members, such as Mabel Hees (wife of federal politician George Hees), Robert Laidlaw, Arthur Gelber, and Eddie Goodman. They invited Celia to their homes. The Woods and the Laidlaws also invited Celia and Kay to their summer cottages, a Canadian pastime that never appealed to Celia. Perhaps as a reaction to her short-lived experiences at Port Union, she never took to the pleasures of Ontario rustic life. She hated bugs and wasn't keen on swimming. Life at the Laidlaws' family compound at Roches Point, Lake Simcoe, reminiscent of an English manor home, was more to Celia's taste. Along with cottage visits, Robert Laidlaw,[124] known to intimates as Bobbie, occasionally took Celia and Kay to hockey games at Maple Leaf Gardens, cheering from front-row seats.

Among the board members, Celia's staunchest supporter and consistent champion was Eddie Goodman. Joining the board in spring 1951, he met Celia while she was still working at T. Eaton. His love of ballet stemmed from the days when his sister had studied at the Boris Volkoff School and he had attended recitals. It's possible he and Celia had an affair. He was a most attractive man, sophisticated and witty. Goodman and Franca did take a trip together to New York in 1953 to talk to Antony Tudor about *Lilac Garden*.

As did others, Goodman took it for granted that cottage life would relax Celia. In his memoirs, *Life of the Party*, he wrote about taking Celia fishing one weekend at his Lake Couchiching cottage. When a huge muskellunge hooked on her line, she screamed and threw the rod back to Eddie, who fought for twenty minutes unsuccessfully to bring the muskie into the boat.

Doris Margolis's first cousin Pearl, Pearl's psychiatrist husband, Dr. Ben Geneen, and the couple's two children, Lucy[125] and son David, emigrated from Glasgow to Toronto in the 1950s. Through Doris, Celia had become a friend of the Geneen family while still in England. They were among the few non-ballet friends Celia had in Toronto. Lucy Geneen and Gail Oliphant became friends and enjoyed spending time with "Auntie Celia." Years later Dr. Geneen commented that he felt Celia was basically shy. He also described what he called her "façade of self-confidence," perceptively diagnosing that Celia had worked hard to create her persona.

Façade or not, Celia had convinced Canadians that she had the ability to create a national ballet company.

EIGHT

Constructing a Ballet Company

THE MINUTES OF THE National Ballet Guild meeting in May 1951 recorded that the directors had agreed they should alert "the proper authorities in Ottawa that an attempt was being made in Toronto to form a national ballet." Since no ministry or department concerned with the arts and culture then existed, Syd Mulqueen wrote directly to the prime minister, Louis St. Laurent. Back from an aide came the blandest possible reply: "Mr. St. Laurent has noted the views set forth and he has asked me to assure you that they will be kept in mind." Eddie Goodman got a more committed response from an unnamed member of parliament. His reply was, "I'm not going to give any money to a bunch of sissy boys in long underwear."

All fundraising had to come from the private sector. While far from easy, it was not impossible. By August 1951 the Guild had raised sixty-five thousand dollars, today about half a million dollars, to underwrite the National Ballet's debut to be held that fall at the Eaton Auditorium. The Three Ladies nagged their husbands and did their best to get their Rosedale friends interested. While miniscule compared to philanthropy in the United States, some generous cultural patrons had long been supporting the arts in Canada. Byron Walker, president of the Bank of Commerce, did a great deal for the Royal Ontario Museum, the Toronto Conservatory of Music, and the Toronto Mendelssohn Choir. The Massey family built Toronto's Massey Music Hall, among many other projects. In Winnipeg, the Richardson family propped up the Royal Winnipeg Ballet for over half a century.

In addition to her duties as the artistic director and a dancer with the company, Celia worked as a fundraiser — perhaps more accurately as a flatterer of potential donors. Just days after arriving in Toronto, she spoke to a group of over one hundred at a cocktail party at the Woods' home. She told Doris, "I was terrified as I had for various reasons no news to give them but it went off alright." But it was uphill work. The prevailing tone of cultural activity in Toronto at this time was that of conformity. In 1951, a group of professional artists in the city protested the inclusion of abstract works in a show at the Art Gallery of Ontario to be opened by the governor general. This was half a century after the emergence of Modernism and years after abstract painting had developed in New York and in Quebec with the Automatists.[126] Still, there were signs that a metropolitan city was beginning to emerge.

If the National Ballet was to survive, it needed, besides money, an audience. Attracting one in Toronto was challenging. Luring people in the rest of the country to ballet performances — an art form few had had the opportunity to experience, with perhaps the exception of having seen the film *The Red Shoes* — was a far greater challenge. From the start, Celia was determined that the company would be what its name said it was: a national ballet company rather than a company in Toronto that simply used that name. Without knowing the consequences — no newly arrived

British immigrant could have any idea of the immensity of the country nor of the fierceness of its winters — Celia committed herself to staging coast-to-coast tours. The first two general managers, James and Homburger, as well as quite a few of the board members, had serious reservations about going on tour in a country without a theatrical circuit and only a handful of legitimate theatres.

But Celia, having said she would do it, insisted. In the fall of 1952, the company set off by train from Toronto to Calgary and then criss-crossed the western provinces, appearing in Edmonton, Red Deer, Lethbridge, Vancouver, Victoria, Nelson, Saskatoon, Regina, Winnipeg, and Fort William (the latter now part of the amalgamated city of Thunder Bay).

The audiences, initially small, loved having a ballet company come to their town. The greater achievement of that first tour was to start to turn the National Ballet company into a team who looked out for each other. During the three days and nights it took to reach Calgary, the company's first destination, its members began to draw together. Celia and Kay entertained their mostly young dancers by singing the famous ditty made popular by wartime troops travelling on British trains:

Passengers will please refrain
from passing water while the train
is standing in the station ... I love you.

Men who're working underneath
will catch it in the eye and teeth,
So hold it in — or do it in your shoe.

In Moose Jaw, some of the dancers smuggled aboard a cat found on the platform. For several months the feline became the company's mascot, Salome. This train tour, which included sleeping berths, was a luxury never again to be experienced.

Thereafter, to keep costs to the bare minimum, they toured in old buses. The trials and tribulations helped bond the company together and fostered several romantic affairs.

This first tour had to have brought back memories to Celia of her wartime rail tours with the Sadler's Wells Ballet company. This time, though, she was den mother to twenty-eight dancers, some of them underage. The inconveniences and the backstage melodramas were tame compared to those she, and many others, had endured during the war.

Not that touring peacetime Canada was easy. Ambrose described the experience to Cyril in a letter sent on Boxing Day 1953:

We try to tour and no-one has ever tried this on a professional, regular scale in Canada. So there is no ready-made style of advertising, which so far has only terrified me but I think will become a real danger to the company. Then very, very few people know how to work, and I suppose Celia, myself and the stage manager, an excellent lad called David Haber, do the entire staff work between us and, because we are only humans, a good deal isn't done — like sending regular articles to papers and magazines, which should be my job, I suppose. But I only have time for the mean essentials.

By the end of 1953, however, the company had managed to stage fifty-five of their sixty-three performances outside of Toronto.

Celia needed few lessons to give her audiences what they wanted. Her basic program always contained a "white ballet" — meaning a romantic classical ballet such as *Les Sylphides* with an ethereal-looking corps de ballet in long, pale-coloured tutus, their bodies covered in wet-white, a body makeup that added to the other-worldly atmosphere. Changing pace, she would also include a rousing dance such as the Polovetsian dances from *Prince Igor*, or, after 1954, Antony Tudor's *Offenbach in the Underworld*, of which the highlight for men in the audience had to have been the cancan

Celia and Jury Gotshalk striking a dramatic pose at Montreal's His Majesty's Theatre, where the company performed in early 1952. Courtesy of Dance Collection Danse

dance, with dancers chosen especially for the length of their legs to maximize the impact of sheer black stockings and suspenders with a carefully measured five inches of firm flesh showing above the stocking top.[127]

Celia tried to appeal to national pride by staging repertoire with Canadian themes.[128] But her own first piece of Canadian-inspired choreography, *Le Pommier*, which depicted Quebec village life, caused offence by seeming to show *habitants* of years past as

Kay Ambrose's costume designs for the baker, his wife, and the cobbler for Franca's ill-fated dance, *Le Pommier*. Courtesy of Library and Archives Canada, e008439040

village simpletons. She wrote in her 1978 memoir, "In all innocence, having not digested very much Canadian history I proceeded quickly to fabricate a naïve, but well-intentioned pastiche.... From the lyrics [from selection of French-Canadian folk songs arranged by Hector Gratton] I made up a gentle scenario incorporating the activities of a fiddler, a milkmaid, an old man, a cobbler, a baker and his wife and children, a miller and his wife and daughters and two labourers." Its opening in Western Canada went well enough, but not so well when presented in Montreal in February 1952. While some critics were receptive, others were not. "But there were some members of the Montreal branch, very sensitive to cultural matters, who surprised me by feeling incensed and insulted that I should portray such a simple *habitant* image of Quebec. So like *Salome*, *Le Pommier* was soon withdrawn from the repertoire. I was learning."[129]

Celia's mention of *Salome* referred to another programming blunder. For the company's first tour in 1952–53, she had included a remount of her BBC dance drama, *Salome,* which had done exceptionally well in England and had been well received at the inaugural performance at the Eaton Auditorium. It could be managed by the inexperienced dancers and the costumes were minimal. Stewart James remembered that Grant Strate, in a burlap costume, looked like a potato sack; Strate said it "itched mercilessly." But some members of the Montreal audience took exception to the depiction of the three Jewish high priests in the ballet as stereotypical. They demanded that the offending scene be removed from the ballet. Jewish board members such as Gelber, Goodman, and Franca herself had no difficulties with the Jewish high priests scene. Celia dropped the ballet entirely.

Original 1949 BBC costumes designed by Stephen Bundy for the "Three Jews" in Franca's made-for-television ballet, *Salome*. Courtesy of Library and Archives Canada, e008439039

Le Pommier and *Salome* were the kind of mistakes inevitable in any start-up period. The achievements of these groundbreaking tours far overshadowed them. In her 1953 artistic director's report to the board, Celia commented, "What we have really undertaken is the combined role of impresario and doctor to Canada's artistic and theatrical future." This self-congratulation was justified. She and her company were pioneers.

An advertisement for the National Ballet's appearance at the Odeon Palace Movie Theatre in St. Catharines, Ontario, in early April 1952. Courtesy of Dance Collection Danse

Celia had to make many adjustments for Canadian audiences. She was warned to deflect resistance to ballet dancing by calling the company in publicity a "dance troupe," which could mean just about anything. After the introduction of television broadcasting in 1952, there became the perennial problem of enticing husbands away from the hockey game. On a tip, likely from either Franca or Ambrose, the popular *Toronto Telegram* columnist, Frank Tumpane, came up with a solution. In an April 1954 column directed at his women readers, he raised the question, "Do you happen to have a husband who holds the view that ballet is strictly for pantywaists and wrist-slappers and who is frightened of being seen within a block of a performance?" Tumpane's solution was the aforementioned *Les Sylphides*. "If the fellow can't get enjoyment from *Les Sylphides* with its charming music and its pretty girls in those short skirts [actually, the skirts were long and filmy], then he just naturally has no feeling nohow and you'd better keep him at home and feed him vitamins."

Celia reading the score of Gustav Mahler's *Kindertotenlieder*, the music for Tudor's ballet *Dark Elegies*. The theme dealing with the death of children, proved too morbid for Canadian audiences.
Courtesy of the National Ballet of Canada Archives

HANDLING THE COMPANY'S BOARD was another challenge. Board presidents, without exception, were taken aback by Franca's imperious attitude. She had made it clear that she alone made the decisions while their job was to find the money. Celia insisted that her fledgling company tour, despite accumulating deficits. As well, she steadily added new repertoire.

In 1953 the National Ballet moved from the Eaton Auditorium to the Royal Alexandra Theatre. Built in 1907, the "Royal Alex" bore a typical nineteenth-century British theatre style, with balconies and private boxes. Celia felt more at home here, especially since, like most of the London theatres in the 1950s, the Alex had lost much of its original grandeur and had a comfortable, shabby atmosphere. It had several disadvantages, including minimal dressing room space at stage level, and no orchestra pit, having been designed as a drama house. With seating capacity of fifteen hundred and professional stage equipment, this was a major step up for the company.

Celia had the pleasure of instructing her dancers on how to first bow to the dignitaries, particularly Lieutenant-Governor Breithaupt and his wife, who were sitting in the flag-draped lower box to the right of the stage for their first Royal Alex performance.

Left to right: Earl Kraul, Marilyn Rollo, Diane Childerhose, Judy Colpman, André Dufresne, and Oldyna Dynowska taking a break to have a healthy snack.
Courtesy of Dance Collection Danse

The extended season at the Royal Alex and the touring created more work for Celia's dancers. If she couldn't keep her dancers employed and stimulated, she risked losing them to the more lucrative dance jobs in television and with large summertime grandstand dance shows.[130]

By the beginning of 1954, though, the much greater risk was that of losing the company entirely. It had acquired a deficit of over fifty thousand dollars with the costs of creating three new dances.[131] Celia justified her expenditures to *Toronto Star* reporter Jack Karr: "We could have strung along doing the same dances with the same sets and costumes. Instead we felt our company, since it speaks for Canada, should be able to follow any ballet group in the world, including Sadler's Wells." The fact that the Sadler's Wells had just taken back to England a profit of $650,000 from a nineteen-week tour of North America must have given the board pause for thought.

On opening night at the Royal Alex, Celia remained on stage after taking her curtain calls for the program's second dance, Tudor's *Lilac Garden*. Recognizing the oddity of Franca still standing on stage, the audience fell silent and became slightly uncomfortable. She pleaded for donations to make up the fifty-thousand-dollar shortfall in order to allow Canada's national ballet company to survive. To make it easy or rather impossible to make excuses, a bevy of young women swept into the auditorium distributing forms in envelopes addressed to "Save the Ballet Fund." While some spectators found Celia's entreaty déclassé and distasteful, many wrote out cheques. Then, to remind the audience of what they would be missing if the company folded, she carried on to present the rest of that evening's program.

She won over the *Toronto Star*, which printed an editorial, "Save the National Ballet."[132] A few days later, the paper reported that Franca's campaign had already raised over twenty thousand dollars.

Celia's direct appeals for money for a national ballet company provoked Gweneth Lloyd of the Royal Winnipeg Ballet to respond by placing an advertisement in the rival *Toronto Telegram*. Enraged by Franca's presumption that there was only one national ballet company in Canada, Lloyd reminded readers that the Winnipeg company was thriving. She then went on the attack. "While it is regrettable that one company finds itself unable to remain solvent despite generous public support, it would be more regrettable that the hard-working young dancers should be misled and disillusioned regarding their opportunities in the future."

While it is certain that members of the Toronto National Ballet's Women's Guild and some board members would have known in advance of Celia's plans for her opening night, it was decided that she should stop making the pitch. This did not stop her from making "the direct ask" to keep her company going. Celia and Betty loved to tell a story of when they resorted to a ploy to talk the Royal Alex's general manager, Ernest Rawley, and its box office manager, Edwin de Rocher, into deferring the rental fees that week in order to be able to pay their dancers. The two women, still very much a team, paid a visit to the administrative office and plied the managers with Scotch and charm. The dancers were paid that Friday.

Despite support from Oliphant, Celia often felt isolated in her constant struggles in those early years. "I was working alone, pushing alone, begging alone, fighting alone, yes, it was lonely, I didn't consider that though, you do what you have to do. I was never sorry for myself."[133] She never gave up.

WHAT THE BOARD FAILED to acknowledge was Celia Franca's feat of introducing new pieces of repertoire without spending a single cent on performance rights fees. Mainly, she chose excerpts from classical ballets she herself had performed in England. As well, she coaxed English choreographer friends to donate works.

In the summer of 1953, Celia's friend Antony Tudor invited her fledgling company to come to Jacob's Pillow, a summer school

Celia with the legendary pioneer of modern dance Ted Shawn, who established the Jacob's Pillow Dance Festival.
Courtesy of Library and Archives Canada, e008406975

and festival in Massachusetts established by the early pioneer of modern dance, Ted Shawn, for a residency. During this time, Tudor set his ballet, *Lilac Garden*, on the company. It starred Lois

Smith, David Adams, Jimmy Ronaldson, and Celia herself. Giving eight performances in the famous Barn Theatre, it provided some of America's most influential dance critics with the opportunity to check out the young Canadian ballet company. On August 17 *Newsweek* magazine ran a story under the heading "The Canadians Come," while Walter Terry, dance critic for the *New York Herald Tribune*, described their performance as "a stirring program of dance by a highly promising and already gifted new company." Very early in the game, Celia had shrewdly figured out an important part of the Canadian character: a cultural endeavour needed to receive praise from the United States or Great Britain before Canadians themselves would give it any recognition.

Lois Smith, Franca, and David Adams in a costume fitting for *Gala Performance*, one of six Tudor ballets that have been in the National Ballet repertoire over the years. Courtesy of the National Ballet of Canada Archives

Celia had gambled by taking her dancers to a festival primarily devoted to modern dance. And she had to endure Shawn's admonishment or as she described it, "his usual disgusting speech to students and audience that it was shameful that Britain and its Dominion had no modern ballet."[134]

Franca and Ray Moller in *Dark of the Moon*, choreographed by Canadian Joey Harris, with an original score by Louis Applebaum. This version made a brief appearance in 1953, but returned in 1960 with a new name, *Barbara Allen*, and new choreography by David Adams. Courtesy of the National Ballet of Canada Archives

HAVING BEEN WELL RECEIVED in Jacob's Pillow, and after touring extensively throughout Canada in 1954, Celia raised the bar. In 1955 she convinced the board to sign up with the New York-based William Morris Concert Agency to tour through the United States

every second year, mostly on the circuit of college and community centre venues. But she had had to fight hard.

Earlier that year the board had provoked a showdown over finances and insisted on cancelling several bookings including one at the Brooklyn Academy of Music (BAM). Celia rushed back to Toronto to confront the board, arguing that the engagement at the prestigious BAM was too good to be missed. She berated them, 'The theatre is all gamble, and if you don't gamble you're through." One board member commented, "We won't die if we don't go to New York." Celia shot back, "That's just where we disagree. I think we'll die of slow rot if we don't expand. If we get good notices in New York we'll get other bookings and more people at home will come to see us when they see we're accepted in the States."[135]

The board, unconvinced and unprepared to gamble away any more money, challenged Celia to raise nine thousand dollars in two days. The target was virtually impossible. But Celia, with Betty Oliphant as her ally, set out to get that money. Over two days, the pair cold-called everyone they could to solicit a donation. As *Maclean's* magazine reported afterwards, Oliphant phoned a woman she had never met who asked, "Don't you think you have a nerve taking the company to New York?" Betty retorted, "No I don't. I think they'll be a credit to you and to me." The stranger donated five hundred dollars. The dancers themselves turned in ten dollars of their own pittance of a salary, while various members of the Canadian Association of Dance Teachers chipped in. In all, five thousand dollars was raised. At this point, Eddie Goodman asked a senior executive at Cadillac Constructing and Developments Ltd. to make a matching donation. As Goodman explained in his memoirs, "I pounced upon its president, Eph Diamond and his partners, Joe Berman and Jack Kamin, and extracted $5,000 of their meagre profits, which got the company to New York and back."[136] The target had been exceeded by one thousand dollars.

The tiny but formidable Celia Franca, with the help of Eddie Goodman, had called the board's bluff, but the episode had exasperated Celia. Tolerance and patience were not her strong suits, as she would demonstrate time and again. A *Maclean's*[137] article touched on Celia's short fuse. "After one such meeting a guild director complained to Betty Oliphant: 'I've had just about all I can take from that woman. Today she called me a bloody fool.' Betty reproached Celia. Celia denied the charge. 'I didn't call him a bloody fool, I'm sure,' she said. 'Maybe I called him a fool.' 'Bloody fool sounds more like you,' Betty Oliphant observed. 'Well, I wouldn't call him that unless I really liked him,' was Franca's closing defence."

Celia's triumph in getting the nine thousand dollars meant that her company did go to New York's Brooklyn Academy of Dance in March. As an added coup, Celia presented Tudor's *Offenbach in the Underworld*, with the choreographer sitting in the audience. The National Ballet's two appearances attracted other notable ballet luminaries, including Lucia Chase, co-founder of the American Ballet Theatre, along with ballerinas Alicia Markova and Nora Kaye. The major New York dance critics came to check out this upstart Canadian company. Celia had proved to her timid board that their company could compete in the international ballet world. This success led to the company going to Washington D.C. that June to open the season at the Carter Barron Theatre, a large outdoor stadium.

These ventures below the border paid off, certainly in terms of recognition. Writing to Cyril Frankel on February 24, 1957, Celia enclosed several positive reviews, and told him that a theatre manager in Dallas had commented that the National Ballet may bring about a ballet renaissance in the U.S. But some nights were less successful. In late March 1959 in Beaumont, Texas, Yves Cousineau, peeking through the curtain before performance time, and told the dancers already on stage that the entire audience had "come in the same cab."[138]

Donald Mahler, Franca, and Yves Cousineau stretching their legs in the Smoky Mountains while on tour in the southern United States in 1957. Courtesy of the National Ballet of Canada Archives

Attempting to educate her directors about the hardships their dancers endured, Celia, in her 1957 artistic director's report, described a typical tour day. When the dancers got on the bus early in the morning, the first order of the day was hanging their damp tights and undies on the overhead luggage rack so that they dangled to dry in the passengers' faces. She talked about the gruelling travel schedule: arriving in a town, going to the theatre to unpack makeup and shoe bags, taking class in the theatre's lobby or corridor, most times on an unyielding hard floor because the stage crew was moving the sets onto the stage, then posing for photographers from the local media, later putting on costumes and makeup, performing, finding a place to eat a late dinner, returning to the hotel, sleeping for four or five hours and then going back on the bus at eight a.m. to start the entire process over. All this for a weekly salary of around forty-two dollars, with the employment period not long enough for the dancers to qualify for unemployment insurance.

Still performing, Celia had the added tasks of actually running the company. While her dancers at least could sleep or mentally prepare themselves for their upcoming roles on the bus, Celia would be occupied with paperwork such as programming and casting roles for future performances. Once they arrived at the theatre, she would teach a class and conduct a rehearsal, provided there was adequate time. Only then could she turn her attention to concentrating on the roles she herself would be dancing that night. Costume cutter Cynthia MacLennan, who doubled as Celia's dresser while on tour, said that when Celia dressed for a role, she remained quiet, focused, and self-contained — always with a cigarette in her hand.

The weather — something Celia had badly underestimated — was often a hazard. The rehearsal pianist, Mary McDonald, a devout Catholic, prayed their bus through one especially bad blizzard in Nova Scotia. At one small theatre in Nova Scotia, the janitor's wife and children all had mumps and managed to pass the disease to several of the dancers. At another Maritime town, the theatre's stage door was too low for the scenery to be brought in. The locals insisted it could be done. Kay Ambrose recounted, "So we opened the stage door to show them the truck with the scenery and in walked a cow.... It wasn't a professional cow either, because it had no stage presence at all. It looked very embarrassed and it went out backward, without any inducement."[139]

Among Kay's numerous duties while on tour was promotion. A confident presenter, she spoke to a wide variety of groups from service clubs to children in school auditoriums. Her quick, clipped English accent left her audiences charmed, if somewhat bewildered. Dancer Lillian Jarvis observed, "She never really opened her mouth a great deal, she was usually smoking and the words just sort of tumbled out over each other."[140] She carried a large suitcase with dolls dressed in miniature ballet costumes. The *Winnipeg Free Press* on May 10, 1958, featured a photo of Kay with two of her ballerina dolls with movable joints, demonstrating a variety of ballet poses. When it could be arranged, Kay appeared in the front window of large department stores. Standing elegantly dressed in black with her artist's apron holding her drawing tools, she would create a series of sketches of ballet dancers on oversized paper. While Kay drummed up audiences, Celia would be back at the hotel doing paperwork, giving interviews to journalists, or arguing with theatre managers.

Kay posting a hand-lettered sign announcing "Capitol Theatre Tonite!! 8:30 pm. These costumes were worn last night." She was in the midst of drawing a high-kicking ballerina. Courtesy of Library and Archives Canada, e008406973

FOR THE COMPANY, WHEN back at their home base in Toronto, things were almost as rough and ready as on tour. Their temporary home remained St. Lawrence Hall. In the first years, during the winter months when the Hall was a men's hostel, alternative rehearsal space was found in a bowling alley, or in the hall of St. Margaret's Church on Burnaby Boulevard, where resin was not allowed on the floor, making it impossible for the girls to go en pointe. Several Canadian Association of Dance Teachers ballet instructors, such as Bettina Byers, continued to allow the company to use their dance studios usually in the morning when they were not giving their own classes.[41]

The vagabond life for the dancers came to an end when the National Ballet was able to rent rehearsal space in Toronto's east end at Pape Avenue and Gerrard Street. This cold and primitive space was over a warehouse that stored feed and grain. As Celia told her board in 1958, "When I and my family move over to Pape Ave. in the winter, we have to put up with even smaller quarters. The roof falls down, the rain comes through the walls, the heating system fails to justify its existence, there is no hot water, and there are but two horrendous washrooms."

The resilient young dancers didn't mind these uncomfortable conditions. As one of them, André Dufresne, recalled, "296 Pape was our first real home. We used a large studio space, one toilet room in the front, another small room for the boys to change in, a large space as a changing room for the girls, a small office for Franca. The girls' room was not curtained off. Their privacy was assured by placing most of the large wardrobe touring armoires to make a sort of wall."

Dufresne added, though, "Pape Ave. is where the company coalesced, where Franca could put her feet on the edge of a desk, hang up her coat and put down her galoshes, where anyone could carry his or her own ashtrays from corner to corner, where Jimmy [James Ronaldson, a charter member dancer who became the company's longtime wardrobe supervisor] could permanently install his sewing machines and where members of the Board could come with cakes and coffees and chat with the dancers."

Yves Cousineau, who joined the company in 1954, had a less

poetic take on the Pape Avenue studio. He remembered its bitter cold with the dancers wearing thick woollen hockey socks. Classes or rehearsal always began with the dancers running briskly around the studio to get the blood circulating in their chilled limbs. Cynthia MacLennan recalled the cramped workshop with sewing machines perched wherever there was a spot and the mice nightly leaving their droppings on their favourite fabric, the netting for the tutus.

Myrna Aaron, Sandra Francis, and Lilian Jarvis in cramped quarters preparing for a performance. The dancers used fishing tackle boxes because of the convenient compartments to carry their makeup and hair pieces. Courtesy of Library and Archives Canada, e00843019

While Celia called Pape Avenue "miserable," it was not all that different to conditions with the Ballet Rambert in the 1930s or travelling through war-torn Britain. What was surprising was the readiness of the young Canadian dancers to work in these surroundings.

Occasionally, some of the dancers who had enough money would go to the local greasy spoon and wolf down pork with mash, or beef in gravy, or fish and chips on Fridays. Most likely it was the boys. Betty and Celia kept their eagle eyes on the girls' weight. On tour there was less opportunity to avoid their surveillance. Celia, in particular, disapproved of all starches, regarding that wonderful comfort food, mashed potatoes, as the worst offender.

When the audience arrived, dressed in their Sunday best clothes, and the curtain opened to reveal a fairyland setting with ballerinas seeming to float across the stage, few of those watching had any idea of the crude and makeshift conditions these dancers endured to create their art and the beautiful illusion.

BEGINNING IN 1956, CELIA found another way to build audiences without leaving Toronto. Every Christmas season from then to 1962, the National Ballet presented a full-length ballet on CBC Television.

The Canadian Broadcasting Corporation (CBC) had made its first television broadcast in Toronto and Montreal on September 8, 1952. Television, however, was not new to all Canadians. Over one hundred thousand viewers living near the American border had been picking up television signals and enjoying popular programming for well over a decade. But apart from *Hockey Night in Canada* and the news, Canadian programs attracted less attention than American game shows and comedies such as *I Love Lucy*. CBC programming was patterned on the British Broadcasting Corporation model, which emphasized cultural education with plays, orchestral music, theatre, and dance. Very shrewdly, Celia capitalized on the CBC's early bias towards the arts. From 1956 on she collaborated with producer-director Norman Campbell[142] in producing ballets for television. Eric Till, a fellow Brit who had worked with BBC before emigrating to Canada, contacted Celia to ask if her company could perform an adaptation of *Swan Lake* for the CBC arts program *Folio*. Her response was, "Of course I can!" It aired on December 12, 1956, starring Lois Smith and David Adams.

Franca and Donald Mahler in Brian Macdonald's ballet *Post Script*. During the 1956–57 season, Celia allowed Grant Strate, David Adams, and Donald Mahler to choreograph short dances. Courtesy of the National Ballet of Canada Archives

During Celia's tenure as artistic director of the National Ballet, her dancers appeared in twelve full programs of dance and took part in numerous variety shows.[143]

Celia boasted to Cyril on Boxing Day, 1958, about the success of *The Nutcracker*, again staring Smith and Adams. "Our TV *Casse* fantastically successful on Dec. 23rd. N.Y. City Ballet did it last night on CBS network — ghastly — no imagination, very American in the worst sense & unforgivably boring."

From the start, Campbell realized that Celia, because of her earlier experience in presenting dance on television in England, understood what he was trying to do. The admiration was mutual. Franca remarked, "I cannot recall one cross word ever passing between us — which must be some kind of record considering the tensions inherent in the television business.... He was so secure in his talent that I could put forth my own suggestions without fear of being misunderstood."[144]

Their mutual musicality created a particular bond between them. After familiarizing himself with the narrative and choreography, Campbell worked from the musical score, actually marking his camera angles and moves directly onto the score. In her study of Campbell, Cheryl Belkin-Epstein described the result of his use of the score as the script; "The camera work parallels the music, providing a natural flow to the unfolding spectacle on the screen."

Celia trusted Campbell for his sensitivity in presenting dance through the medium of television, saying,

> I lived in dread of what I call 'crotch shots' when, for example, the male dancer lifts the ballerina high in the air with her legs in the splits. The lift may be carried from audience (or camera) right to left, the choreography, obviously having been designed to be seen from centre front. The producer, because the action travels left, is liable to have the camera in the left corner of the studio take the shot (and from a low angle!), so that what is seen by the viewer is a crotch advancing towards him at a rate of knots and filling more and more of the screen.[145]

These television appearances earned her dancers extra money, while the company itself received a small fee. In a time when the company's advertising budget was miniscule, these programs also whetted some television viewers' appetites to see a live performance in advance of the company's arrival in their city or town.

BECAUSE OF HER DEMANDING schedule, Celia had little time for her personal life. And although she had Kay Ambrose's companionship, she missed her other London friends and the ballet and theatre gossip. She missed the buzz of a cosmopolitan city offering art gallery shows, plays, theatre crush bars with red flocked wallpaper, pubs, red double-decker buses, BBC Television, London's shops, and the smell of English cigarettes.

In her first seven years in Canada, Celia managed two trips back to England. Newspapers had been tipped off about her return in April 1953. The *Evening Standard* ran a photo with Celia quoted as saying, "I've lost a lot of weight." Packing in as much as she could during her ten-day vacation, she visited with her dance friends, spent time with her parents, and dropped in on her former in-laws, Muff and Puff.

She returned again in 1957, this time taking along Grant Strate. Together they learned the choreography of Walter Gore's dance, *Winter Night*. Strate accompanied Celia to the Franks' Golders Garden home for dinner one night. "She became a vulnerable young woman in their presence, addressing them as Mummy and Daddy. This was a side of Celia I had never witnessed before and I was touched by her genuine show of affection."[146] On their flight back to Toronto, Celia burst into tears without explaining the reason for her distress. What Strate did not know was that Gertie had created a scene, accusing Celia of abandoning her family in order to focus entirely on creating a Canadian ballet company. Back in Toronto Celia wrote to Doris, "Had a frightful row with mother — usual business — stop the ballet — never see my children." No matter how successful her daughter may have become, Gertie viewed Celia as thirty-six years old with two marriage failures, no children, and living thousands of miles away from home.

Just a year after being criticized by her mother for disappointing her, Celia received the Bnai B'rith's Woman of the Year Award, her predecessor being Olive Diefenbaker, wife of Canada's prime minister. Celia told the *Toronto Telegram*[147] that giving her the award showed that Canadians had lost their inferiority complex about their culture.

"My hands speak for me on stage so I use Trushay to prevent red, dry hands," reads the caption for this hand lotion advertisement. The ad appeared in *Chatelaine* in 1956. Courtesy of Library and Archives Canada, e008439031

Celia's celebrity status continued to grow. She appeared in full-page advertisements for the Morgan's department store wrapped in a royal pastel mink, and for Trushay hand lotion in an ad showing her sitting at her dressing room table dressed in a ballet tutu.

In these, and in her innumerable social appearances, she was promoting herself, but also every bit as much promoting her ballet company.

NINE

Finales and Overtures

C ELIA'S CAREER AS A ballerina came to an end in 1959. On Saturday, February 28, at Toronto's Royal Alexandra Theatre, she officially danced for the last time in *Giselle*, a role she had made her signature piece since coming to Canada. Celia poured everything she had into the performance, first portraying the tormented young girl and then revealing her as a supernatural being. After a standing ovation and prolonged applause, her dancers presented her on stage with a silver cigarette case (an apt present for a chain-smoker). The stage crew sent a basket of flowers winging down from the flies. After thanking her backstage crews, Celia confided to the audience that sometimes on the last night, the props people put real champagne in the stage glasses for *Offenbach in the Underworld*. Governor General Vincent Massey came backstage to add his personal best wishes.

Changing into a white evening dress with flowers appliquéd

at the waist and neckline, Celia was driven to the Toronto Club
for a reception arranged by the board, and was presented with a
jewelled evening bag plus a most-welcome cheque. Celia blew out
the candles of a three-tiered cake marking both the eighth anniversary of the company and her retirement as a dancer. Among
the numerous well-wishing telegrams, Celia particularly cherished the "warm greetings to add to the tributes of your farewell

Celia's farewell reception was held at Toronto's oldest private social club,
the Toronto Club, bastion to Canada's most powerful businessmen and home
to several National Ballet board members. Courtesy of the National Ballet of Canada
Archives

performance" from Russian ballerina Tamara Karsavina, who had danced with the Ballet Rambert in the early 1930s (and who had been one of the Imperial Russia's greatest ballerinas, as well as one of the stars of Diaghilev's Ballet Russes, where she partnered Nijinsky).

The *Toronto Star* ran five photos under the headline "Few Dry Eyes As Celia Franca Ends Dance Career." The front page of *The Globe and Mail* had a photo of Celia curtseying while holding hands with David Adams and George Crum, with the cutline "A Ballerina's Farewell." Critic Herbert Whittaker praised her final performance, saying "It is unlikely that ballet history records a famous dancer's farewell performance that was as fine, for Miss Franca leaves the stage at the peak of her powers, still a young woman."

Celia had always known that the day would come when she would have to hang up her ballet shoes. Coming to Canada had extended her performance career by almost a decade. She always insisted that the lack of principal ballerinas forced her to take on such roles herself. It was hardly a coincidence that she cast herself in the lead of *Giselle*, the same role de Valois had once refused her. And she was not defensive about her decision, saying, "I don't think I was that bad in *Giselle*." Still, she was realistic about her limitations: "I didn't have the classical legs and feet to be a swan queen, but I knew I could do *Giselle*."[148]

Unlike such dancers as Rudolph Nureyev or the Russian Maya Plisetskaya, who danced far beyond their prime, the thirty-eight-year-old Celia bowed out gracefully. But retiring from the stage opened up a large hole in Celia's life. Dancers experience a deep feeling of loss as they come to the end of their career. By necessity, it has been their all-consuming life. Little exists to match the experience of standing alone on a darkened stage bathed in a bright spotlight with the audience on its feet, hearing applause and cries of *bravo* and receiving lavish bouquets of flowers. Celia had craved that kind of attention since the day she waltzed around at the family wedding as a little girl. Retiring meant giving up celebrity status. Star power only lasts as long as the performer is in the public eye. An even greater sorrow, though, is the loss of the major means of expressing oneself. Dancers use movement the way artists use paints or writers use words.

In answer to a question from Herbert Whittaker, Celia said, "Will I miss dancing? Of course. I know I shall be very bad-tempered for about a year. And I'm afraid all this muscle will turn to fat." She also admitted that she would miss the flowers principal ballerinas always receive during their curtain call. Forever after, those who knew her well never came to visit Celia without bringing a huge bouquet of flowers.

What she didn't miss were the daily aches and pains most ballet dancers endure. Since her school years, when every minute was taken up in her busy day, Celia was used to being perpetually on the go. Now that the time taken up by performance was gone, Celia, who always moved at high speed, ratcheted her life up to fast-forward.

Outlining her impending schedule in a letter to Cyril in early February, even the unrelenting Celia recognized the craziness of her life. "1) Fly to England around April 5th or 6th immediately following the US tour to get Mermaid and Death [dances by Andrée Howard: *Mermaid and Death and the Maiden*]; 2) Fly to Canada around April 17th or 18th in time for our tour of northern Ontario and Quebec (I can't leave the co alone — personnel problems); 3) Fly to England around May 11th to get Pineapple Poll although I haven't found out yet if Cranko [choreographer John Cranko] can give me time then; 4) Fly to Canada around May 28th to receive Honorary Degree of Doctor of Laws at Assumption University of Windsor — it seems I can't send a representative & Carman [Guild] thinks the publicity is too valuable to forego. 5) If business unfinished in England, fly to England around May 31st. 6) Fly to Canada for summer school around June 14th or perhaps a couple of days later; 7) Pass out."

What Celia hadn't included in this list, and what she hadn't mentioned to the journalists in Toronto, were the details of plans that looked like anything but "retirement." Immediately following the official end of her stage career at the end of February, she planned to go back on the road with the company to finish off the season, dancing in twenty-two towns and cities in the U.S. from Michigan to Louisiana. One by one, she danced her last performance of the pieces in the 1959 repertoire. While stuck by a blizzard in Cedar Rapid's Iowa that March, she wrote to Cyril that she had danced her last *Winter Night*[149] accompanied by lightning flashing through the auditorium windows. After dancing through the Blitz and the V-1s, a blizzard seemed pretty tame.

In April, Celia travelled to England with Grant Strate and visited several choreographer friends to refresh her "brain box" and collect more of the short pieces she had danced during her England years, managing to get them either for free or for a pittance in royalties. She and Grant went to the studio of her old teacher, Stanislas Idzikowski, to learn Fokine's *Carnaval*. Frankel, working as the middleman, convinced Andrée Howard to give *Death and the Maiden* and *The Mermaid* to the National Ballet of Canada.

Upon her return in mid-April, Celia went straight out on the road to shepherd her dancers through a month of one-night stands in northern Ontario.

Following her self-prescribed hectic schedule, by May 10 Celia had returned to London to begin work with John Cranko to learn his popular comic ballet *Pineapple Poll*, intended to be the highlight of the National Ballet of Canada's ninth season. Cranko had come from South Africa to Britain in 1946 to study at the Sadler's Wells Ballet School and first joined the Sadler's Wells Theatre Ballet when Celia cast him in *Khadra*. Shortly after joining the Royal Ballet, he stopped dancing at the early age of twenty-three, but went on to become a highly regarded choreographer.

Grant Strate notating while Celia and John Cranko mark the steps for Cranko's ballet *Pineapple Poll*, which entered the NBC repertoire in the 1959–60 season.
Courtesy of the National Ballet of Canada Archives

Celia and Grant had arranged to meet up with Cranko at the Royal Opera House before a performance of his ballet *The Prince of the Pagodas*. To their bewilderment he didn't show up and also failed to answer his phone. Eventually they discovered he had been arrested for "persistently importuning men for immoral purposes" on a Chelsea street. Humiliated and refusing to leave his home, Cranko allowed Celia and Grant to come to his flat to learn the choreography. Strate recalled those sessions: "In view of his embattled position with the English justice system, John was remarkably focused. Possibly he was grateful for the

Grant Strate and Celia on a London street looking more like tourists than ballet dancers. Courtesy of Library and Archives Canada, e008439021

opportunity to concentrate on his choreography rather than his personal problems."[150]

Back in Toronto by the end of May, Celia didn't even have time to unpack her bags before getting on a train for Windsor on May 30 to receive an honorary degree at Assumption University. Arriving at the station, she stepped out into a wall of heat and humidity. She nearly blacked out during her speech, likely the result of the heat plus exhaustion. To make matters worse, she was attacked by mosquitoes at the subsequent garden party. She wrote the next day to Cyril, "There was no spiritual uplift to ease the physical discomforts if you know what I mean."

Celia Franca after receiving her honorary degree at the Assumption University.
Courtesy of the National Ballet of Canada Archives

Another person may have requested the postponement of receiving an honorary degree in light of such a heavy schedule. Celia claimed that it had been the general manager, Carman Guild, who had insisted that she attend the convocation for the sake of the company. In truth, Celia was so keen on receiving an honorary degree that she had been prepared to interrupt her London rehearsals to return to Canada. Acutely aware that she had left school at the age of fourteen, she was a sensitive to having no academic credentials. Even if it was only honorary, she could now put "LL.D." after her name.

Celia was also honoured with invitations to two royal dinners when Queen Elizabeth and Prince Philip came to Canada at the end of June. The first, in Toronto on June 29, crammed fifteen hundred people into a banquet room at the Royal York Hotel, where guests feasted on Lake Erie pickerel accompanied by three selections of wine. The *Toronto Telegram* reported that Franca had one of the longest talks with the Queen, who had been well briefed on the National Ballet. "She's heard about it from Mrs. George Hees last week at the seaway opening"[151] said Celia. "Imagine her remembering with all the people she's met and all she's done since." Celia added that Prince Philip also knew about ballet in Canada and had asked her if there was any exchange of dancers between the National and the Royal Winnipeg.[152]

A day later, Celia found herself in Ottawa's Rideau Hall, residence of the Governor General, as one of a group of select guests chosen to represent a variety of Canadian business, cultural, and sports interests. Other women invited included singer Lois Marshall and skiing champion Anne Heggtveit. For Celia, almost as exciting as attending dinner with the Queen was being at the same event as the hockey star Maurice "Rocket" Richard. Seated at a dining table decorated with silver candelabras and dark pink carnations, the guests were served chicken consommé, salmon with cucumbers, saddle of lamb accompanied by tiny potato balls sautéed in butter, and, for dessert, a pineapple shell filled with a mixture of fresh pineapple, and ice cream in a sugar basket. This time four wines were served.

The *Ottawa Citizen* featured a photo of Celia in an elegant, sweeping, floor-length cape with a high stiff collar, an outfit that could only be carried off by a woman of high drama. In this sophisticated costume, she was in a league of her own, outshining the other women, some in European designer dresses, while others were wearing homemade creations reminiscent of high school prom dresses. Celia had agreed to pose in the dress before the event. The *Toronto Star* ran her photo with the cutline, "Celia Franca, artistic director of the National Ballet, will dine with Queen and Prince Philip in Ottawa." The *Toronto Telegram* had convinced her to hold up her official invitation to Government House. Luckily for her, the picture of a grinning Celia, as more groupie than grande dame, was not published.

Celia posing with her invitation to the dinner with Queen Elizabeth at Government House, Ottawa, on July 1, 1959. Courtesy of York University Libraries, Clara Thomas Archives and Special Collections, *Toronto Telegram* fonds, ASCO5307

Solly and Gertie Franks were overcome with pride while going through the newspaper clippings sent by Celia. Not only had their daughter been in the company of Queen Elizabeth and Prince Philip, she had actually talked to them. By this time, Celia's parents had emigrated to South Africa to join their son and Celia's brother, Vincent, who had moved there before the war. In 1957, their Camden High Street dress shop had been expropriated for redevelopment. They had also found a buyer for their Golders Gardens home, so they had been distressed when their first application for emigration to South Africa was turned down, for reasons unknown. It seems the Franks had never considered joining their only daughter in Canada, no doubt because Vincent had by now married and produced three grandchildren — David, Michael, and Jayne.

IN HER 1958 ARTISTIC director's report, Celia insisted to her board that a National Ballet of Canada school was "a dire necessity." As she put it, "Obviously students trained in our own school can best be fitted into our company: an angular, affected little Swan can make our whole *Swan Lake* look like a 'Duck Puddle'." At this time no pre-university residential ballet schools that also offered an academic program existed in North America. In fact, there were still only a few college-level dance programs in the United States and none in Canada. The residential school she planned was to be an incubator for hatching her own brood of highly trained dancers.

A school had always been an integral part of Celia's grand plan. Her model was the Sadler's Wells School, which, besides its dance training, had a first-rate academic program. Those who stayed in the program until graduation either went on to become dancers and actors or possessed the educational qualifications to pursue another career.[55] In the natural order of events, the Canadian ballet school should have been established first, followed by a company. But the Three Ladies and their supporters wanted a ballet company immediately.

Since arriving in Canada, Celia had been running summer schools, which included a five-day concentrated teacher's course. She viewed these programs as part of her mandate to raise the standard of teaching throughout Canada, by which she meant promoting the British Royal Academy of Dancing and Cecchetti syllabi. At a meeting of the Quebec Teachers' Association in May 1953, Celia had been brutally blunt, lambasting inferior teaching and criticizing teachers for going to dance conventions in the United States to pick up cookie-cutter dance routines and costume patterns to bring home for their annual dance recitals.

The forceful rhetoric she used in her 1958 report won her an important, although far from conclusive step forward. The board agreed to set up a committee headed by John Osler (a judge who served on the board from 1957 to 1966 and 1969 to 1972) to study the feasibility of such a project. Much to Celia's annoyance, progress was slow and erratic. In May 1959, while Celia was in London collecting repertoire, Betty Oliphant wrote,

> Celia Darling, ... the school situation is very bad, company finances are such that we need $56,000 to clean up this year's mess — caused mainly by the most recent U.S. tour and northern Ontario. The Baptist church seems to have fallen through and Carman was too depressed to discuss anything as you can imagine ... I hate to worry you with all of this. We are back to our usual problem of the company's survival being the first and most important item on the agenda. I have wild dreams of you asking Bobby [Laidlaw] to buy Sherbourne and we could rent it from him. At least we could start a school this way.

These setbacks only spurred Celia on. The day she returned from receiving her degree in Windsor, she focused on an all-out effort, applying her formidable willpower and ability to concentrate intensely on a single objective. Although she was personally running a summer school, she set out to win over both the board and the provincial government. Together with board chair Eddie Goodman, general manager Carman Guild, and John Osler, Celia met with the provincial deputy minister of education, Stanley Winters. The meeting went exceptionally well, it helping considerably that Winters had received an honorary degree from Windsor's Assumption University on that same muggy day as Celia. As well, Goodman lobbied his personal friend, John Robarts, then the minister of education and later premier.

With the provincial government ready to grant accreditation to the private school, Celia's remaining challenge was to convince the board that the project really was necessary and feasible. This, with the extra financial risk involved, wasn't easily done. Adroitly, Celia cited the recommendation in the Massey Report: "in ballet, as in surgery, there can be no amateur status."

Arthur Gelber, the most important member of the committee, and highly regarded by all the others, remained dubious. During a key meeting of the feasibility committee in Goodman's office on June 11, Celia did her best to answer and assuage Gelber's objections and concerns, yet her passionate arguments still left him unconvinced. Celia fought as never before to get her way, but at one moment she succumbed to the pressure. As Gelber persisted with his cool queries, Celia burst into tears. "Don't you trust me after all these years?" she shouted at the group. Goodman, normally her strongest ally, was unimpressed by her theatrics, coldly suggesting that if she didn't like this board, she could go out and find another.

Goodman's bluntness broke the deadlock. The feasibility committee faced a simple but consequential choice: either Celia got her school or the National Ballet might well have to find a new artistic director. The board passed a resolution approving the creation of a residential, and also of a day, ballet school.

The following day Celia described the scene to Cyril Frankel, her sounding board for so many years:

The big news is that at yesterday's board meeting the permanent school was passed. Unfortunately the fight for it, the strain, the heat and the beating I got from the directors got me into such a state that I broke down and couldn't regain control for the next 5 hours. I've never behaved like that before and was thoroughly ashamed. But I find it disheartening that to get new ideas across I must fight as hard now as I did 8 years ago.

In fact, what the board thought of as Celia's usual dramatic temper tantrums to get her way, had this time been her heartfelt despair at the thought of the school being turned down.

IMMEDIATELY AFTERWARDS CELIA GOT herself into more hot water by making unwise comments about the Bolshoi Ballet company, then performing for the first time in Toronto at Maple Leaf Gardens with the Russian prima ballerinas Galina Ulanova and Maya Plisetskaya. The Bolshoi dancers were using St. Lawrence Hall for classes and rehearsals. After attending all three programs, Franca offered her opinion to a *Toronto Star* reporter, criticizing the company for its lack of musicality, limited range of dance vocabulary, and mannered style. While complimenting ballerina Galina Ulanova, Franca offered her corrections to Maya Plisetskaya in her *Swan Lake* role. "There was not sufficient contrast between her second and third sets. She is sensuous rather than poetic in the second, and while secure and technically brilliant in the third, in which she is the wicked Black Swan, she did not hide her evilness from the Prince whom she is supposed to deceive." Shocked by Franca's audacity, Boris Volkoff, himself Russian-trained, rebuked Celia in the *Toronto Star* the next day. "All I can honestly say, and I say it without passion and malice," remarked Volkoff, "is that anyone who was not genuinely moved by the performances of the Bolshoi, is ready for the embalming fluid, because they must be dead." Celia hastily wrote a personal apology to the director-general of the Bolshoi Ballet, claiming she had been misquoted. "I regret that these remarks did not appear in the paper as they were outlined by me and that there was unfortunate publicity given as a result of this misunderstanding. I must add my personal admiration of your work which I find both exciting and satisfying."[154] Writing to Cyril a few days later, she gave a brief mention to the fact that she had gotten herself in trouble with the press over her Bolshoi comments.

All this battling exhausted the seemingly indestructible Celia to the point that she momentarily lost faith in herself. "In fact, I wonder whether I am strong enough to continue the job," she confided to Cyril. "Being somewhat emotional by nature, it actually was an achievement that I have managed to generally adopt a calm exterior during times of stress."

While Celia, with her mastery of makeup and hair along with her choice of clothing, could create an elegant image, the past eight stressful years had taken a toll on her health and appearance. Although always perfectly groomed, media photos sometimes caught Celia looking haggard, painfully thin and with a spotty complexion. She had developed epiglottitis, a reoccurring and debilitating throat condition. Rarely seen without a cigarette dangling from her lips (the preferred brand, Craven Menthol), her heavy smoking did not help. Even she recognized that she needed to relax. Cyril Frankel, who had taken up meditation as a disciple of the Maharishi, encouraged Celia to try it herself. She dabbled with the idea for a few months, but unsurprisingly found the concept of spending time absolutely still impossible. Celia's method of unwinding, as was common in the 1950s and 60s, was to have a few drinks at the end of the day.

With incredible speed, newspaper notices appeared across the country announcing that a National Ballet Residential school, providing an academic program up to and including Senior Matriculation, Grade XII, with a comprehensive ballet training, would be accepting students for that September. By acting this rapidly and publicly, Celia was taking good care to ensure that the board could not change its mind.

At the end of September, the National Ballet School opened its doors with an inaugural class of twenty-seven full-time students (all girls), with a supplemental 202 after-school students. Celia Franca was to be the overall school director, while Betty Oliphant was the principal of the ballet school, and Anna Haworth principal of the academic school.[155]

It must have wounded Oliphant deeply to open the November 7, *Toronto Star Weekly* to find a photo spread on the new ballet school in which her name was mentioned only briefly as the principal while there were two photos of Celia Franca attractively attired in a pale, fitted dress with a large shawl collar and a string of pearls. One had the caption, "Miss Franca, seen here assisting a young charge, is internationally famous as the founder and artistic director of The National Ballet of Canada," while the second showed Celia and Anna Haworth with three students.

Carmen von Richthofen, one of the first students, still remembers arriving at the school's residence and sharing a third floor room with two Americans.[156] Celia came into their room in the early evening and gave all three girls a warm hug and encouraging words. Von Richthofen, along with several other early students, sensed that those selected by Franca were ostracized by Oliphant. Richthofen said, "Betty Oliphant told me almost right from the start that I would never be a professional dancer." This proved to be the case.

The school premises consisted of an imposing building in downtown Toronto at 111 Maitland Avenue with broad stairs and columns. Once a former Quaker Meeting House, it had been purchased by the National Ballet Guild for eighty thousand dollars. The ground floor auditorium made an ideal studio, with wooden floors and natural light coming in through large windows. A house around the corner on Jarvis Street was rented to accommodate the initial fourteen female boarders. A year later, a house on the west side of the church at 105 Maitland was bought for seventeen thousand dollars. All the administration moved to this premise, providing more classroom space in the main building.

The girls wore uniforms featuring pleated skirts in the Ancient Irvine tartan of light moss green and beige, and dark green monogrammed blazers. The school week was five and a half days with a full academic program as well as seven classes of ballet, classes in notation, Spanish dancing, and eurhythmics (a method of teaching music and movement). High school level science classes were taken at nearby Jarvis Collegiate, and there the National Ballet School's female students received a fair amount of ribbing for their "bunheads" and their distinctive turned-out walk.

The rules and regulations during the first years at the National Ballet School were patterned on those of British boarding schools. Residential students were expected to wear their uniforms from Monday to Saturday noontime, never to appear in public in unsuitable clothing, have all homework completed on time, and to write a letter to their parents once a week.

In those early years, there was a weekly weigh-in with all the students lining up together. Oliphant wrote in her memoirs, "My motives [for the weigh-ins] were good. I wanted to help those students who had weight problems by supporting them in controlling their weight, but it was a grave mistake, one that I quickly discontinued." While in hindsight recognizing that this practice was inappropriate, Oliphant and Franca had been quick to pounce on a dancer putting on weight. Today, although the ballet world pays lip-service to healthy eating, thinness continues to be the ideal aesthetic for a female dancer. As depicted in the film *Black Swan*, albeit in exaggeration, diseases such as anorexia nervosa and bulimia still plague the ballet world.[157]

One month after the official opening of the school, Franca reported candidly to the company's board on the stresses creating the ballet school had posed. "Things were so tough at times that

Betty Oliphant and I took refuge in floods of feminine self-pity; when it looked as though the projected buildings were either unavailable or totally beyond our means. When at last the buildings were secured, we gazed at the limitless forests of red tape with horror — but never with despair; and succeeded in chopping out a narrow passage through which renovations eventually began." In thanking all those people who had made the school possible, Celia stated, "As for the school principal — Miss Betty Oliphant — we can only state that she IS the school."

For Franca, the school was an essential component in creating a world-class ballet company. For Oliphant, the school was her identity. Soon after the school opened, she sent Celia a typewritten letter explaining that she could not speak to her in person because she would become too emotional. She objected to Celia, in newspaper articles, referring to "my students" and failing to mention Oliphant's name. The fact was that, as principal of the school, all the students were Betty's, and she staked her claim: "The implication when you say "my students" is that you have been actively responsible for their training which is not true nor could it ever be true as long as you are the Director of the National Ballet. I am sure that you would agree with the following facts: — you and I are co-founders of the school. I already had an established school which formed the foundation of the N.B.S."

Betty was particularly possessive of Veronica Tennant and Nadia Potts, who had directly transferred from her prior private school. Once they graduated and had become members of the National Ballet Company, they became Celia's dancers.

In the early years of the school, Oliphant relied on Franca to come to the last rehearsals for school recitals to put "the polish" on the dancers. She recognized that Celia had that intangible knack of turning a dance from a set of technically proficient movements into a dramatic and artistic performance. Celia passed onto these young students the lesson given to her by Antony Tudor, the secret of going completely into the character, imagining the feelings, the smells, and the sounds surrounding the situation.

The issue of who had been the key founder of the school rankled Oliphant more than Franca at first, but as the years passed, both women became mean-spirited over who had been the primary initiator. When Rasky reminded Celia that she and Betty in the early days had a common goal of establishing a school, Celia snapped back, "No, it was my goal. Let's get that one straight. Betty was helping me. She approved of what I was doing. She could see what I was leading to and she was helping me achieve that goal."

WHILE CELIA FOCUSED NARROWLY on the National Ballet, around her in the wider world the conservatism of the past decade was being shaken up by pop culture. Arriving from south of the border were Barbie dolls, hula hoops, and flashy American cars with chrome bumpers and elongated tailfins. On Sunday nights, families watched Elvis Presley gyrating on the Ed Sullivan Show. Young people were listening to Chubby Checker telling them to do the twist and were glued to the television after school to watch Dick Clark's American Bandstand and study the latest dance moves. Their parents were singing the catchy lyrics from Broadway musicals, many of which now had a movie version.

In Canada, a big political issue in the late 1950s was the Diefenbaker government's abrupt termination of the Avro Arrow interceptor aircraft project. People were fixated on the trial of the fourteen-year-old Steven Truscott, convicted (wrongly) for the rape and strangling of his twelve-year-old schoolmate. Mordecai Richler brought out his irreverent book *The Apprenticeship of Duddy Kravitz*. Radios blared out the whiny voice of Paul Anka singing *Put Your Head on My Shoulder*.

Occupied as she was with the growth of her company and the advent of the new school, few of these outside events penetrated into Celia's consciousness. Moreover, she no longer had anyone with whom to discuss current affairs, or more to her taste, cultural matters, when she came home from the office. Instead she returned to an empty apartment. By this time, after living together for seven years, Kay Ambrose and Celia Franca had moved into separate accommodations.

No clear explanation exists for why Kay and Celia decided to stop living together. It may have been that they were simply fed up with communal living, or it may have been that the long daily commute from the west end of Toronto by streetcar had become tiresome. Kay, by far the more outgoing of the pair, may have felt isolated so far away from midtown. Her interests went far beyond the ballet world. She began a passionate affair with Canadian hockey and kept like-minded dancers up-to-date by sending sports clippings to be posted on the bulletin board next to rehearsal and travel schedules. *Globe and Mail* sportswriter Scout Young became one of her friends. She followed current events. Thus, 1954's Hurricane Hazel — which dropped torrential rains, swelled the Humber River, and resulted in deaths and property destruction in Toronto — was the inspiration for her sets in Tudor's *Dark Elegies*. She created a brave little tree standing firm and straight, unbeaten beneath gold-lit clouds in the calm aftermath of the hurricane.

Ambrose always had a high-spirited enthusiasm to soak up foreign cultures, be it in India or the North American West. She became enthralled with the Calgary Stampede, making notes and quirky sketches with titles such as "Bronc Rider Comes to Grief" for a proposed book on Canada and began wearing cowboy-style plaid shirts and blue-denim pants with matching plaid on roll-up cuffs.[158]

It could have been that Ambrose's innate ebullience became too much for the more serious Celia Franca. Or it may have been the simple fact that Kay Ambrose was yet another person who had outlived her usefulness. Years later, when questioned by Rasky, Celia was reluctant to discuss Kay, but did say, "She was getting a little too forceful and some of the dancers were objecting." By the end of the 1950s, Ambrose was designing many fewer ballet sets and costumes.

Inevitably, with two adult women living together, there had been backstage whispers about the relationship between Kay and Celia. Leo, naturally bitter about his broken marriage, said that Kay was "batty" about Celia. It seems most unlikely that Kay and Celia were lovers. It was just practical for two career-oriented single women to live together, sharing expenses, especially in the 1950s when there were fewer unmarried women. Each had her own bedroom and separate friendships. Years later in an interview, Betty Oliphant dismissed any talk of them being lesbians as "nonsense." Rather, as she put it, "They were just two sensitive people who were comfortable with one another."[159]

Kay moved into a cozy, old house downtown at 25 Bellair Street, sharing with a cat called Mrs. Duncan. Here she continued to have her Sunday evening dinners and bring home injured dancers in need of feed and care. Celia moved into an apartment that Betty Oliphant found for her, a new square-box, yellow-brick high-rise at 166 Carlton Street across from Allan Gardens and within walking distance of St. Lawrence Hall and the National Ballet School.

AT THE START OF January 1960, the company began a month-long bus tour of the United States, starting in Baltimore then wending down to Florida and finishing back up in Rochester. On January 3, an American musician, hired for the tour, asked Celia if the empty seat beside her was spoken for. This breached the unspoken rule that no one sat beside the artistic director on the bus. But clarinetist James Morton was allowed to sit down and the two of them talked all the way from Washington to Baltimore.

Something about travelling by bus in the dark night can lull strangers into intimate conversations. At the end of the ride, as they were pulling on their coats and gathering up their belongings,

Morton asked Celia if she might go out with him one night. By now, he undoubtedly knew that he was talking to the artistic director of the National Ballet of Canada.

James Morton, better known as Jay, was a thin, bespectacled, serious-minded, somewhat taciturn man with a wry, sardonic sense of humour. Born in Oklahoma in January 1929, he was eight years younger than Celia. He had gone to the University of Michigan and obtained a master's degree in music. For three years, he had taught music at Wisconsin State College. He had moved on to New York City and worked as a freelance performer from 1955 to 1959. By all accounts, he was a very talented clarinetist.

After the January tour, Morton came to Canada to join the ballet company orchestra as principal clarinetist and later personnel manager. Sometime in February Morton repeated his invitation to Celia to go out with him on a date taking her for drinks at a jazz club on Yonge Street, a milieu not familiar to Celia. When they were again together on tour in March he asked her out to dinner. Eventually the clarinetist made lasting claims to the bus seat next to Celia. Travelling romances of this kind were common enough, and developed more easily when one member of the couple enjoyed the privilege of a single room in a hotel, as was certainly the case with Celia.

Although Celia was still officially married to Bert Anderson, they had long ago gone their separate ways. After working for *Maclean's* for a time, Bert moved on to the National Film Board, first in Peterborough and later in Ottawa and California, before retiring back to Ontario.

Sometime in 1960, Celia and Jay began plans to make their relationship permanent. On November 22 she obtained a quickie divorce from Anderson in Juares, Mexico, although, oddly, her personal diary makes no mention of going to Mexico. (On that date, the ballet company was, in fact, performing in Montreal.) For a second time, Celia wrote to Leo Kersley to ask for their divorce papers.[160] The ever-affable Leo sent the newlyweds a Christmas card addressed to Celia and erroneously to "George" and included his costs of £2.27 for obtaining and posting the divorce documents, along with the cryptic message, "and wasn't it worth it." On December 7, 1960, James and Celia crossed over the border to Erie, Pennsylvania and got married.[161]

The public announcement of their marriage came on January 10, 1961, when the *Toronto Star* featured a photo of the couple with the cutline, "Artistic Director of the National Ballet of Canada, Celia Franca was married to James Morton, contractor for the ballet's orchestra on December 7 during the company's tour of the U.S. It was the second marriage for Miss Franca." (Actually, it was her third marriage.) The wording in this cutline set the pattern for their marriage. Celia Franca always came first with Jay standing beside her.

Celia left out one person when sharing the news of her marriage. In April 1962, Cyril Frankel (by now a successful film director) sent her a letter saying, "I haven't heard from you for ages, and some months ago, I did hear that you were married. So you have a lot to tell me." Clearly, after meeting Jay she had broken off communications with Frankel. It seems Celia felt guilty towards Cyril when she fell in love with other men, such as the mysterious Mortie during the war and now Jay.

Frankel said that when Celia went to Canada in 1951, the plan was that if she failed to start a company, she would return and marry him.[162]

During her visits to London in the 1950s, Celia had met Cyril's companion, an artist by the name of Stephen Andrews (who, coincidently, was Canadian). Whether Celia and Frankel ever spoke about the nature of his relationship with Andrews is unknown. She remembered him in her letters to Cyril, usually ending with "Love to Stephen" and "Love to you as always Celia."

After their marriage, Jay moved into Celia's third floor Carlton Street apartment. Official photographs of the newlyweds show a rather tense and very thin couple. More informal photos of the

couple were taken by a photographer from the *Toronto Telegram* at
Celia's apartment. Awkwardly posed sitting together on the piano
bench, fingers on the keys with a music stand in the background,
Celia and Jay displayed their common love of classical music.

Celia and James Morton in a *Toronto Telegram* publicity shot emphasizing the
newlyweds' common interest in music. Courtesy of York University Libraries, Clara
Thomas Archives & Special Collections, *Toronto Telegram* fonds, AS05309

As a married couple with two incomes, they moved into a
three-storey brick and stucco house at 187 Glenrose Avenue in
upper Rosedale. Their decor was shabby chic with a collection of
castoffs, including a dining room set and a colour television. Celia
shared little in common with the women of the Ballet Guild, who
filled their days with shopping, lunching, and good works. She
had neither the time nor the interest to decorate her home or to
entertain with dinner parties.

Celia at her home office at 166 Carlton Street, demonstrating that her work never ceased. Note the black dial phones, books, photos, mementos, and, dangling in front of her, cast lists. Courtesy of York University Libraries, Clara Thomas Archives and Special Collections, *Toronto Telegram* fonds, ASC05310

With Celia now forty, it was likely too late for her to have children. From several cryptic diary entries, it appears she was taking the pill but also having gynecological problems, perhaps even the beginning of menopause. On the first of March, 1961, she went into Women's College's hospital for an unspecified procedure. Years later she discussed her childlessness with Rasky: "I never wanted the responsibility of having a child of my own because of my work. The idea of giving up any time at all of my work was appalling to me. So I never wanted children…. I've always loved them, I still love them. I work well with children." Instead, Jay and Celia lavished their affection on a growing number of cats.

It was a happy relationship, with the two of them sharing a passion for their cats and for classical music. Celia was especially proud of the fact that her husband was a university graduate. Besides playing full-time for the ballet orchestra, Jay took freelance engagements with the Canadian Opera Company Orchestra, the Toronto Repertory Ensemble, and the CBC Studio Orchestra. Although Celia was frequently away on business, they were together when the ballet company was on tour. Their letters to each other were both domestic and affectionate. He called her by her family's nickname, Cele, and spoke of missing her and loving her very much. She called him Darling J and, in a letter written just before one of their early anniversaries, she ended with "I love you darling, very, very much."

Despite all of Celia's professional achievements, she knew her parents rated her status as a wife as the pinnacle of their daughter's success.

TEN ✍

"The Ballet Problem"

I N 1951, BY COINCIDENCE the same year as the National Ballet's founding, Vincent Massey and his colleagues on the Royal Commission on National Development in the Arts, Letters, and Sciences handed over their massive, multi-volume report to the St. Laurent government. During its two years of inquiry, the commission had held 114 public hearings across Canada with twelve hundred witnesses along with 462 formal briefs and hundreds of letters. Because of the scope of the investigation, only three pages of the over five-hundred-page report discussed the future role of ballet in Canada.[163] The commissioners commented, "We are beginning to discern the fallacy in the ancient maxim, 'no sober man ever dances,' on which our attitude toward the dance has for so long been based." The committee had been surprised to discover the extent of the public's hunger for professional ballet and cited as an example a ticket demand seven to eight times the seating capacity for the Sadler's Wells Ballet's second tour to Toronto in January 1951 — just a month before Celia's arrival in Toronto.

The core conclusion of the report was that the government had a responsibility to care about the state of the nation's artists and to nurture its emerging cultural institutions. It called for the creation of the Canada Council "for the encouragement of the Arts, Letters, Humanities and Social Sciences." This would require a great deal of money.[164]

Several years passed before anything happened. Then, in 1956, a politically acceptable way around the concern of taxpayers and bureaucrats about such an expenditure happened by pure accident. That year, the government's coffers were bolstered by $100 million generated by the death duties collected on the estates of two exceptionally wealthy Maritime businessmen.[165] This entire windfall was applied to creating the Canada Council.

The Canada Council's inaugural meeting was held on April 30 and May 1, 1957, in the prime minister's office in the Parliament Buildings.[166] The first day was taken up by opening ceremonies, the passing of bylaws and preliminary discussions on creating granting policies. The members were then presented with a letter from the National Ballet's president, Antony Griffin, a prominent businessman, asking for immediate funding of one hundred thousand dollars to save the company from bankruptcy. He ended his letter, "We realize that the amount we have asked for is not inconsiderable but the only alternative would be to accept a much lower standard and a lesser goal. That, we feel sure you will not expect us to do." Griffin's blunt language had the sound of having been dictated to him by Celia. It was certainly her sentiment. And Griffin freely admitted that the board was putty in her hands. They all recognized that she was one "who must be obeyed" and he attributed their compliance to a combination of her "very firm speech and absolutely indescribable body language."

Griffin said, "I knew that she was a hard person to tangle with, but I didn't tangle with her. I was right on her side." He continued,

"Celia had this principle. If the ballet required a certain amount of money, then the board had to supply it — quite the reverse of what these good people had been used to — here's the money, see what you can do with it. Celia would have none of this at all." It wasn't just Celia's fierceness that overpowered the predominantly male board. Griffin admitted, "Bobbie Laidlaw was in love with her in that slightly distant way that elderly people are, including myself."[167]

Taken aback by this scarcely veiled blackmail, the Council informed Griffin that "no grant could be made before an adequate study was completed."[168] The Council's initial response was a flat no and the announcement that money for dance would be allotted to individual scholarships. Some board members immediately gave up and suggested economizing with a season of only eight weeks in Canada and no new productions. Their capitulation enraged Celia. She told Cyril Frankel that she foresaw a tremendous fight because she had to keep her dancers in performing shape and their interests up with new choreography. Refusing to take no for an answer, Celia convinced Griffin and another board member to press on with their fight. "Our president with one of our directors goes to Ottawa for a conference with the uneducated bastards. It's going to be a hell of a year," she told Cyril.

The face-to-face meeting resulted in the Council agreeing to give the National Ballet an initial grant of fifty thousand dollars for 1957 and another fifty thousand dollars for 1958, providing a number of conditions were agreed upon. Council members grumbled internally that they were miffed by the company's aggressive sense of entitlement. The National's next president, Eddie Goodman, responded to the 1959 grant of eighty thousand dollars by asking for it to be raised to one hundred and twenty-five thousand the next year with the assurance of a multi-year commitment at that funding level.

Celia was taking it for granted that the National Ballet was the only real professional ballet company in the country. This had never been true. The Massey Commission had singled out Winnipeg, stating that the city "in particular is fortunate as a centre of ballet, with its high standards of music and with its thousands of people of Slavic and Central European background to whom the dance is a natural and habitual form of self-expression." Characteristically, Celia refused to acknowledge any competition. She paid little heed to the fact that the Royal Winnipeg Ballet presented lively, light-hearted works along with original choreography, such as *Shadow on the Prairie*, which spoke to audiences. Likewise, she ignored the spunky, newly formed Les Grands Ballets Canadiens in Montreal, where founder and choreographer Ludmilla Chiriaeff charmed Quebec audiences with dances such as the French-Canadian themed *Suite Canadienne*.

Comparative artistic merits aside, the core cause of this spat was inevitably Canadian regionalism. To westerners, the Royal Winnipeg, which toured, was their company; by comparison the National Ballet, even with its token western dancers such as David Adams and Lois Smith, belonged to Toronto, no matter its name.

The fundamental Canadian divide was, of course, always marked out by the Ottawa River. Despite the Catholic Church and the repressive Duplessis government, modern dance had come much earlier to Quebec with the works of such dancers as Francois Sullivan and Jeanne Renaud, members of Quebec's 1940s cultural Automatist movement. Gerard Crevier's Les Ballets-Québec (which included Francois Sullivan) made a brief appearance on the scene from 1949 to 1952. In the winter of 1951–1952, an intense, Berlin-born, Russian dancer, Ludmilla Chiriaeff, a survivor of a Nazi labour camp, arrived in Montreal. Within a few weeks, the formidable thirty-seven-year-old had set up a ballet school and begun to choreograph and dance in productions for the CBC's French-language Radio-Canada TV service. Chiriaeff's company, Les Grands Ballets Canadiens, arrived on the scene just weeks before the establishment of the Canada Council.

High-handedness did work for the National Ballet of Canada. In the first three years that the Canada Council gave grants to ballet companies, the National Ballet received one hundred and eighty thousand dollars, compared to forty-five thousand dollars to Canada's oldest company, the Royal Winnipeg Ballet, and eighteen thousand dollars to Les Grands Ballets Canadiens.

Such a disparity between the grants given to each of the ballet companies inevitably raised regional resentments. That the preferred company should have been located in Toronto, home of Bay Street, multiplied the dissatisfaction. One key factor in the allocation of the ballet funds was that the head of the Council's Arts Division, Peter Dwyer, was an erudite Englishman; his knowledge of ballet was based on London-based ballet companies. It certainly did not hurt the National Ballet to have a dance style and repertoire based on the Sadler's Wells Ballet Company. In fact, the Massey Commission had gone so far as to state that the country needed a national company modelled on the Sadler's Wells Ballet company. Dwyer's credentials for being hired in 1958 as the first supervisor for arts programs are rather murky. His prior career, both in his native England and afterwards in Canada, was in counter-intelligence. He was appointed Director of the Canada Council in 1969.

The inequality in funding and uncertainty over the relative merits of the three main Canadian ballet companies became known in Council circles as "the ballet problem." Dr. A. W. Trueman, the Canada Council's first director, went to New York to seek advice from dance experts. He talked to John Martin, dance critic of *The New York Times*, who described the National Ballet as "not yet a really good company on the international competitive scale." Anatole Chujoy, editor of *Dance News*, whom Celia had befriended at the 1950 Ballet Festival in Montreal, disagreed, saying the National "had reached a very good standard indeed." He described the Royal Winnipeg Ballet, on the other hand, as "beyond hope."[169]

With the Council no closer to a solution, it commissioned a report detailing the financial conditions and operational problems of the three companies. By now, the Royal Winnipeg had an accumulated debt of $1,847 (just under fourteen thousand dollars in today's values) while that of the National Ballet of Canada had climbed to $109,986 (today slightly over eight hundred thousand dollars). A major reason for this was that the National Ballet toured with a twenty-three-person orchestra whose union-rate weekly payment was $155, while the dancers earned $77.50, including their extra touring allowance. The report's author, Kenneth Le Mesurier Carter, a leading Toronto chartered accountant,[170] recommended that the National Ballet continue to receive the major share of the funds until it had achieved the nirvana of being able to make its tours self-sufficient. In effect, Carter was endorsing the idea that the National Ballet was, indeed, the "national" company.

Carter's report, while thoroughly examining the issue, did no more than support the status quo. To reach a final verdict, the Council decided to call in outside adjudicators. A 1961 Council media release summed it up: "The funds available to the Council, scarcely adequate for a single company of any size, must be distributed among three."

After considerable searching, the Council assembled a trio of experts to view performances by the three companies and submit a report recommending how the available funds should be allocated. The group consisted of the American patrician Lincoln Kirstein, who had brought George Balanchine to New York and established the New York City Ballet; Richard Buckle, dance critic for Britain's *Sunday Times*; and Guy Glover, a Canadian director and producer at the National Film Board.

When first approached about the problems confronting the Council, Lincoln Kirstein wrote to Dwyer on August 16, 1961:

The persons responsible for the three companies you have may have excellent moral capacities, historically, they have played an important role in the development of the art in Canada, but on an absolute basis, they are quite incompetent to deliver anything that would be interesting on a normal international level. They are also incompetent to teach, and their prime energies are spent in survival on a rather pitiful level.

Referring to the companies as "three sickly fruit," Kirstein, sounding like a devotee of Ayn Rand, suggested withholding support to allow all of them "to wither on the limb, pending reorganization and consideration." He implied that Canada was a provincial country and that any talented dancers would naturally want to leave. "As you know, we have three first-rate Canadian dancers in our company,"[171] he wrote. He finished by suggesting that the Council's allotted ballet money be spent on setting up a training school. "Count on our aid; we will be grateful for you training good dancers who would like to be 'loaned' to our company."

In his final report, though, Kirstein struck a more thoughtful and respectful tone. His highest marks went to Les Grands Ballets Canadiens, with the Royal Winnipeg second and the National Ballet of Canada a distant third. Kirstein, however, was well-known to have a strong dislike for the British tidy style of ballet. In his 1959 *American Glossary*,[172] he had criticized British ballet for its lack of vitality and innovation and had attacked the Royal Ballet's "self-satisfied parochialism" and "sweet moderate graciousness."[173] In comparison, the New York City Ballet's Balanchine style stressed athleticism with high leg extensions and overall line, boldness, and difficult combinations. Kirstein had particularly harsh words for Celia Franca. "The artistic direction suffers as much from complacency as from ignorance, but it is doubtful if it can be much altered by the mere palliative of temporary guests."

Glover attended a program of original Canadian ballets by the National Ballet in Montreal. He called *The Remarkable Rocket* (choreography by Don Gillies) a "downright turkey," *Antic Spring* (Grant Strate) "slight in content," *Pas de Chance* (David Adams) "a lovely *pas de trois*, encumbered with a fragmentary comedy element, which neither I or the audience found funny," *Aurora's Wedding* (Franca) "a bargain basement rendition of the Petipa-Tchaikowsky original, with only slightly kinder words," and *Pas de Deux Romantique* (David Adams) "a pleasing work."

Buckle (commonly referred to as Dicky) attended four performances by the National Ballet of Canada, a company class, several classes at the National Ballet School, and a screening of the film version of *Giselle*. He also attended a board meeting and had a private interview with Arthur Gelber.

His comments about the National Ballet were particularly personal and nasty. He dismissed the Canadian company as a copy of the conservative Royal Ballet with Franca pandering to the tastes of the audience. "The National Ballet is certainly dowdy, and people in Winnipeg say that Franca gives the Ontarians just what they want." Buckle gave his vote to the Royal Winnipeg but did not differentiate between the other two Canadian companies.

Buckle's duplicity is evident from his personal letter to Celia, sent after reviewing her company.

> I admire your pioneering spirit which has already achieved such results in this country. And how clever or rather how lucky you are to have been able to inspire the devotion of so many helpful and enthusiastic people, not least among them Arthur Gelber. I am sure Canadian ballet must go from strength to strength and I wish you all the most glorious future.
>
> Yours very,
> Dicky

Reading over his letter, Buckle added a P.S. to say that his choice of the words *clever* and *lucky* may have sounded unintentionally rude. His comments could be construed to suggest that he was aware of how Celia attracted acolytes and then dropped them when they were no longer useful.

Discussing Buckle and the report many years later with retired general manager Carman Guild, Celia said that Dicky had been intentionally mean-spirited, refusing to acknowledge her achievements and having the preconceived idea that she had created a company based on de Valois's Royal Ballet. What she didn't admit to Guild was that Buckle had been absolutely right.

The collective reports, under the title of Canada Council Ballet Survey, were so harsh, particularly regarding the National Ballet of Canada, that the Council decided they could not release the full version but only one that had been judiciously edited. Director Trueman warned board members, "I am sure members will appreciate that Mr. Buckle's report contains a great deal of information which would be extremely painful if it were to be read or known by a number of people in Canadian ballet. For this reason, we would particularly ask members not to allow its contents to become known in any way." As was a minor miracle, no word of these opinions leaked out to the general public at the time.

What the Council and the three consultants had failed to recognize was that Celia's objectives were far more ambitious than those of either the Winnipeg Company or the emerging Les Grands Ballets. Her goal had always been to create a dance company that could compete on international stages, hence her insistence on touring the United States, which was ruinously expensive (not to mention gruelling) to gain experience and wider international attention. What Celia failed to see was that her aspiration was at cross purposes with the Canada Council's mandate to promote and develop culture across and within the country.

The reputation of the National Ballet of Canada had been thoroughly rubbished. A memorandum by the Council staff summed up the trio's report in cautious bureaucratese:

> If we have seized correctly on the essential points of what
> has been said about the three companies, it would appear
> that Les Grands Ballets Canadiens should command the
> Council's particular attention; that continued support is
> justified to the Royal Winnipeg Ballet, and that while we
> should not abandon the National Ballet, it has been weighed
> in the balance and found in a number of respects wanting.[174]

The National Ballet appeared to have been edged off its
pedestal. At the very least it had been recognized officially that
there were three professional ballet companies, all with their own
merits. In a speech in 1963, Peter Dwyer admitted that regional
and linguistic concerns in Canada virtually obliged the Council to
support all three companies.[175]

Yet, amazingly, nothing changed substantially. The next year
the National Ballet still received the largest grant, seventy-five
thousand dollars, even if this was well below their request. The
other two companies received more than in previous years —
forty-five thousand dollars for the Royal Winnipeg, and forty
thousand dollars for Les Grands Ballets Canadiens. In general,
it was a pittance for all the companies. In succeeding years,
the National Ballet continued to be the largest recipient of the
Council's dance funds.

There were a number of reasons for this preferential treatment, the major one being that Celia took no notice of the report's
conclusions. She soldiered on with her ambitious tours in Canada,
the United States, and Mexico. She courted Council officers
sending personal notes with press clippings showing her dancers
as Canadian ambassadors of culture. When in Ontario, Celia
— along with her board and advisory council, a large group of
socially and financially prominent citizens — invited Council officers to performances and entertained them at receptions. It was

exciting to be in the company of this exotic celebrity who called everyone "darling" in a cultivated English accent. She added dash to the company by hiring the flamboyant Russian-trained ballerina Galina Samsova, who had come to Toronto in 1961 after marrying a Canadian. She introduced neo-classical Balanchine works to counter criticism of the company's predominately British ballet repertoire. It became recognized belatedly that Celia Franca's mission to create an international calibre ballet company entitled it to special considerations.

This unquestioning British bias repeated itself when Peter Brinson, an Englishman affiliated with the Royal Ballet, was hired by the Canada Council in 1974 to conduct a survey of the country's professional ballet training programs. By this time, the National Ballet School had competition on a number of fronts, including newly created university dance departments and several regional schools, the largest being Montreal's L'Ecole Supérieure de Danse and the Royal Winnipeg Ballet School. Brinson's assumption that the Royal Ballet School model was the superior one meant that Toronto and the National Ballet School came out the winner in his assessment. He went so far as to recommend that the National Ballet School "be the national centre of excellence and guardian of standards" for Canadian professional ballet training.

The result was that the next year, the National Ballet School received six hundred thousand dollars — more than double its previous grant — while the Montreal and Winnipeg schools were offered ten thousand dollars if and when they submitted a teaching plan. To make matters more contentious, the advisory board evaluating their submission included the National Ballet School's Betty Oliphant. While the Brinson Report fortified Franca and Oliphant's absolute conviction of the superiority of the British ballet style, it caused alienation and resentment in the rest of the national dance education community.

ᗩ

THERE WAS, NEVERTHELESS, ONE clear loser from the Canada Council's 1961 ballet survey: Kay Ambrose. Dicky Buckle went out of his way to ridicule her sets and costumes. "Visually, Franca seems to have no taste at all. It seems deplorable that so feeble and chocolate-boxy a designer as Kay Ambrose should have been entrusted with the majority of productions, however loyal and devoted to the cause she may be or how admirable in interpreting other artists' work as a scene painter or dress maker." In his meeting with Gelber, Buckle had suggested that the National Ballet gamble by mounting a really superb production of a big classical ballet, adding that it should not be designed by Kay Ambrose.

Guy Glover had also criticized Ambrose's work. "Miss Ambrose

In one of the earliest productions, Kay is helping Natalia Butko adjust her costume. Kay, jack of all trades, taught the young dancers how to apply their stage makeup. Courtesy of Library and Archives Canada, e008439035

especially has a poor sense of colour — conspiring to be sugary and ugly at the same time; her costume detail is fussy as if she saw the whole body through a milliner's eyes, and her scenic designs are derivative and even, on occasion, preposterous."

Kay Ambrose never read the Canada Council report, but she seems to have sensed its condemnation of her work. Even before the report came out, Grant Strate had refused to use her as a designer for his works. In late May 1962, a luncheon was held at Toronto's Hy's Restaurant, to celebrate Kay's upcoming "sabbatical" in England. She never came back.

Kay Ambrose is an unsung hero in the history of the National Ballet of Canada. Almost single-handedly, she created decor and costumes for over thirty ballets, including full-scale productions of the classics *Giselle*, *The Sleeping Beauty*, *Coppelia*, and *The Nutcracker*. And she did it with almost no budget for materials. Defending Ambrose and those early costumes, Franca told dance historian James Neufeld, "Kay did that stuff and whether people liked those sets or not, we had sets, whether they liked the costumes or not, we had costumes; besides which she knew how to sew them." This was the blunt truth.

In Toronto, Kay had been the den mother of the company, cooking up vast pots of nourishing stews and soups, tending to dancers' injuries, and listening to their anxieties. She did all this for a pittance of a salary. Like Celia, who contributed her choreography free of charge, Kay, whose official job title was "artistic advisor," accepted no additional money for her costume and set designs.

Kay did have some private income from royalties for her books. Her textbook, *The Ballet Student's Primer*, was published in 1953. Her other books included 1949's *Ballet Lover's Companion: Aesthetics with Tears for the Ballet Lover*, which she had dedicated to Celia.

In 1987, Franca was interviewed by James Neufeld for his history of the National Ballet, and she perhaps revealed more than she intended in her account of Kay's departure from the company:

Kay Ambrose's efficiency and steadfastness enabled Franca to shoulder the burden of being artistic director. Courtesy of the National Ballet of Canada Archives

There wasn't anything she couldn't do. She was so kind to me — I mean really kind. But you see I had to be kind to her too, and that was energizing. It was also exhausting because when people were complaining about her, I had to protect her from all that. I suppose mainly I needed her. Also, I loved her. But she did in the end get too difficult. You see by this time she was having terrible headaches which turned out in the end to be a tumour which killed her. I didn't know what was wrong with her — she didn't know — she was taking aspirins and vitamins and painkillers and smoking and not getting enough sleep, because of the headaches, living on nerve, and it really just became too much, in the end, for all of us.

As the company matured, though, and when Celia had found a companion in Jay Morton, she needed Kay less.

When Kay returned to England, Celia's contact with her close friend and artistic collaborator since the early 1940s dwindled quietly away. After Kay sent a Christmas hamper to Canada, she had to write several months later to inquire if it had ever arrived. Celia had not bothered to send a thank-you note. The pattern was repeating itself. Celia simply had no spare time for anyone who could not help her further her own goals.

Outwardly, Kay bore no grudges. While quickly reintegrating herself back into London life, she continued to keep in touch with her Toronto friends and colleagues. In letters written to Celia and Aileen Woods in July 1963, Kay apologized for not being able to produce five costume designs for the company. She explained, "I have more work of many kinds than I can cope withal. And I'm being forced to refuse any extra work, whether I want to do it or not, at the present. I have, in fact, been converged upon as Sir Winston would allow me to put it. But I am really sorry, Perhaps later ???"

Living together enabled Celia and Kay to work from home. In just over a decade, Kay Ambrose single-handedly designed sets and costumes for over thirty ballets. Courtesy of the National Ballet of Canada Archives

Whenever Celia or Betty Oliphant visited London, they met with Kay. In the summer of 1963, Oliphant reported back to Celia, "Kay is well and affluent — has made money on the stock exchange, is having a 'Kind to Ambrose' campaign, will tour Europe soon, is not quite so vitriolic and still for you and the company." During the 1960s Ambrose turned her enthusiasm to Russian ballet. Returning in the spring of 1964 from the "Soviet Onion," as Kay gleefully called it, she reported to Celia, "I got sent there on an investigatory trip, not pursuing ballet only but dancing and theatre in general, and did some touring around on my own which started off in Moscow." She also became interested in circuses and gypsy life.[176]

The combination of the Canada Council report and of changing aesthetic tastes, however, meant that Kay Ambrose's career with the National Ballet of Canada was over. As for Celia, the survey in no way left her, at least visibly, demoralized. Rather, it prodded her into proving how wrong the critics were. She remarked, "Despite the Dicky Buckles of this world, the National Ballet has done alright."

ELEVEN

New Stages

C ELIA'S JOB AS ARTISTIC director involved an endless merry-go-round of finding new ballets, negotiating performance rights from choreographers, hiring costume and set designers, preparing budgets, teaching class, rehearsing, setting cast lists, giving corrections to the dancers, talking to the press, and chatting up potential donors. At all times she had to constantly justify her actions to her Board of Directors. In the company's first decade, she did all this virtually single-handedly scribbling pencilled notes to herself on any available scrap of paper.

As with any ballet company, the National Ballet had an insatiable need for new repertoire to entice audiences back and also to challenge its dancers. By the beginning of the 1960s, Celia's own sizable "brain box" had been emptied. She had called in most of the favours from her English choreographer friends, eventually acquiring five dances from her mentor Antony Tudor (*Lilac Garden, Gala Performance, Offenbach in the Underworld, Dark Elegies, The Judgment of Paris*), but only one, *Les Rendez-vous*, from Frederick Ashton. She and Strate had done very well on their English "repertoire hunting" trips.

Her 1961 artistic director's report warned that after meteoric progress (Celia had presented over fifty ballets in the decade), the company had finally hit a brick wall. Empty coffers meant that she had nothing available for new repertoire. As a result, only two new ballets debuted in the 1961–62 season: Balanchine's *Concerto Barocco*, which he donated to the company (the only cost being for the coaching by the *répétiteur*, Una Kai), and English choreographer Ray Powell's *Five in One*, a light piece featuring clowns and balloons.[177]

As well, by the beginning of the 1960s, Celia's family of charter dancers had started to leave the nest, some having retired, while others pursued their careers elsewhere. At the same time, David Adams and Grant Strate began to openly challenge Celia's authoritarian style. Unlike the young ballerinas — all in awe of "Miss Franca" — Adams and Strate, both of whom she relied on for support and original choreography, bristled under the weight of her domineering manner. David's younger brother, Lawrence Adams, who had joined the National in 1955, also broke ranks to become a dissident.

In 1961 David Adams abandoned Toronto to return to England, ostensibly for a break. Once there he signed a one-year contract with London's Festival Ballet. For the next three years, he divided his time between England and Canada. Although neither he nor Celia was willing to admit it, Adams was making a break from the company, and from his wife, Lois Smith. This ballet couple had been Canada's romantic "icon" throughout the 1950s. Adams, however, had become involved with a young dancer, Leila Kovacevic (stage name Leila Zorina), who had joined the National Ballet in 1957. They had gone to Europe together in 1961, although their relationship had fizzled out by 1962.[178]

Letters flew back and forth between Adams and Franca. In response to one from Adams, Celia sent a five-page typed letter addressing his complaints. She was, as usual, brutally frank but fair:

> When I first came to Canada, I saw you dance in Montreal. Your work was understandably undisciplined — untidy in technique, and unpolished and unsophisticated in presentation. Later you attended one or more of my classes — I forget where, possibly Toronto; you told Lois you couldn't stay where you were (was it Vancouver or Winnipeg?) when my classes were available. So both of you came to Toronto. Lois, too, was very talented, and born with a lovely body. You both had a lot to learn, and most certainly you did learn and improve to the point you became idols of the Canadian ballet public. Not once, either in public or privately, have I ever heard either you or Lois give credit to the National Ballet organization for this.[179]

She remained receptive to accepting Adams back in the company, but by 1964 his break from the National Ballet and Lois Smith had become permanent.

Likewise, Grant Strate, originally chosen for his potential as a choreographer, had long chaffed under Franca's rule that he must take five years to learn the full classical ballet code before he could create. Only seven years Celia's junior, he was the company's best educated member, having qualified as a lawyer before joining the company. Quiet, usually puffing away on a pipe, and with his dog, Kirby, nearby, Strate had become Celia's indispensable assistant. She relied on his maturity and administrative capabilities. On their trips to England to gather repertoire, he had proved himself invaluable.

Strate eventually grew restless. He had an open, inquiring mind about the field of dance. In the early 1960s he went to New

York to study the works of Balanchine as well as those of modern dance innovators Paul Taylor and Merce Cunningham.

During one of Strate's stays in New York, Celia asked him to see if George Balanchine would donate one of his works to the National Ballet of Canada. At that time, she was not a fan of Balanchine's neoclassicism with its non-narrative dances and stripped-down black-and-white costumes and sets. When Balanchine graciously offered Strate a choice of two of his seminal works, *Serenade* or *Concerto Barocco*, Franca knew little about either; nevertheless, both of these dances eventually entered the National Ballet's repertoire.

It's not surprising that Celia would have such a negative attitude towards Balanchine's works. When Balanchine took the New York City Ballet to London in 1950, the English dance critics met him with misunderstanding, if not downright contempt, considering his choreography little more than impersonal exercises in gymnastics.[180] Whether it was fear of the unknown or an ingrained sense of British superiority, Celia, at that time, was focused totally on making her dancers and company a technically superb classical ballet company in the British ballet style with the emphasis on a clean, precise technique and the avoidance of any exaggeration. In contrast, Balanchine was happy to forfeit a complete finish to a step in an effort to create faster footwork and a sense of speed.

Strate's increasing curiosity in other dance forms took him to Europe on a Canada Council scholarship. Writing to a friend in 1963, he vented his frustration at British ballet: "We must no longer look back to mother England for supplemental dancers and artistic inspiration. There is NOTHING here which could possibly set a new trend and we must not be content to follow any more.... British ballet can sink into the ocean for all of me. Saccharine romance and pretty dancing still seems to be the standard."[181] Strate was rebelling against all the works Celia valued.

ℬↄ

IN 1964 THE ISSUE of the National Ballet's repertoire became more urgent when the company left its Toronto stage home at the Royal Alexandra Theatre to move into the O'Keefe Centre (today the Sony Centre). This modernistic granite, glass, and limestone building in the international style opened in 1960 and was designed by architect Peter Dickenson. Arriving in Toronto from England in 1950, Dickenson, with his modernist high-rise office designs, managed to change the city's skyline during the 1950s and early 1960s.

The O'Keefe Centre became a destination theatre — a place to be seen — and brought a new buzz to theatregoing. Attendees passed under the centre's distinctive canopy, which jutted out over the Front Street entrance, before moving into the open-space lobby of wood, brass, and marble. On the north wall, artist York Wilson's vast mural *The Seven Lively Arts* dominated the lobby. The multi-purpose performance venue opened on October 1, 1960, with a pre-Broadway production of the musical *Camelot*.

While the O'Keefe Centre provided a state-of-the-art new performance venue for the National Ballet of Canada, it also provided competition. The O'Keefe strove to book two international ballet companies each year. Foreign ballet companies including the Royal Ballet, the Kirov/Leningrad Ballet, and the New York City Ballet performed at the centre, giving audiences an opportunity for comparison.

Because the centre had a seating capacity of over three thousand, double that of the Royal Alexandra, Celia had to redesign not only the choreography, but all the sets to accommodate the capacious stage. She had to teach the company to dance "bigger" in order to project out into the huge auditorium. Such efforts by those staging theatre at the facility led to the expression "O'Keefe-centred choreography."

Celia outlined to her board in no uncertain terms why it had been necessary to relocate to the O'Keefe Centre. The facility would provide enhanced technical productions and the opportunity to build new and much larger sets. The company's orchestra would finally have an orchestra pit. The bigger stage would allow her dancers to show off their growing confidence. Most important, the bigger theatre meant that the company was one step further in its development as a major classical ballet company.

And yet, the move to the barn-like O'Keefe Centre never truly pleased Celia. In response to New York critic Clive Barnes, who had referred to the O'Keefe Centre as the company's "home," she tartly reminded her board, "The O'Keefe Centre is *not* our home — we just rent it just as we rent those abominations in Ottawa, Hamilton and elsewhere for a very limited period of time."

What Celia wanted was her own theatre. The year following the move into the O'Keefe, she told the board, "Ladies and gentlemen — one learns to cook better in one's own kitchen. At Canada's current snail's pace of cultural progress we are unlikely to acquire one in our earthly lifetime." In fact, this wouldn't happen until 2006, long after Celia had retired, with the construction in Toronto of the highly praised Four Seasons Centre for the Performing Arts, though even then the National Ballet would only be a tenant, since the board made the decision not to take the financial risk of going into joint ownership with the Canadian Opera Company.

BEFORE LOOKING CLOSELY AT the National Ballet's debut at the O'Keefe Centre, it's necessary to step back to take in a wider view of the state of Canada's cultural affairs in the 1960s. After her initial insistence on tours across Canada, Celia Franca admitted in her 1953 artistic director's report that she had had no idea that there was what she described as a "formidable array of material difficulties [across the country]." In plain language, she was referring to the lack of professional theatres with modern staging equipment throughout Canada. The prosperity of the 1950s, however, together with increased leisure time and the growth of the entertainment industry — including the popular Broadway musicals south of the border — made Canadians increasingly aware of the cultural vacuum in their own country.

In the late 1950s and early 1960s, several Canadian cities had built theatres, such as the Jubilee Auditoriums in Calgary and Edmonton, the Queen Elizabeth Theatre in Vancouver, the Cleary Auditorium in Windsor, the O'Keefe Centre in Toronto, the Stratford Festival Theatre in Stratford, Ontario, and Place des Arts in Montreal. The decisive force for change, however, was the approach in 1967 of the one hundredth anniversary of Canadian Confederation. Performing arts centres would be built in five provinces, with the jewel in the crown being the National Arts Centre in Ottawa. Celia joined a distinguished group of Canadian cultural experts in the fields of theatre, music, and dance to advise on the National Arts Centre.[182] Already recognized as an authority on performance spaces, she had been consulted for several earlier projects, including the Stratford Theatre and Toronto's O'Keefe Centre. Builders of the latter had failed to heed her advice of not making the stage floor rigid. Initially, the construction, with steel girders spanning the entire width of the stage and a wooden floor laid on top, made it an unyielding floor for ballet dancers.[183]

In addition to these major venues, Centennial funding contributed to the construction of over two hundred other cultural facilities, including museums, art galleries, and libraries, along with 428 community centres, many of which were multi-purpose and designed with basic theatre facilities. Along with bricks and mortar, the Centennial Commission paid for cultural events from the grassroots community level right up to a roster of major performances at Expo 67 in Montreal.

A Centennial project close to home was the National Ballet of Canada's quarters at St. Lawrence Hall. By 1959 it had become the company's year-round rehearsal and administrative centre. The city of Toronto undertook to completely renovate the interior of the historic hall. When completed, the 1850-era building's interior had been transformed. Nearly all the company's func-

A fur-clad Celia stands inside the gutted St. Lawrence Hall. The photo editor at the *Toronto Telegram* had requested photos of "little Celia looking up at the big hall kind of thing." Courtesy of York University Libraries, Clara Thomas Archives and Special Collections, *Toronto Telegram* fonds, ASC5311

tions were now accommodated within it — two large rehearsal halls, smaller coaching studios, offices for artistic, technical, and administrative staff, a library and lounge for the dancers, a scenic workshop, a properties shop (with space for eight artisans), and wardrobe vaults in the basement (where costumes were made). Instead of the broken-down staircase, dancers used the newly installed elevator to get to the studios, air-conditioned for steamy summer rehearsals.

NOW THAT CANADA WAS beginning to catch up with the needs of the National Ballet, Celia felt challenged to present ballets to match the splendour of the new stages. With the move to the O'Keefe Centre preceded by an engagement at the new Place des Arts in Montreal, Celia chose, with her unshakable belief in the superiority of British ballet, Ninette de Valois's 1935 ballet *The Rake's Progress*. (Its six scenes are based on a series of Hogarth paintings.)[184] The plan was to bring Ninette de Valois to Toronto to rehearse the dancers and to invite, as a guest star, Lynn Seymour, a Canadian who had gone to England and worked her way up to a principal dancer with the Royal Ballet.

Despite having lived a decade and a half outside of Britain, Celia had altered none of her core convictions about ballet. She knew *The Rake's Progress* well, having danced in it herself. She may have just been playing it safe hoping that de Valois would donate the ballet, thus saving the company performance rights fees. Further, de Valois and Lynn Seymour, with their association with the Royal Ballet, still possessed drawing power.

Celia may have been digging in her heels in resistance to demands from board members, company dancers, and the audience for diversity in the repertoire. She had already made concessions, such as acquiring some Balanchine works. She had given in to pressure and presented three Canadian choreographed dances — *Arctic Spring* by Grant Strate, *The Remarkable Rocket* by

Don Gilles,[185] and *Barbara Allen* by David Adams — in the tenth-anniversary program in 1961. She described it as "disastrous."[186]

De Valois pulled out of the project in 1963, giving illness as the reason. Celia found herself with less than one year to find a spectacular, yet affordable, ballet, to assign costume and set designers, and to rehearse and mount in unfamiliar new venues. Grant Strate came to the rescue. Having seen John Cranko's *Romeo and Juliet*,[187] a brand new, full-length story ballet with music by Prokofiev in Stuttgart, he wrote to Celia raving about it. He had recognized that Cranko was choreographing cutting-edge ballet that appealed to a younger audience.

Celia immediately asked Strate to mail over a house program and, after counting the number of scenes and dancers, calculated a rough budget. She sent a telegram outlining her proposal to general manager Carman Guild, vacationing at his Georgian Bay cottage. Celia lowballed the estimated costs at $19,735 (close to $150,000 today). Without consulting the board, the general manager wired back, "Proceed, Guild."

It soon became evident that Celia's estimate was grossly short of the mark. In a letter to Cranko on September 17, she came up with a new estimate of $34,750 (nearly a quarter million dollars today). She continued, "As you can imagine we are all still reeling from the shock. If you remember I was originally given permission to spend $20,000 inclusive." Nevertheless, she and the show went ahead.

The result was a major coup for the National Ballet, an accomplishment for which Celia always gave Strate full credit. The company was the first in the world to acquire *Romeo and Juliet* and the only company besides the Stuttgart Ballet to have Cranko himself rehearse the production. In early March, 1964, he arrived in Toronto to begin rehearsals. Yves Cousineau, forever remembered for his dashing portrayal of Tybalt, recalls that Cranko was a breath of fresh air and gave the dancers "the coloring, the spirit, what we needed to know." The Russian ballerina Galina Samtsova[188] was cast as Juliet, while Earl Kraul won the role of Romeo. On April 14 at Montreal's Place des Arts, the hard-to-impress Quebec audience gasped at the opulence of the Capulets' ballroom scene with all of the dancers resplendent in black and gold costumes. On the opening nights in both Montreal and Toronto, the lead roles of *Romeo and Juliet* were danced by the Stuttgart Ballet's stars Ray Barra and Marcia Haydée.

Earl Kraul watches John Cranko demonstrate a difficult lift with Galina Samtsova in rehearsals for *Romeo and Juliet*. Celia Franca's "brain box" is noting every move. Courtesy of the National Ballet of Canada Archives

The dramatic mime role of Lady Capulet was played by Celia herself, who later remembered, with a dramatic rolling of her eyes, "Johnnie [Cranko] wanted me to do Lady Capulet, and he started to teach me a bit of it, and I loved it. I thought it was a wonderful role. Talk about meaty! And I'm sure I overdid it tremendously."[189] Celia made her entrance into the ballroom scene costumed in a gown of black velvet and gold brocade with voluminous, floor-length sleeves, which she brandished around. The day before the premiere, Arthur Gelber, Canada Council director Peter Dwyer, and theatre director John Hirsch attended the final dress rehearsal. Gelber described their response to the ballet:

> In the pivotal scene, after Tybalt is killed by Romeo, we watched in fascinated horror as his body is carried out on a stretcher with Celia as Lady Capulet riding astride her dead kinsman, weeping and tearing her hair, and raising her arms to heaven in a curse on the Montague clan. It was a moment of electrifying theatre! At that point in the rehearsal, John Hirsch leapt up from his seat and shouted "Bravo" at the top of his lungs!

The National Ballet had at last achieved not just Canadian success, but genuine international success. As former principal dancer Yves Cousineau put it, "Cranko put us on the map and brought us from a C company to a B company."

BEHIND THE SCENES NOT all went so smoothly. Being good friends, Strate and Cranko had agreed on the performance rights on a handshake in Stuttgart. In a 1964 letter to Grant and Celia, Cranko wrote, "My management are agreeable to my doing Romeo only on the condition that you don't play it in number one U.S.A. dates. Naturally we hope to come to the States one day to earn lovely dollars and Romeo would be a main attraction."

Only after the National Ballet had already presented the ballet in Montreal was a formal letter of agreement drawn up by the company and co-signed by Cranko and general manager Carman Guild. The agreement deliberately fudged the issue of performance rights.

Romeo and Juliet was a guaranteed audience pleaser. Celia therefore scheduled it for 1965, and again in 1967, at the Carter Barron Amphitheatre in Washington, D.C. As she well knew, this was in clear contravention of the agreement. In mid-May 1967, Celia wrote a scribbled letter to Strate, then in Belgium: "I feel we should make a final stab at our level (ie. Johnnie and us) in getting permission to perform R & J anywhere.... After the last fuss re: Washington we probably should get permission to do R & J there but my instinct tells me to just go ahead and play it and face the music, if any, afterwards. Knowing how Johnnie procrastinates I'm afraid we wouldn't get an answer until the day before we are due to perform — then if the answer is negative we'll be sued." On June 16 she followed up with a night cable warning Strate: "Please tread carefully with John re: Washington. Romeo already advertised there. Use judgment but perhaps wiser not mention it."

Later Celia gave the issue a Jesuitical spin by saying it was her understanding that the National Ballet was not to perform *Romeo and Juliet* in first class theatres. Since Carter Barron was an outdoor amphitheatre, she argued she was complying with the agreement. This was specious enough, but it wasn't the limit to Celia's deviousness. She put *Romeo and Juliet* on the program for the company's performance at the 1970 Expo in Osaka, Japan. This time the Stuttgart Ballet management adamantly insisted that the National Ballet did not have the rights to perform Cranko's ballet anywhere outside of Canada. Facing potential humiliation, Celia wired Cranko, pleading with him to sort out the problem, since cancellation could bankrupt the company. She ended her telegram with, "I implore you as friend and colleague to bestow your blessing."[190]

Cranko convinced his management to grant that permission to the National Ballet, but he never again considered Celia a friend. When Yves Cousineau and Karen Bowes later broached the idea to Cranko of getting the rights to his *Poeme de l'extase*,[191] Cranko refused, calling Franca "amoral."[192]

WITH *ROMEO AND JULIET* now in the National Ballet repertoire, Celia was back to square one — looking for new works for the end of 1964 at the O'Keefe. To save money, she undertook herself to create a new production of *The Nutcracker,* based on the nineteenth-century Russian version by Petipa. Using costume designer Jürgen Rose, who had scored such a success with *Romeo and Juliet,* she created a Christmas holiday ballet. It was so successful that her version of *The Nutcracker* would remain in the company's repertoire until 1995, and Celia would return every year to serve as répétiteur. A production of *The Nutcracker* was, and still is, a cash cow for ballet companies, with families making it a part of their annual holiday tradition.[193]

Having finished Toronto's run of *The Nutcracker* on December 31, 1966, Celia and the dancers had only a couple of days to rest before flying to Vancouver to repeat the ballet twice daily to sold-out audiences, bringing much needed money into the coffers. Early on Monday morning, January 2, Canada's Minister of Defence, Paul Hellyer,[194] received an urgent call from the National Ballet's artistic director. Recognizing the desperation in her voice, Hellyer[195] listened as Celia Franca explained that the hastily packed freight train car carrying the company's sets and costumes had been sidetracked on its way to Vancouver. Commercial airlines and the Canadian National Railway were unable to guarantee delivery on time. Unwilling to accept the situation as hopeless, Celia had phoned the only person in Canada with the power to save the situation by sending out an air force plane on a rescue mission. Hellyer agreed to dispatch a Hercules transport plane from Cold Lake, Alberta, on Mission National Ballet. On January 4, the curtains opened at Vancouver's Queen Elizabeth Theatre to full sets and costumes.

With 1964 successfully dealt with, Celia needed another show-stopper for the next season. This time a prince came to her rescue. He was the great Danish dancer Erik Bruhn, a regal danseur noble trained in the Bournonville style. Moreover, Bruhn was somebody Celia knew well, as both had been members of the Metropolitan Ballet in the late 1940s in England. She invited him to mount *La Sylphide* (not to be confused with *Les Sylphides*, Fokine's one-act ballet) with the National Ballet of Canada.

Erik Bruhn recognized Celia's unending quest for perfection. Courtesy of Library and Archives Canada, PA210128

Bruhn was nervous at the prospect of staging his first major Bournonville ballet.[196] As he said later,

> I went to Toronto and was faced with a company that had no notion of what Bournonville was all about. But I managed to work with the dancers and while they looked nothing like

the Danes — how could they — they somehow responded to my direction and to my ability to demonstrate the style without stifling them. It was a happy time for me and I think that the company, under Celia's direction, was really first rate.[197]

On December 31, 1964, the curtains at the O'Keefe Centre opened to reveal Erik Bruhn, as the Scottish character James,

Erik Bruhn (foreground) rehearsing Rudolph Nureyev and Rebecca Ryan in *La Sylphide*. Photograph by Courtney G. McMahon, courtesy of the National Ballet of Canada Archives.

asleep in his chair on the eve of his wedding but about to be visited by a sylph, danced by guest ballerina Lynn Seymour. Once again, Celia was back on stage, this time in the dramatic mime role of the witch, Madge.

Five nights later, the curtain arose once again to reveal the character James, asleep in his chair. But this time, James was played by the Russian dancer, Rudolph Nureyev, without doubt the greatest international dance celebrity of the time. He had come to Toronto to celebrate New Year's with his lover, Erik Bruhn.

After defecting to Paris in June 1961, the Russian dancer from Leningrad's Kirov Ballet had sought out his idol, Erik Bruhn. For a time he and Bruhn lived together in Copenhagen (along with Bruhn's mother, who never liked this messy, temperamental younger man who had left his own mother behind in the Soviet Union). Although both men were extraordinarily gifted ballet dancers, their personalities and dance styles could not have been more different. As Erik Bruhn's biographer, John Gruen, has described it, "The raw energy of the Dionysiac Nureyev might be tempered by contact with the Apollonian Bruhn."

In 1962 both had been invited by de Valois to guest-perform with the Royal Ballet for three months. During this time the most famous ballet partnership of the twentieth-century began between twenty-four-year-old Nureyev and the Royal's indomitable ballerina, forty-two-year-old Margot Fonteyn. The intensity yet tenderness of their partnering in ballets such as *Giselle* and, later, *Marguerite and Armand*, led audiences to believe the couple were offstage lovers as well.

Erik Bruhn, the real offstage lover, was completely overshadowed at the Royal Ballet by Nureyev. Although the media never questioned the integrity of Bruhn's dancing, he was constantly compared to Nureyev. Bruhn never blamed the press for the break-up of his relationship with the Russian dancer.[198] Nureyev's wild promiscuity was the major cause of friction.

Bruhn suffered a further blow to his pride when at the end of the three-month period de Valois and Frederick Ashton did not renew his contract. Bruhn was not alone in being eclipsed by Nureyev. Someone likened Nureyev to the Great War, in the sense that he wiped out a whole generation of male dancers at the Royal Ballet.

Nureyev had been to Toronto before on a North American tour with the Royal Ballet in June 1963. After a reception, the inebriated Nureyev stumbled from the party around three a.m. and had been found pirouetting down the middle of a downtown street. After executing one of his showy high kicks too close to a Toronto police officer, he was arrested, handcuffed, and taken into a police station. Being detained had unnerved the defector.

Nothing was going to stop Nureyev from joining Bruhn in Toronto. Whether or not Bruhn feigned a bad knee, the story has always been that Nureyev stepped into the role of James in *La Sylphide* in order to help his injured friend. The more likely explanation is that the duo had planned in advance to give Nureyev the opportunity to dance James and add the role to his repertoire. Suddenly, the young dancer Rebecca Bryan, who played the bride-to-be, Effie, found herself in rehearsal with Rudolph Nureyev. He had failed to show up to rehearsal with the full cast. This may have been because he had slipped on an icy street, spraining both ankles. Recklessly, Nureyev performed anyway to a packed audience at the O'Keefe Centre. He and Lynn Seymour took nineteen curtain calls that night. Franca, never a fan of Nureyev's dancing, thought he had not mastered the Bournonville Danish style, but recognized that the audience had loved him.[199]

That holiday season, Celia's dancers found themselves in company with some of the greatest dancers of the day. At the barre, besides Bruhn and Nureyev, were the Royal Ballet's Lynn Seymour, who Celia described as pleasingly plump; the Royal Danish Ballet's Frank Schaufuss; and his dancer son, Peter. The

repertoire was by some of the best choreographers of the time —
Balanchine, Cranko, and Bruhn.

MORE THAN STARS, THOUGH, are needed to make a ballet company.
While *La Sylphide* had been a great success, Celia faced an empty
repertoire cupboard again. With money available from the Centennial celebration funds, she was under pressure to produce a
crowd-pleaser for Expo 67.[200] For some unknown reason, Celia
selected a ballet by Heino Heiden. Heiden was a naturalized
Canadian citizen who had emigrated from Germany in the early
1950s to co-found the British Columbia Ballet Company and who
had choreographed ballet for television. His hour-long *La Prima
Ballerina* told a fictional tale of Marie Taglioni, the most famous
dancer of the nineteenth-century Romantic era, being captured by
bandits. Lois Smith danced the lead role.[201]

Celia also turned again to Erik Bruhn and asked him to
mount his own version of *Swan Lake*. Celia's 1955 version, with
Kay Ambrose's sets and costumes, had been retired due to fatigue.
Bruhn created a two-act ballet composed of two scenes in each
act and changed the evil magician von Rothbart into a Black
Queen. Although the Black Queen's character was never really
developed by Bruhn, Celia, who played the role, strode around
the stage with a malevolent menace.

Swan Lake opened on March 27, 1967, at the O'Keefe Centre
with Lois Smith as the Swan Queen and Earl Kraul as the Prince.
Occasionally, Bruhn took the role of the prince himself. Martine
van Hamel, a National Ballet School graduate who had won first
prize at the Varna International Ballet Competition in 1966,[202] also
danced in the role of the Swan Queen.

This was not only another critical success for Bruhn; it was a
financial success for the company. Indicative of the lack of enthusiasm for televised ballet, Norman Campbell's production of *Swan
Lake* attracted not one advertiser. As Celia wrote to Bruhn, "The

TV show was aired on December 27 and was *very* well received but can you believe it — no sponsor would buy it. The spaces we left for commercials were quietly filled with an intermission sign." Ballet was still a very hard sell in Canada.

TWELVE

Annus Horribilis

O N NOVEMBER 12, 1968, by coincidence the seventeenth anniversary of the founding of the National Ballet, Celia battled her
way through Ottawa's first snowstorm of the year to Rideau Hall
to receive from Governor General Roland Michener the medal
of Officer of the Order of Canada. It had been awarded to her in
recognition of her unique pioneering contributions to Canadian
culture. This would be, for her, the single truly happy and trium-
phal moment of the year.

CELIA GAVE AN INTERVIEW to the *Toronto Star*'s cultural critic, William
Littler, in which she briefly lowered the guard she normally held
up so high. She compared the National Ballet to the stock market,
remarking that there were years of fantastic acceleration and years
of setbacks. She said, "You have to have the fortitude, the guts,

to keep pushing." She seemed to be revealing an uneasy awareness that despite some good years in the 1960s with stars of such
calibre as Bruhn and Nureyev appearing with the company, her
own ventures might experience the equivalent of a market crash.
At any rate, once the euphoria of Canada's Centennial year and
Expo began to fade, Celia steeled herself to face a test of her "fortitude" and "guts."

An inkling of her troubles ahead had already occurred in early
1968 when Erik Bruhn let Celia know that he would not be available to continue the kind of huge contributions he had recently
made to the company by mounting *La Sylphide* and *Swan Lake*.
In no way was Bruhn withdrawing his friendship and support
of the National Ballet or from Celia personally. Rather, he had
accepted the post of artistic director of the Royal Swedish Ballet
in Stockholm and would be fully occupied elsewhere. While
congratulating him on his new job, Celia threw in a jab at her
own board's constant nagging over the company's compounding
deficits. She said that she hoped that in his role of artistic director,
Bruhn would avoid much of the "rot" her board heaped on her.

With Bruhn gone and time and money in short supply, Celia
still had to produce new repertoire for the spring 1968 season. She
made a choice that was brave, risky, and thoroughly unselfish,
but, as events would prove, thoroughly unwise. Celia decided to
mount her own version of the story ballet *Cinderella*.

Her choice was one of desperation. She undoubtedly would
have dearly loved to have staged Ashton's version of *Cinderella*,
it being the first full-length ballet he had staged for the Royal
Ballet in 1948 with an all-star cast. She did not know, however, if
the money would be there. Celia's version, with the same score
by Prokofiev, would be compared not only to Ashton's but also
to those of both the famed Russian ballet companies Moscow's
Bolshoi and the Kirov of Leningrad.

As if such competition wasn't already more than enough,
only a scant four weeks of rehearsal time was available to Celia

— one week for each of the three acts and one week for technical rehearsals at the O'Keefe Centre.[203] As well, Heino Heiden ate up valuable rehearsal time trying to salvage his 1967 Centennial production La Prima Ballerina, to be presented in the same run as Cinderella. (It bombed as badly then as it had at Expo.)

Franca pushed her entire company beyond its endurance. Thy had arrived back in Toronto on March 13, having been on tour in the United States and Mexico since January. The high altitude in Mexico City had made performing particularly difficult, with the dancers experiencing nausea and weakness from the lack of oxygen. Exiting offstage, the dancers took in gulps of air from oxygen cylinders. Upon their return to Toronto, the exhausted dancers began rehearsals immediately at St. Lawrence Hall, working six days a week with Celia, who was flying by the seat of her pants, revising as she went along.

Despite the board's concern about the deficit, Celia had budgeted an exceptional amount — one hundred thousand dollars (today well over half a million dollars) — for the sets and costumes to be designed by Jürgen Rose.[204] Perhaps she was relying on the look of the ballet to distract the audience from the weak choreography. Crossing her fingers, Celia was gambling that her Cinderella would be a resounding success and eventually recoup its costs.

Celia admitted to Littler that she was scared. She had good reason to be. On April 15 at the O'Keefe Centre, Cinderella opened.[205] One member of the audience, Carol Roach, Betty Oliphant's youngest daughter, remembers, "Cinderella was terrible — it was long, it was boring, the humour was not even there for the ugly stepsisters, it was plodding, it was just a really bad ballet. She was not a choreographer."[206] Celia herself, coming off stage after the first performance, ran into ballet mistress Joanne Nisbet in the wings and told her calmly, "We have a prize flop on our hands."

Celia's original risky decision to stage so inadequately rehearsed a production was now magnified by the most extraordinary piece of bad luck. No doubt motivated by the excitement

Bruhn had generated in Toronto, *New York Times* dance critic Clive Barnes, then the most influential critic in North America, came northwards to review the National Ballet's 1968 spring season. His April 29 review was brutal:

> This "Cinderella" with its scenery and costumes by the German designer Jürgen Rose, is the most sumptuous-looking ballet ever produced in North America. But never judge a sausage by its skin — the eye catching look of this "Cinderella" is the best thing about it. The worst thing about it is the choreography.

Barnes went on: "The choreographer rarely enchanted or amazed. It had, of course, classroom competence, but little theatrical magic." *Toronto Star* critic Nathan Cohen was of the same mind, ending his review with, "Poor Cinderella, Poor Miss Franca, Poor National Ballet of Canada. Poor muse of the dance."

Nathan Cohen had, in fact, been a thorn in Celia's side almost from the moment she first arrived Canada.[207] Within weeks of her coming to Toronto in 1951, he had invited her out for dinner. Celia found the over-six-foot-tall, fleshy man terrifying; he was very intellectual, had an enormous vocabulary, and was unctuous and pompous. During the meal, which was really an interview, Cohen quizzed Celia on what she planned to do. When she told him she planned to create a national ballet company, he shot back, "You'll never do it."

In the company's first years, Cohen was actually supportive. "There is no doubt whatever in my mind," he wrote, "that it has the shape, the bone and muscle of a great ballet company, still in the formative process, but very much aware of its destiny." As the years passed, though, his willingness to make compromises of judgment was overtaken by his distaste for what he saw as ongoing provincialism and a lack of rigour in the Canadian arts community. He measured Canadian culture against European standards.[208]

While keeping a wide berth around Cohen, Celia felt no qualms in bossing around more compliant critics such as *The Globe and Mail*'s Herbert Whittaker, whom she called Herbie, or the *Toronto Star*'s William Littler. One evening Celia literally ordered the critics backstage to reprimand them for criticizing George Crum and the National Ballet orchestra. Littler said she didn't mince words, telling them that their thoughtless disparagement might cause Crum to quit. She explained that the orchestra sounded thin because there was not enough money to hire the proper number of musicians, and that the O'Keefe Centre acoustics were beyond bad. Littler, somewhat taken aback, thereafter became more understanding about how fiscal restraints impacted the company.[209]

The critics were right about *Cinderella*. After being performed an unlucky thirteen times, it quietly disappeared from the repertoire. The ultimate misfortune befell Franca's *Cinderella* in October 1973, when a fire on the fourth floor of the St. Lawrence Hall storage unit destroyed almost all of the elaborate Jürgen Rose costumes. The one bright spot in the disastrous endeavour came when Norman Campbell's December 1968 CBC Television version of *Cinderella* — with the choreography adapted by Franca — went on to win an Emmy Award for Outstanding Variety or Musical Program (Classical Music).

Later, Celia made a surprisingly candid admission about her abilities as a choreographer:

> There's the thing with choreography — if you don't use it, you lose it. I don't believe I had a great talent for choreography, but I never really had the opportunity to develop it because if you are running a *new* [her emphasis] ballet company, you are pioneers, you've started something from scratch. I can tell you that just about takes every ounce of energy — emotional, intellectual, and otherwise — especially when you're working with a group of dancers who

Left to right: Veronica Tennant, Norman Campbell, (unknown), and Celia Franca pose with the Emmy Award for the televised version of the Franca-choreographed *Cinderella*. Courtesy of the National Ballet of Canada Archives

have little or no experience — most of them — you have to give them everything you know. And there isn't time to indulge yourself in creative work.[210]

Although Celia was referring here to the early 1950s, her comments applied equally to her choreographic abilities in the 1960s. She had stretched herself beyond the limits of her strength.

NOT LONG AFTER THE professional embarrassment of *Cinderella*, Celia had to cope with a personal blow. In early May 1968, news arrived that her father was seriously, possibly terminally ill from a bleeding ulcer. Celia flew immediately to South Africa expecting to witness her father's death. Thankfully, Solly Franks had started to recover instead. Aside from the extreme stress she'd undergone, the hurried flight forced Celia to cancel a vacation she and Jay had planned to take to South Africa to spend real time with her parents and with her brother's family. Celia's family, most particularly her mother, Gertie, resented Celia's infrequent trips and refused to accept how difficult it was to make regular, long, and expensive flights to visit them.

During the Franks' retirement years in South Africa, Gertie still faithfully sent her daughter blue aerograms filled with news about herself, Solly, and their grandchildren. She could never resist an element of nagging in these letters. On February 9, 1964, she wrote, "If you are very busy, we don't expect long letters from you, just a few lines to say that you are well." She went on to ask if Celia would be able to come to South Africa for her and Solly's golden anniversary in February 1965. Celia didn't make it, though she saw them for a few days in June 1964 when they visited London to spend time with Aunt Lena and her husband, Harry. Celia, on a business trip to London, Paris, and Stuttgart, was able to spend a couple of days with her parents and other family members.[211]

REASSURED THAT HER FATHER was on the road to recovery, Celia returned to Toronto. Relaxing with *The Globe and Mail* on Saturday, June 8, 1968, Celia found herself described in an article as "a black dominant force who was now being made to allow other people to show their artistic taste." This comment, unattributed, was contained in an interview by cultural journalist Wendy Michener with three National Ballet School students — Ann Ditchburn, Timothy Spain, and David Gordon. The trio were members of the 1960s counter-culture movement and due to enter the company in the fall of 1968.[212] The three offenders were summoned to St. Lawrence Hall to talk to Celia and Wally Russell, who had been named general manager of the National Ballet in 1967 (a position he would hold until 1972). They had already agreed among themselves not to tattle on the person who had called Franca a "black dominant force." Even though she had been forewarned of their rebellious attitude, Celia accepted all of them into the company. It may well have been that she saw something of her younger rebellious self in the threesome.

DURING THE 1960S A dance boom had taken place in North America. In the United States, ballet companies began popping up all across the country from Boston, Massachusetts; to Austin Texas; to Tulsa, Oklahoma; to Cincinnati, Ohio. In 1963 the Ford Foundation gave over seven and a half million dollars to several American ballet companies to build up their standard of training in classical ballet.

The same expansion took place in Canada. In 1966 the Alberta Ballet Company acquired professional status. While modern dance had been growing in popularity in the United States since the turn of the twentieth century, in English Canada it began to compete for dance audiences around the mid 1960s. Patricia Beatty founded the New Dance Group of Canada in 1967. She then banded together with two other Martha Graham–trained dancers, David Earle and Peter Randazzo, to form a modern dance company, the Toronto Dance Theatre, and a school in 1968. With the construction of modern performance venues such as the O'Keefe Centre, foreign modern and classical ballet companies began to make Canada part of their touring circuit. Dance audiences now had a far wider choice of where to spend their ticket money.

Celia appeared to either not recognize or avidly reject the social and cultural changes rapidly taking place in Toronto. Her crisp British accent, which had once engendered deference, now began to grate on the ears of both Canadians and new immigrants. The city, with its increasingly multicultural population, no longer looked reverentially towards what had been called "the Mother Country." The dissenting trio she'd had to deal with in 1968, in fact, represented the new 1960s generation rejecting their parents' materialism and conventionality. The slogan "Don't trust anyone over thirty" encompassed the forty-seven-year-old Celia. She had balked at Grant Strate's attempts to introduce avant-garde choreography. She seemed impervious to the second-wave feminism that encouraged young women to be less compliant to authority figures. Having previously been in total control of her dancers and her boards, she found it disturbing to be suddenly challenged.

AS 1968 PROGRESSED, CELIA needed to decompress and restore her energy and balance. The July trip she and Jay had planned to take to South Africa had been nixed by the emergency visit to Celia's family that May. Her diary, however, has a notation of a midsummer, two-week vacation from July 9 to 25, but with no record of where she and Jay went. It's unlikely they went to a cottage. Celia never took to that quintessential, quasi-sacred Canadian activity of "going to the cottage," summing the tradition up to Erik Bruhn as "rain, hail and misery.... My four cats hated it so my husband carted us all back to Toronto after a couple of weeks."

AFTER THE HUMILIATION OF the public and critics' response to *Cinderella,* Celia told William Littler that she never dwelled on past failures and never went home to her husband feeling sorry for herself. Except that's exactly what Celia proceeded to do.

At the seventeenth annual board meeting on November 15, 1968 (three days after Celia was made an Officer of the Order of Canada), president John Godfrey informed board members that the accumulated deficit now amounted to $344,000 (today more than two million dollars). Drastic action could no longer be avoided.

Earlier that year, Hilda Neatby, one of the commissioners of the Massey Report, had given a speech to music educators in Saskatchewan, where she declared that cultural events of all kinds "may be uneconomic subjects, but they do lie at the centre of life and its central purpose to know truth and enjoy beauty." Godfrey,

a member of the old Toronto elite and soon to gain great influence with Prime Minister Trudeau as his chief fundraiser, either
didn't believe this view of the role of the arts in the life of the
community, or had come to the end of his readiness to accept
either the National Ballet's fiscal excesses or Celia's high-handed
assumptions that the board existed to raise whatever amount she
decided needed to be spent. Either way, Godfrey had had enough
of the deficits and Celia's demands. The existing system could no
longer continue, he said. Instead, from now on, "if the artistic side
is not prepared to make realistic recommendations for retrenchment, then in my opinion it is the duty of the General Manager
to do so, and if the Artistic Director is not prepared to accept his
recommendations then, and only then in my opinion, should the
Executive Committee or the Board of Directors have to step in
and arbitrate." There had undoubtedly been extensive consulta-
tion with board members before Godfrey read Celia this riot act
about her overspending.

Celia's response to this direct challenge to her authority was
at least as direct. She rose to her feet to deliver what she called
"the shortest artistic director's report in our National Ballet's
history." That report consisted of her immediate resignation. She
said that as nearly everyone seemed to have lost confidence in
her, she had no choice but to resign. She added icily that she would
finish out the current season. "However, as from today, I renounce
responsibility for any actions I may be pressured to take against
my better judgment."

She then went up to her third floor office at St. Lawrence Hall
where her assistant David Walker was waiting, had a good belt
of Scotch, called a taxi, and went home to Jay. They took their
telephone off the hook. "What are you going to do?" Jay asked.
"Cook," was her reply.

Celia's announcement shocked the board. Godfrey himself
was devastated. Some of the women members wept. Over that
first weekend, board members Hamilton Cassels Jr. (son-in-law

to Aileen Woods) and Arthur Gelber (who had missed the board meeting), independently came knocking on her Glenrose Avenue door and managed to talk to her. Cassels told the *Toronto Star*'s Nathan Cohen, "We had a long chat ... she felt stunned by the criticism she had been meeting on all sides."[213]

In fact, Franca had had fair warning that her method of running the company — making all of the decisions herself while ignoring the ever-increasing deficits — was coming to an end. The National Ballet had grown from a tight-knit group of pioneers to a corporate entity. In 1967 a board subcommittee, headed by Gerry Townsend, had submitted a report that recommended the general manager take over financial responsibilities to free Celia to deal solely with artistic matters. In June 1968 Godfrey had written to Celia asking her to respond to Townsend's report.

More pointedly, Godfrey had asked her to comment on how the artistic side could best function with the administrative side. This was a direct reference to the growing animosity between Celia and her general manager, Wally Russell. Years later Celia reluctantly discussed Russell, saying that he had been an empire builder. She had trusted him at first, although others had warned her. Celia had also made a tactical error in relying on Russell to attend board meetings to free her from what she saw as a waste of time. It is likely that Celia, in the midst of rehearsals for the CBC Television taping of *Cinderella*, simply ignored Godfrey's request for her views on the recommendations of the Townsend report. As was so often the case, what Celia didn't like, she ignored.

Several knowledgeable types inside and out of the National Ballet, as well as a number of board members, assumed Celia's resignation was a ploy to melodramatically bring matters to a head. This may have been the case. She was, though, utterly dispirited and genuinely exhausted. She felt pulled in all directions. The dancers wanted bigger and better challenges and guest teachers; they were resentful that Franca appeared to have little time for them. The Women's Committee requested what Celia called "snappy ballets that didn't cost anything" for their fund-raising endeavours. The board fretted over the deficit.

In a private letter to her lifelong supporter, Aileen Woods, Celia explained her resignation.

> I know you must be feeling awful at the turn of events. Please believe me — I thought over my horrible decision very carefully before I made it. I thought particularly of you and the many friends who have supported me in building our beloved National Ballet. The truth is, dear, that life with the ballet has become intolerable for me and I feel I cannot continue the struggle.

A factor Celia did not disclose was that the equilibrium of her personal life had been shaken when Jay quit his job with the National Ballet Orchestra sometime in the early fall of 1968. In a letter dated November 2, 1968, Gertie responded to her daughter's news: "How long has Jay left the Ballet Company? I suppose he can make a living away from Ballet; as you say, he can do some teaching." Her husband's dissatisfaction obviously would have affected her own thinking about the company.

The board responded to Celia's abrupt walkout with the classic bureaucratic device of setting up a committee. Its three members[214] were mandated to come up with a solution that would please everybody, or, at least, displease everybody more or less equally. All the relevant parties were interviewed by the committee.

The most important group of all, that of the dancers themselves, was divided by the news of their artistic director's resignation. At the time, the company was halfway through a tour of the Maritimes. Celia flew down to meet with them. Later, in a vote, some three-quarters of her dancers cast their support in favour of Franca, though some, among them Lawrence Adams, expressed their relief that with Franca gone, the company would be able to branch out into more experimental and edgy directions.

The best guess is that while far from all the dancers loved her — she was old-fashioned, dictatorial, and exceptionally grudging with praise — most of them admired and respected her for her unwavering dedication to the very highest of standards, and could see no one else who could do her job half as well.

After Celia resigned, the company was basically rudderless for the following four weeks. The dancers continued on their tour in the Maritimes and then on to the United States. Returning to Toronto, they began rehearsals for the annual program of *The Nutcracker*, while box office sales experienced a drop. After the special committee submitted its recommendation to the full board of directors on December 20, 1968, a media release went out announcing that Celia Franca would continue as the artistic director of the National Ballet of Canada. As board president, Godfrey told the media, "To accept Celia's resignation would be to cut the company off from its entire history, and this would be foolhardy in the light of the splendor and success of that history."

John Godfrey, as usual, behaved the gentleman. He had written to Celia immediately after her resignation, saying he could not remember a time when he felt quite as depressed. He apologized if his overly blunt tone had been personally offensive to her. After Celia's reinstatement he remained board president for another year. For all Godfrey's talk of fiscal responsibility and retrenchment, the deficit rose to four hundred thousand dollars (over two million dollars today) under his watch.

And he apologized publicly. Years later, on the occasion of the company's twenty-fifth anniversary in November 1976, Godfrey, then a senator, stood up in the Chamber to pay tribute to Celia Franca.

> As everyone knows, the National Ballet was Celia Franca. Without her artistic standards, ability, energy, guts and sheer unmitigated gall, the company would never have survived, nor would it have reached its present stature as one of the

great international ballet companies.... It is the Celia Francas of this world who accomplish great things, not the cautious, pragmatic, timid types like myself.

It had been a pyrrhic victory for Celia. While still the artistic director, the committee had recommended the establishment of an artistic management committee consisting of Celia, Grant

Celia with the artistic management committee. Left to right: Grant Strate, George Crum, Betty Oliphant, and Wallace Russell. While the group appeared cohesive in public, behind the scenes there were struggles for power. Photograph by Anthony Crickmay, courtesy of the National Ballet of Canada Archives

Strate, music director George Crum, general manager Wally Russell, and Betty Oliphant. Oliphant took on the thankless task of associate director — a role that made her a mediator between Franca and Russell. The artistic management committee assured the board they would work more co-operatively in the future. Memos were dutifully copied to each committee member. In fact, nothing had been settled.

In the meantime, Celia was back in fighting form. In a March 1969 *Toronto Life* magazine article, she blamed the federal government's arts austerity program for her company's financial woes. She urged the grant givers to "get off the pot and give us some bread."

THIRTEEN

"Well, Dear, You Did It"

WHILE PUTTING ON A brave public face, Celia had been chastened by her resignation experience. At home on Glenrose Avenue, she stared into an empty future, an experience that forced her to do some hard thinking. Her presumption had always been that she alone called the artistic shots and that it was up to her board of directors to dig the company out of financial holes. Board member Lyman Henderson, though a great ally to Franca, had been struck at her dismissive attitude, writing in his memoirs,

> I took my glass of wine and approached this modern Boadicea. "I'm just a new Board member, Miss Franca. My name is Lyman Henderson. My expertise, if I have any, is in business. The Treasurer presented a disastrous annual statement, yet you have these grand ideas for the future. I confess, I just don't understand." I could feel her appraising

eyes checking me out. "Lyman, I can afford to die financially. I can't afford to die artistically."

To Celia, nothing mattered other than her art. She gave her entire body and soul to ballet. As she herself summed it up, "The whole thing really is a search for the best quality production one can achieve — a search for perfection which one never achieves, but it's an ongoing process. I absolutely can not abide imperfections. I want to see everything right."[215]

While never abandoning her perfectionism, Celia now realized she had to come to terms with economic realities. Her 1969 artistic director's report was a conciliatory effort to demonstrate that she recognized the need for fiscal restraint and was on side in trying to save money. She broke the company down into smaller groups. Ballet Concert toured though northern Ontario and Quebec, while dancers in the Prologue program appeared in schools. In the fall, forty-five dancers with the company's main repertoire toured in Ontario, Quebec, the Maritimes, and the United States.

CELIA'S BRUSH WITH JOBLESSNESS was quickly superseded by the honour given the National Ballet of Canada of being chosen to open Ottawa's National Arts Centre (NAC). Given all the other cultural institutions competing for such recognition, this was a clear mark of national distinction. It had certainly helped that the NAC's director of programming for the two-week festival was David Haber, stage manager with the company in its early days and a long-time friend of Celia's.

On June 2, 1969, the NAC's curtain opened to Grant Strate's eight-minute, neo-baroque curtain-raiser with original music by Canadian Louis Applebaum. The feature dance had been a nightmare for Celia. She had commissioned Antony Tudor, but after several months he had come back empty-handed. In his later years, Tudor suffered the equivalent of writer's block and choreographed almost nothing. In a panic, Celia contacted the French choreographer Roland Petit, whom she had known since the war years, and gave him a virtual carte blanche.[216] He created *Kraanerg*, a seventy-five minute avant-garde ballet with jarring music by Iannis Xenakis, black-and-white sets by op-artist Victor Vasarely, and white tights, leotards, and cincher belts for the dancers. It was non-narrative dance, though in the program notes the composer alluded to the student uprisings of 1968 and the "evolutionary significance of inter-generational clashes."

Afterwards, Prime Minister Pierre Elliot Trudeau, accompanied by his long-time partner, Madeleine Gobeil, went backstage to congratulate the performers. Still in their white leotards, the excited ballet dancers stood in a long line to meet the debonair Trudeau, probably one of the only prime ministers in Canada's history who actually appreciated ballet.

During the one-week engagement at the NAC, the National Ballet also performed Cranko's *Romeo and Juliet*, Bruhn's *Swan Lake*, and Royal Ballet choreographer Kenneth MacMillan's *Solitaire*, enabling Celia to demonstrate the company's versatility and abilities in performing both classical and modern ballet.

On evenings when *Kraanerg* was performed, Celia could pinpoint the exact moment when thirty or forty patrons would walk out, unable to take any more of the dissonant music, which at times sounded like whale calls. It was so unmusical that the ballet master, David Scott, had to stand in the wings and loudly count out the beats to help the dancers mark the choreography.

During one performance, a technical glitch resulted in the orchestra suddenly ascending out of the pit mid-performance while Franca, as Lady Capulet in *Romeo and Juliet*, was onstage in the ballroom scene. She rushed off to stop the performance. As the platform sank back into the orchestra pit, one of the violinists tied his handkerchief to his bow, either in a gesture of truce or a friendly wave to the audience.[217]

One of the musicians nearby was James Morton, now the lead

clarinetist of the National Arts Centre Orchestra. Celia's husband had left Toronto to accept this job in Ottawa in 1969. In a new city, he was no longer known as "Celia Franca's husband who played in the National Ballet Orchestra"; he became a full-time member of a well-regarded group of musicians who, under the baton of Mario Bernardi, had been given a mandate to create the premier orchestra in the country. Along with in-house concert series, the orchestra toured and recorded. Now forty years old, Jay had taken longer than his orchestra colleagues, of whom the average age was twenty-six, to become established. But at last, he was his own man.

At first Jay rented an apartment in Ottawa's Glebe area. In 1973 he bought a small, one-and-a-half-storey, grey, stone-faced house at 250 Clemow Street, across from road from Bernardi. He began teaching students in his home studio and later joined the music faculty at the University of Ottawa.

The Mortons were now in a long-distance marriage. No one dared ask, nor did Celia choose to disclose, what was going on in their relationship. For the next five years, she made every effort to go to Ottawa on weekends to take care of her husband. She told a magazine writer, "God, I spend most of my salary just flying out to see him."[218] Celia spoke to Jay on the phone every evening, often rushing home from rehearsals or performances, still in makeup, to make her call. People noted that very seldom did Jay make the journey from Ottawa to Toronto. Company pianist Mary McDonald remembers that for years Celia would leave on Friday night and come back either late Sunday night or early Monday morning; "But she was so much in love with him that she wanted to make him happy, and they had a pretty house."[219]

It may have been that the couple had decided that, for a time, both needed to pursue their own careers, even if this meant living apart. It may have been that Morton made the decision arbitrarily, moving to Ottawa and waiting to see what his wife would do. Celia chose the most difficult solution of commuting, a solution that satisfied neither of them. All that is certain is that their relationship had changed profoundly, with Celia now in the role of the pleaser.

Alone now in Toronto, Celia had sole responsibility of taking care of the large Glenrose house and her and Jay's four cats: Smokey, Tweetie, Bobbie, and Missy. She was only able to go to Ottawa by engaging a young woman, Mary Ann West, as a live-in cat sitter. West had the dubious experience of living with Celia Franca while at the same time having a day job as the assistant to Betty Oliphant at the National Ballet School. Occasionally, Celia and Mary Ann would, with guilty pleasure, order in *Swiss Chalet* chicken, washing it down with a whisky while they watched TV. Mary Ann remembers the cats with fondness, though it is with less fondness that she recalls Celia's instructions to feed them raw horsemeat, which she had made into little packages and stored in the freezer.

Celia further needed her cat sitter in 1971, when she had to make a special trip to South Africa. In late June, Celia flew to sit shiva for her brother, Vincent, who had died in a car crash.[220] After her return to Toronto, Gertie sent a newspaper clipping from Port Elizabeth's *Evening Post*. "It was lovely to have you with us, dear, even for so short a time. Hope you haven't been put to too much inconvenience. I suppose you must be very busy to make up for your absence. Thought you would like to see this reprint of your interview — not a very flattering picture of you, I'm afraid." It was a terrible photograph of Celia looking old and tired with dark bags under her eyes. Gertie's letters frequently were untactful, showing her lack of emotional closeness with her only daughter.

Suddenly, Gertie's blue airmail envelopes stopped arriving. On the eve of the National Ballet's twentieth anniversary in mid-November, Celia once again flew to South Africa to sit shiva, this time for her mother. Celia wrote to Erik Bruhn in early December, telling him about her mother's death and describing how she had to fly to South Africa to help her eighty-one-year-old father get settled. Solly Franks moved in with his son's recently bereaved wife and her children.[221] A South African relative writing to give Celia news on how her father was coping reported that she had seen, prominently displayed in Solly's room, a photo of Solly and Celia as a little girl with her bobbed, black hair.

Celia's father, Solomon Franks, kept this photo of himself and his daughter on top of his television set. Courtesy of Library and Archives Canada, e008439030

Returning to Toronto, Celia discovered that her friend Kay Ambrose had died on December 1 at the age of fifty-seven. An obituary in the London *Times* described Kay's impressive professional life as only part of the picture: "No one was ever more ready to help anyone in need, her home was a veritable almshouse filled with those on whom she could bestow her kindness and warmth. Always there was at least one stray cat to be cared for."

Celia wrote a brief message to Kay's family saying, "Ballet has lost one of its most talented and best-loved artists." This impersonal sympathy note showed that, in her highly focused way, Celia had simply moved on from the friend she had known since the mid-1940s. Ambrose had bequeathed a number of items to Celia (several of which Celia had still not collected three years later), as well as the royalties on one of her books, likely *Beginners Please*, the ballet primer the two of them had written together.[222]

At the end of a year of passings, one might expect that she would turn to the National Ballet to fill the holes in her life. For the first time in her career as artistic director, however, she was not present for the after-Christmas week of performances of *The Nutcracker* at Toronto's O'Keefe Centre. Instead, she and Jay left on Christmas Day for a much-needed Caribbean holiday. Just before leaving, Celia may have been momentarily comforted by a condolence message she received on December 23, 1971: "I sincerely hope that you have overcome your grief and that 1972 will be a happier one for you and your father." It was signed by Pierre Trudeau.

IN THE SPRING OF 1972, after having founded a national ballet company and established a residential ballet school, Celia would realize her third ambition of taking the ballet company she had created to England. She had been lobbying for years to tour abroad, knowing full well it could never be a financial success.

Before achieving this third ambition, Celia had to endure what has entered the National Ballet lexicon as "Palace Revolution Number Two." The five-person artistic management committee had always been a band-aid solution to attempt to clip, or at least to constrain, Celia's artistic director's wings. After the drama of her resignation and return in 1968, the offices, hallways, and rehearsal rooms of St. Lawrence Hall were filled with whispered connivances, and endless gossip and allegations of petty slights. Fingers were pointed every which way; it was Betty Oliphant's fault, it was Wally Russell's fault, it was specific board members' faults, it was Celia's fault. Some wanted Celia out, some wanted Celia in. Everyone was unhappy. The blame of all this infighting was assigned to just about everyone.

All this dysfunction affected Celia's health. In February, she was laid low by a virulent attack of flu. Alone that weekend in her Glenrose house, she phoned the ballet master and mistress, David and Joanne Scott, to ask for help. Arriving at the house on Sunday morning and realizing that Celia was very unwell, and with no doctor on call, they phoned a veterinarian friend who came over and gave Celia some medication. One of the positive outcomes was that she finally gave up smoking.

In mid-February, all the paranoia and plotting to get rid of Celia Franca came to a boil. Board members had split into factions. Then-president Lyman Henderson was faced with a meltdown. He wrote in his memoirs, "When I got wind of the plot, it was already well formed. Inasmuch as the ringleaders had been drumming up support, the Directors were now divided into three groups." Those wanting Celia to continue as artistic director included Henderson, Jock McLeod, and Veronica Tennant. The anti-Celia group was led by general manager Wally Russell, along with board members Leighton McCarthy and a married couple, Bernard and Patsy Protter. Indeed, the Protters were alleged to have travelled to Sweden on their own accord to ask Erik Bruhn if he would be available to take Celia's job. Other board members were confused, undecided, or apathetic.

The wild card was Betty Oliphant. So far as it's possible to determine, in 1972 she was still ambivalent about getting rid of Franca. The issue of who had founded the ballet school continued to eat away at her. In July 1989, speaking to Frank Rasky, Oliphant, in her soft-spoken, languid voice, heaped abuse on her former friend:

> The biggest difference between us is that I was always keeping morale up and she was always destroying it. I think it was insecurity. As long as the kids in the company were calling her Auntie Celia and bowing down to her, she was happy. The minute they were independent or thought that they ought to do a role or they'd go and say they thought it

was time they got a promotion, the way she dealt with them was quite horrible. She's very destructive.

The highly opinionated Oliphant felt free to offer to the board her judgment on who should be hired and fired. She thought the ballet master, David Scott, had been brutal to dancers and advised them not to renew his contract. Her unsought advice was ignored.

Celia remained convinced right to the end that, as well as being a major conspirator in the "get rid of Celia" campaign, Oliphant coveted the artistic director job herself. In that 1972 Palace Revolution, however, Oliphant voted to keep Franca.

Meetings were held to allow all sides to express their views. Celia's opponents presented a litany of complaints — she lacked creativity, she had no clear sense of direction, she didn't support Canadian content, she went over budget, she didn't heed her general manager. When it came to Celia's turn to have her say, she let fly, spewing out all her grievances and examples of Russell undermining her authority.

After nearly eight hours of discussion on Friday, February 10, 1972, the vote gave Celia Franca unanimous support to continue as artistic director. Henderson said, "I nearly wept. I went out of the meeting to tell the outcome to the waiting staff and dancers."

That same afternoon, Wally Russell marched out of St. Lawrence Hall, leaving behind a handwritten note: "In my capacity as the senior administrator of the National Ballet, I decided to terminate my employment effective immediately rather than Aug. 31st, 1972. This decision I feel deeply is in the best interests of the National Ballet in view of recent events."[23]

In the *Toronto Star*, Marci McDonald, writing about Palace Revolution Number Two, quoted an unnamed former ballet official who had summed up the issue: "It was the case of two powerful personalities in a ferocious pas de deux to the finish over who would control the company — the lady who had built it from nothing and gradually watched her power over every detail erode by its very size and success; or the one-time production manager turned chief administrator who has been accused of wanting to be artistic director himself." McDonald's article was accompanied by a wickedly clever cartoon of Celia, costumed as Lady Capulet, with tiny ballet dancers huddling under her long black gown while a long sword brandished by Celia stabbed the prostrate Wally Russell.

Celia had won another round. That she needed to keep winning was demonstrated by a spiteful letter sent to *The Globe and Mail* in November by her board adversary Patsy Protter. Commenting on an article by dance critic John Fraser, Protter wrote,

> The company was neither founded or kept alive by Miss Franca — it has been kept alive in spite of her.... While we allow a dictatorship that grew out of hero worship to plague the Company, the same old problems will continue. No one, of course, including me, would dispute the great contribution Miss Franca has made — the company has indeed been her whole life and she has put all she had into it. But this in itself is not, today, enough.

ONE CONSEQUENCE OF WALLY Russell's abrupt departure was that Celia found herself without a general manager two short months from the company's first European tour. Former stage manager David Haber stepped into the breach, being seconded from the NAC to take over the management duties on the tour. Since Haber had left his stage manager position with the National Ballet back in 1955, he had gained extensive artistic management experience, first with the William Morris Concert Agency in New York (the agency that had managed the National Ballet's American tours), then as a theatrical producer at Expo 67 and a consultant to the World Festival for Osaka's Expo 70. He played a part in setting up the Canada Council's Touring Office, and by 1972 was programming director at the National Arts Centre.

With the problem of finding an acting manager solved, Celia, who arrived in London a week before the company, was able to revel in the publicity and social events surrounding the National Ballet's visit. She gave many press interviews and addressed the London Ballet Circle and the Royal Overseas League. She attended a Sunday evening reception at the flat of Belle Shenkmen — a Canadian socialite and chairperson of the gala evening — and mingled with guests who included London ballet friends and the Canadian High Commissioner.

The opening performance at London's Coliseum Theatre on May 17, 1972, was[224] attended by Princess Anne and Prime Minister Edward Heath. Along with these influential guests, most of Celia's London ballet friends, including her old teacher Stanislas Idzikowski, were in the audience. They were entertained with a mixed program that included Peter Wright's *The Mirror Walkers* and Bruhn's *La Sylphide*, in which Celia Franca cast herself as Madge, the witch.[225]

Celia had been ambivalent about having European guest dancers for the first-night gala performance. While they were intended to entice a larger audience, the National Ballet did not have the money for these foreign artists, and their addition would overshadow her own dancers. Celia managed to limit the competition to a single number of John Cranko's *Legende*, performed by his own Stuttgart dancers, Marcia Haydée, and Richard Cragun.[226]

Celia was equally concerned about the size of the venue, as the Coliseum had a seating capacity of well over two thousand. She worried about empty seats. Taking advantage once again of Cyril Frankel's obliging nature, she asked him to round up all of her old friends and persuade them to buy the expensive seats. She also made sure that all of the people who were instrumental in forming her career were among the invited guests. She added, "I will be dancing myself incidentally — the witch." Beyond any

Celia, in character as Madge the Witch in *La Sylphide*, backstage at the London Coliseum with her teacher, Stanislas Idzikowski, and his companion. Note Celia's misshapen feet from the years in pointe shoes. Courtesy of Library and Archives Canada, e008439038

doubt, Celia wanted everyone to see what she had managed to accomplish in Canada.

At the crowded champagne reception on the stage following the performance, the elegantly gowned Celia made sure to be photographed with de Valois. Five words of respect and praise from de Valois — "Well dear, you did it" — were undoubtedly the pinnacle of Celia's professional career.

Celia's dressing room had been filled with flowers and telegrams of welcome and good wishes from her former British

At the backstage reception at the London Coliseum, Dame Ninette de Valois extols the success of her protégé, Celia Franca. Photograph by Anthony Crickmay, courtesy of the National Ballet of Canada Archives

dancing colleagues. Ninette de Valois wrote, "All my good wishes and love to you and the company." Frederick Ashton wrote, "All love and best wishes for a successful season." Other congratulations and greetings came from Sol Hurok, Governor General Roland Michener, Prime Minister Trudeau, Rudi Nureyev, and Arnold Spohr and Ludmilla Chiriaeff, the two artistic directors of Canada's other ballet companies.

The London reviews were generally positive. Writing in the

Financial Times, Clement Crisp described the National Ballet's style as "clean, elegant and with a certain frankness of demeanour that seems specifically Canadian, and very appealing," while the *Guardian's* critic stated, "This company is a feather in the Canadian hat." Celia's performance as Madge received mixed reviews. Critic John Percival of *The Times* found that Franca played "the witch Madge in an inappropriately comic way," while the *Guardian's* Philip Hope Wallace wrote "Celia Franca, guiding spirit of the whole splendid enterprise, earned the cheering." The *International Herald Tribune* faulted the National Ballet of Canada for lacking "the ebullient joie de vivre of the best Americans or Russians," as well as not featuring any homegrown stars.

In a lengthy article in the July issue of *Dance and Dancers*, Peter Williams, who knew Celia personally from her time with the Metropolitan Ballet, stressed Celia's obsession with the classics as the backbone of any true ballet company. In his summation he wrote, "She has gone about it the only way possible, which was to form that classical basis from which she can now move out in other directions. It was something like a crown of triumph that the London public, still I think the most discerning public in the world, took the company to its heart."

In the run-up week to the engagement at the Coliseum Theatre, Celia got together with her relatives. Uncle Alf held a party in her honour at his central London apartment with several family members present, including his partner Rosa, aunts Lena and Annie, and cousins Trudy, Marian, and Esther. Esther remembers going with her mother Annie and sisters Marian and Trudy backstage after a performance to see their famous cousin in her dressing room. One audience member proudly attending had been indirectly responsible for Celia's dance career. This was Aunt Bessie, whose wedding reception with the live band had inspired the little Celia to twirl around entertaining the guests.

For some reason Alf and Lena didn't make it to the Coliseum Theatre. Auntie Lena, who was less intimidated by Celia than many other of the other relatives since she had grown up in the Franks household, sent her niece a letter in October, scolding her for not writing a thank-you note to Alf for the party.

> I hope you won't mind me saying this but I feel he's disappointed that you haven't written to him; he's just said he's surprised that you haven't written. I think perhaps he thinks that you were upset at us not being able to attend the Ballet at that time. It was very unfortunate, but please God, we'll be able to see it another time, all being well.

During the London run, success appears to have gone to Celia's head. She moved from the economy-rate Royal Eagle Hotel, near Paddington station, to the Waldorf Hotel, steps away from Covent Garden. She made the pages of *Harpers & Queen* magazine in a photo at the London gala reception with, by now, Sir Robert Helpmann, both smiling broadly with arms around each other. If only Gertie had been alive to see these photos of her daughter hobnobbing with society.

The National Ballet then travelled to Stuttgart, where they attracted a sellout crowd and earned twelve curtain calls. Afterwards came Paris, where both the weather (the city's coldest in twenty-five years) and the audience reception were cool, followed by Brussels, Glasgow, Lausanne, and, finally, Monte Carlo[227] on July 3.

FOURTEEN

Sleeping "Beauties"

B ARELY TWO WEEKS AFTER their return from Europe, Celia and her dancers were back at St. Lawrence Hall to begin rehearsals for the most ambitious project the ballet company had ever undertaken. American impresario Sol Hurok had invited the National Ballet of Canada to go on tour with Rudolph Nureyev. The catch, though, was that Nureyev would perform as the prince at least six (often seven or eight) times a week in his own version of *The Sleeping Beauty* while all costs for sets and costumes would be the responsibility of the National Ballet. In return, the company would have all its travel expenses paid and be assured sellout audiences across North America. To top it off, the tour would include a three-week appearance at New York's Metropolitan Opera House, one of the world's most prestigious dance venues. After performances in London and Paris, New York was the only goal left.[228]

With a cool eye, Celia summed up the situation in the back of her 1973 appointment book, "Prevailing conditions under Hurok contract. No Nureyev, no job; No new productions for Nureyev, no job; Nureyev has final artistic say because our contract with Hurok dictates that if Nureyev doesn't dance the N.B. doesn't get paid."

The project promised to fill up, to an extent, anyway, the National Ballet's empty coffers.[229] Celia recognized that Nureyev's magnetism would attract full houses. As she put it, "So I knew, bless his heart and cotton socks, that if he had Nureyev dancing seven or eight performances a week, he was going to make money."[230]

Perhaps to justify allowing her company to, in effect, front a celebrity — *Toronto Star* critic William Littler called the National Ballet "the parsley around the salmon of Rudolph Nureyev" — Celia maintained that she had always wanted a *Sleeping Beauty* in the National Ballet's repertoire in order to complete the trilogy of Tchaikovsky's romantic story ballets. The company had already performed Bruhn's *Swan Lake* and Franca's *The Nutcracker*. Frank Augustyn described a troubled Celia, telling Littler and Karen Kain that she had "sold the company" in order to make sure that it would survive.

Celia did all the grunt work in staging *The Sleeping Beauty*. Long before Nureyev arrived in Toronto for rehearsals in August 1972, she had been tirelessly pulling together the production. She laboured at creating cast lists with leads, second and third casts, along with slotting in other repertoire for the tour. Even while in Europe, she had been casting roles and struggling to pare down the number of dancers. Writing to wardrobe supervisor Jimmy Ronaldson from Glasgow in June (and referring to the ballet as "Sleeping Bitch"), Celia reported triumphantly that Nureyev had agreed to reduce the Fairy Attendants from twenty-one to fourteen.

Once the commitment to mount *The Sleeping Beauty* was a reality, board members and Celia could only stand by and watch the production costs escalate to double the projected budget, coming in at a staggering $412,565 (over two million dollars today). Board members, among them Lyman Henderson, obtained personal promissory notes to raise extra cash. The reason some board members had to put their homes at risk was the contemptuous disregard for financial concerns by Nureyev and his set and costume designer Nicholas Georgiadis.[230] His grandiose ideas included a fleet of coaches to cross the stage, and the most expensive fabrics for the production's 340 costumes.

Henderson, in his capacity as board president, wrote to Georgiadis on May 28, 1972, expressing the board's concern at the rapidly escalating costs and urging him to give "thoughtful concern" while warning that "some compromises are going to have to be made." While the costume fabrics remained lavish, the company did manage to get it down to a single coach on the stage, instead of a fleet.

Years later, Frank Rasky asked Celia if she was grateful for the gambles taken by the board. She snapped back,

> Why should I be grateful to the Board? I built a bloody ballet company for the country; they agreed to go through with the Hurok thing — the condition of Hurok was having Nureyev do *Sleeping Beauty*. I was not averse to doing *Sleeping Beauty* since it was the one Tchaikovsky ballet we didn't have ... I don't think they were bloody saints. They had the money to guarantee; otherwise the banks wouldn't have accepted their guarantees.

Celia's pent-up anger was likely not directed at that particular board, but at all the boards she had had to deal with over the years as artistic director. The National Ballet board was still comprised of a clique of very wealthy members of Toronto's mainly Anglo establishment. Over the years Celia had become exhausted and exasperated at forever having to educate new board members to the realities of the ballet world and to defend the repeated deficits.

It's also highly probable that the men on those early boards in the pre-feminist 1950s, if in awe of Celia, were also chauvinistic, delighting in slipping her an occasional allowance cheque to buy some pretty clothes, in wining and dining her, or in having her on their arm at some event like a hockey game. Celia played up to their chivalrous behaviour, but she resented it. "We're always in the position of being grateful servants," she said.[231]

COSTUME MAKING HAD BEGUN months before the first rehearsals. While the dancers were still in England, the National Ballet's head costume cutter, Angela Arana, had flown over and spent three exhausting days grabbing sixty-two dancers to measure and fit for costumes. Some of the dancers were having their costumes basted or snipped in the last moments before they made their gliding entrance onto the National Arts Centre stage.

Partly in jest and partly in desperation, the National Ballet's millinery department began to wear strings of garlic around their necks to ward off evils, including Nicholas Georgiadis. He, on discovering this, thought it was hilarious.

Gilda Majocchi, a ballet mistress, came over in July from Milan to start teaching the dancers the Nureyev version of *The Sleeping Beauty*, which he had first mounted for La Scala Ballet in 1966.[232] When Nureyev first appeared at St. Lawrence Hall on August 3, dressed in a dark, long-sleeved top and woolen hat, he immediately began drastically changing much of what Majocchi had already taught the dancers. Veronica Tennant, a principal ballerina, vividly remembers his first appearance:

> He entered, the grandest of princes, the embodiment of the living legend. His movements were appropriately large and dashing, surprisingly graceful and delicate. What we hadn't expected, was — a *man* who was not tall, oddly dressed in a wool cap and tight leathers — a man — whose eyes twinkled like someone you'd always known and loved — who

chuckled when you were introduced — who made immediate, irrevocable contact with every person in the room and
would notice the instant anyone left.

No one in the company would ever forget those muggy August
days, which started early in the morning with everyone, Rudi
included, taking class. Often the rehearsals would stretch into the
evening, with the exhausted dancers dragging themselves home
at nine or ten o'clock. In the studio, seated on the raised platform,
leaning forward and staring intensely, Nureyev made it nearly
impossible for anyone to sneak out. He insisted that the entire
cast attend every rehearsal, regardless of whether they were in
the particular scene scheduled for practice. And there was no
marking of steps; every movement was to be danced — and
danced well. The dancers had never worked so hard in the short
time available to them to learn a three-act ballet.

Although the National Ballet's male principal dancers were
shut out of the lead role in *The Sleeping Beauty*, the younger ones
were thrilled to be in the presence of the most famous contemporary male ballet dancer. Frank Augustyn, then eighteen years old

Nureyev rehearsing Veronica Tennant and Karen Kain at St. Lawrence Hall in
the muggy August days of 1972. Courtesy of Torstar

and a recent graduate of the National Ballet School, remembers, "From the most arrogant to the shyest and most insecure dancer there — we all felt the same way. Something was happening that we'd never experienced before, and we knew it was going to be a wonderful ride."[233]

Without doubt there was an erotic charge in the rehearsal hall. Nureyev was a proverbial "bad boy" with an outrageous repertoire of swear words while the National Ballet ballerinas were, at least relatively so, "good girls." Rudi's favourite English expression was "shitfuck." Celia's comment was, "We certainly had to get used to it."[234]

That four National Ballet of Canada ballerinas should have had the exhilarating chance to partner with Nureyev was entirely due to Celia. On that first afternoon of rehearsals, Tennant cooled her heels in the studio for nearly an hour waiting for Nureyev to appear. What she didn't know at the time was that he and Celia were upstairs in her office having a screaming match over who would dance Aurora. He wanted international stars such as Marcia Haydée or Natalia Makarova.[235] Celia was determined that it would be her own ballerinas, namely Veronica Tennant, Nadia Potts, and Vanessa Harwood. She won that round.

But Nureyev won the match. The moment he laid eyes on twenty-year-old Karen Kain, he demanded to know why she wasn't one of the Auroras. Celia explained that she was still recovering from surgery and, although still a junior member, had been cast in a number of major roles, including the Blue Bird pas de deux in *The Sleeping Beauty* and lead ballerina in Bruhn's *Swan Lake*.

Celia had, in fact, recognized Kain's star quality from the beginning. She wrote to Bobbie Laidlaw on February 1, 1971, from California to report that the company had a new star, nineteen-year-old Kain. "This is only her second year in the company and she is still officially in the corps de ballet. However she has been dancing *Swan Lake* with tremendous success."

Nureyev demanded that all his Beauties look directly into his eyes in their pas de deux. Tennant remembers, "At the technically difficult points, he would shoot fire into my eyes and be there, gentle and strong.... Always, his eyes demanded connection and beautiful spirit."

While being attentive and nurturing to his Beauties, Nureyev also connived to create jealousy by making critical asides in the wings to one ballerina about another's performance. But the dancers didn't fall for it and would tell each other what he had been saying. Nureyev became bemused when he realized that his ploy didn't work with these Canadian ballerinas.

Celia, cast in the mime role of the wicked fairy, Carabosse, eventually refused to attend rehearsals. Second-cast dancer Victoria Bertram said, "I had to do all the rehearsals and then write it down and take it upstairs and talk to her about the role because she would have to do the full rehearsals."

Although rumours were ripe that Franca and Nureyev couldn't work together, Celia herself said that the stories about their animosity were exaggerated. Franca, by far the more mature and reasonable person, learned to bite her tongue in front of the dancers while saving up their quarrels for the privacy of Nureyev's dressing room.

Celia never knew when the mercurial Russian would turn on her. On one occasion, the two of them were in Nureyev's dressing room talking about ballet training and, in particular, what the training was like at the Leningrad School and the National Ballet School, when suddenly his mood changed and he began to scream at her. "That was the time to get out," Celia said.

Nureyev's petulant egotism made it impossible for Celia to participate actively. Karen Kain recalls,

She had abdicated for her own reasons which I can understand but she had abdicated. There was no fighting with him. She paid a big price — she did what she thought was the best thing for the company — she paid a big personal price for that — because the company, at least for those first years, was almost totally under the control of Rudolf and Sol Hurok and that wave took us to another level internationally. But as soon as he was gone — he wasn't with us all the time, she was in control of the company again — we did a lot of other stuff. She was still picking the other repertoire we had, she was still bringing in the other choreographers, she was still in charge of casting and everything else. But at some time she had decided that it was best if she remove herself from battling in front of everyone. He was who he was — just impossible — and it didn't do her any good or us any good to see them fighting. The whole company would hear him say, "I want that one" and she was very discreet, really, it was very difficult. [236]

THE SLEEPING BEAUTY OPENED at Ottawa's National Arts Centre on September 1, 1972. The day before, *Globe and Mail* dance critic John Fraser spoke to Celia backstage at the NAC. While coping with Nureyev's temper tantrums and refusal to take a photo call, Celia retained, outwardly, her customary composure. She boasted to Fraser, "We're at a peak definitely, for the company and for me. It takes years and years to build a ballet company, and there's a lot of frustration on the way. When we started, we were pretty raw, but there was plenty of excitement. Well, we're past that stage now, we're pretty sophisticated. Performing in Europe gave us the most incredible boost." [237]

Nicholas Georgiadis's set and costume designs were magnificently ornate and, frankly, over-the-top. In the first-act birthday-party scene, he chose the sumptuous costumes of the period of Louis XIII, and in the final act, one hundred years later, copied from the time of Louis XIV, the Sun God, who himself danced in court ballets wearing costumes resplendent with gold. Celia thought many of the costumes were not only impractical but

Words are not needed to describe the friction between Franca and Nureyev backstage at Ottawa's National Arts Centre following a performance of *The Sleeping Beauty*. Photograph by Jean-Marc Carisse

looked foolish. Thus, she felt that the four suitors to Aurora looked "sissy and silly."

Celia, as the wicked fairy godmother Carabosse, made her menacing entrance in the first act. She was dressed in the most magnificent orange and gold brocade gown with a black velvet centre panel, and a frizzy red wig topped with a gold and silver headdress. Reviewing that first night, the *Toronto Star*'s Littler described the production as a mix of Renaissance painting (with

Celia in her role as Carabosse, the wicked fairy godmother in *The Sleeping Beauty.* Courtesy of the National Ballet of Canada Archives

sets dripping in "gold tassels, columns and balustrades") and cartoon: "Celia Franca's portrayal of the wicked fairy Carabosse, complete with a smoke-puff entrance, certainly smacks of Walt Disney, if not of Tallulah Bankhead in extremis, whereas the colour hues of many other scenes quite dazzled the viewer with their burnished richness."[238]

After the performance, Celia, Nureyev, Sol Hurok, and the dancers were visited backstage by Pierre Trudeau and his wife, Margaret. Margaret was dressed in a long, floral peasant-style

Veronica Tennant and Rudolph Nureyev greet Pierre and Margaret Trudeau backstage. Courtesy of the National Ballet of Canada Archives

dress; Pierre had donned a formal white dinner jacket for the evening, which capped what had been a momentous day. Earlier, Trudeau had visited the governor general to ask for the dissolution of parliament and the beginning of a gruelling election campaign.

Thereafter the National Ballet moved on to Montreal's Place des Arts before beginning a tour of the US that began in Philadelphia on September 13. They returned to Canada at the end of November for performances at the O'Keefe Centre. Besides his role in *The Sleeping Beauty*, Rudolph was the star in National Ballet repertoire that included Bruhn's versions of *La Sylphide* and *Swan Lake*, and Jose Limon's *The Moor's Pavane*. Hurok had bought the rights to Limon's work for his Russian star, who wanted a modern piece in the program to show his versatility.[239]

For the Christmas season, this time without Nureyev, the company performed its traditional *Nutcracker* in Ottawa, Toronto, and London, Ontario. Near the end of January, Nureyev rejoined them in Vancouver. After one evening performance, Celia and the National Ballet's general manager, Gerry Eldred, and Nureyev and Hurok's representative, Simon Semenoff, got together over dinner to discuss future plans for Nureyev and the National Ballet. Semenoff and Nureyev suggested mounting a production of *Carmen*. Celia, annoyed at their presumption of deciding repertoire, retorted, "Absolutely not." So strong was her tone of rejection that Nureyev and Semenoff got up and left the restaurant, leaving Eldred and Celia to finish the meal, pay the bill, and return to the hotel. Awaking the next morning, Eldred learned, to his astonishment, that Celia, after leaving him to go to her room, had checked out of the hotel and taken a late plane to Ottawa. She was back on the tour within forty-eight hours, insisting she had simply gone home to see Jay. She later explained to Eldred, "You have to understand that Jay is my third husband and I want to make it work. It's too important, I can't afford to lose him." This explanation caused the general manager to wonder if Celia was not near to some kind of breaking point and might even resign from the company.

The principal cause was, of course, Nureyev. He was temperamental, moody, coarse, self-centred to an extreme, extravagant, and, at times, downright cruel. He was also the most famous male dancer of modern times and an assured box-office attraction. Dealing with him was a wearying and thankless task. Repeatedly, Celia had to intervene in crises that involved Nureyev and one or more of her dancers. But it was much worse with the stage crew. Nureyev was often deliberately brutal to them, screaming and swearing. He once caused a male stage manager to break down and cry. "I had a lot of work to do behind the scenes with some of the staff, trying to keep people from blowing up," Celia said.

In a later season, however, a stagehand managed to score one over Nureyev. Celia wrote of the incident in a diary she kept for a short time in 1974:

Last night Rudi and Lilac Fairy [Carena Bomers] walked through the forest instead of riding in the boat. Norm Dyson explained after the show that Leo the electrician told Rudi the day before that if Rudi didn't stop calling him a "mother fucking cunt" he wouldn't drive him anymore. Dyson persuaded Leo to continue until Los Angeles — in other words finish off the Chicago Beauties. When Rudi and Bomers got into the boat, however, it gave a couple of bumps getting over the wood onto the linoleum [in the wings]. Rudi took fright and thought Leo was up to mischief so he pushed Bomers off the boat and said, "we walk."

The audience must have wondered why the Prince and Lilac Fairy were traipsing along beside the boat instead of being carried in grandeur towards the castle.

At one performance in early March 1973 in Houston, Texas, the Princess Aurora descending the grand staircase was Karen Kain. She recalls, "he decided on tour that I was going to make my debut as Aurora whether she [Celia] liked it or not and he started rehearsing me himself along with David Scott [ballet master] — and even though he was dancing seven or eight shows a week, he would rehearse me between shows. And then I got on and she wasn't happy about it."

At the time the young ballerina was, of course, enraptured to be Nureyev's princess. She admits that she, like many others in the company, was utterly captivated by him. "I was a very innocent, gullible, and shy person and Rudolf wanted my affection for sure, and before I had a chance to have a fully developed relationship with Celia. I mean, I was only in the company two years before this force of nature, who was so passionate, and drove us and inspired us, we were just crazy about him."

Many years later, when Kain herself became artistic director, she was able to look back and fully undestand Celia's feelings:

It must have been very, very hard for her. I didn't really realize the politics that were going on. She wasn't around. I think it was too hard for her. She wasn't on the whole tour with us. I don't remember her being there except in New York. Joanne and David Scott were there, and they were in charge of keeping it on, rehearsing everybody, but I don't recall Celia being there except in certain cities — she was in Ottawa. That's my memory ... if she was there, she made herself completely scarce, and I don't remember her being there.[240]

Chicago appears to have been a nightmare, with Nureyev behaving abominably. On April 7, when a performance was late starting (most likely because Nureyev was acting out), the audience began to clap impatiently. Suddenly, Nureyev appeared from behind the curtain, not yet in costume, with a bare chest and wearing leg warmers, and shrieked at the audience, "You shit-fuckers, shut up."[241]

When Nureyev had been at the peak of his career in the 1960s, Dame Ninette de Valois had been willing to overlook his surly temper. Celia found such behaviour intolerable. She also had doubts about his artistic abilities, saying, "It's a bit of a myth about him as a creative artist. He was not a genius." She felt there were limitations to his talents as a choreographer, finding his production of The Sleeping Beauty too dark, and many of the costume designs impractical and foolish looking. In some cases vanity took over: when Nureyev finally entered in the middle of the second act, he changed the choreography to showcase his incredible athletic strength and virtuosity.

There was, however, a kinder and gentler side to Nureyev. At times he would shower praise upon the whole company, from the principals to the corps. He once took everyone out to dinner at his favourite Toronto restaurant, Barberian's Steakhouse. This warmth was reciprocated: for his thirty-fifth birthday on March 17, 1973, while in St. Louis, the dancers presented him with a fur-lined dance belt made by the company's wardrobe department. This gift was a playful tease, since Nureyev's dance belts (worn by all male dancers) were a particularly prominent feature of his costume.

Nearing the end of the gruelling four-month tour, the company opened in New York's Metropolitan Opera House on April 24, 1973, to good reviews. Clive Barnes of *The New York Times* described the National Ballet of Canada as "a company quite remarkably improved in recent years," giving credit to both Celia and Betty Oliphant: "It has for many years had promise but the hard work of Celia Franca and that of her assistant and head of the Ballet School, Betty Oliphant, together with the special impetus of successful tours in Europe and the United States have all conspired to give the company a new gloss. Miss Franca's taste supplemented by Mr. Nureyev's flair make for a formidable combination." After seeing several performances, Barnes again wrote about the National Ballet, saying, "This is one of the best productions of *The Sleeping Beauty* around. I thought so when I first saw it — with Fonteyn and Nureyev — at *La Scala* and I think so now. But the Canadians dance it better."[242]

The marathon tour ended abruptly, however, on May 13 when the star attraction injured himself. Without Nureyev, the engagement at Washington's John F. Kennedy Center was cancelled. The company's board of directors were well aware that Celia's role over those long months had become that of a troubleshooter. President Jock McLeod sent her a personal letter in May 1973, acknowledging both the artistic and financial success of *The Sleeping Beauty* and at the same time recognizing "the horrible frustrations you have had to put up with." He concluded, "You are truly a gem, and — despite the difficult time we too often give you in Executive committee and Board meetings — we love you dearly." More useful, they gave her a bonus cheque.

BY NO MEANS WAS Nureyev's injury the end of his association with the National Ballet. He toured off and on with the company until

1976. And while his appearances assured a full house, his over-powering aura consigned the rest of the National Ballet to the backdrop of his own performance.

If Cranko's *Romeo and Juliet* had brought the company from a C team to a B team, Nureyev's *The Sleeping Beauty* had made the National Ballet of Canada an A team. He had pushed each and every dancer in the production to dance at their capacity. Nadia Potts remembers watching the ballet from the audience and being amazed at the physicality and electricity emanating from the stage. "It was a very exciting *Sleeping Beauty*, not a pretty-pretty version."

Amidst all the successes, though, the strain had grown between Franca and Nureyev. Without anything being said or admitted, the National Ballet was becoming more Nureyev's company than Celia's. Or more exactly, it was becoming the company of Nureyev and the Hurok organization.[248] Veronica Tennant and Karen Kain were quite shocked when they later realized just how much they had shifted their loyalty from Celia to Nureyev. In particular, Kain, who had been Nureyev's favourite Beauty, revealed that she had been simply swept away by the world of glamour and celebrity to which he introduced her:

> There's no doubt that I was totally enthralled and enamoured with this force and we all were. He was a force to be reckoned with. And he was so obvious in his affection and support of Veronica and I and Frank — you know it soured after some time, he got older and more desperate and did things that disappointed us, but in those first years we were riding this incredible wave.

And by making her partner, Nureyev transformed Kain into a true international star. In a 1997 interview, Celia allowed her resentment to show. "I think she [Kain] goes a bit overboard when she says how much he did for her. I was doing a lot for her, also, thank you Karen. You could mention me every now and then." When Kain was read this quote, she readily admitted, "I think she's probably right. I probably didn't give her enough credit. When I look back on my whole career, I certainly recognize what she did for me and how she supported me. But at that time, no."[244]

In her 1973 artistic director's report, Celia struggled to say something complimentary about Nureyev. She stressed his physical stamina and his insistence that every dancer give the very best of their ability. Veronica Tennant agreed that Nureyev pushed them in directions they had never gone before: "He'd say, 'You must eat up the stage and audience will go wild.' I think we weren't that theatrical a company before Rudolf, and it was after working with him that you realized that this was very much a reciprocal occasion with the audience."[245]

Well aware of the mutual benefits, more tours were organized with the National Ballet of Canada as a backup for Nureyev. Celia could only go along as caretaker. She did, however, use her occasional diary to give vent to her frustrations. Never a fan of Russian-style bravura, she deplored his egocentric stagemanship. She wrote about his performance in *Giselle*:

> His first act until the "mad scene" was excellent — the interpretation that is. Dancing? Forget it. Strained, forced, contrived. He overacts during the mad scene and detracted from Veronica. His second act was embarrassing and posed, phony and that ghastly dirty shit-coloured satin cape he wears and trips over. It's bigger than any I've ever seen in my life and DRAB — tasteless. How he fancies himself in it. After making his entrance, he comes downstage and lets his cape open to show his cuckoo[246] before proceeding.

One incident during a Nureyev appearance in Toronto in *The Sleeping Beauty* gave Celia another opportunity to express her feelings. At the last moment, a tactic Nureyev frequently employed, he asked for lighting changes to allow a follow spot on him descending the stairs and a dim special on the sleeping Aurora. With there being no general lighting, he was left standing in the dark, unable to see where he was going. Instead of traversing the stage waking people up, he stood there and eventually went towards one of the wings and cursed the stage manager. Sensing the coming storm, Celia rushed backstage in time to witness Nureyev throw a chair and knock over a prop box, showering nails all over the floor. She said to him, "That won't help," as he stormed past her into his dressing room, slamming the door.

Night after night the National Ballet was experiencing the heady phenomenon of packed houses and standing ovations. And while fronting Nureyev earned revenue for the ballet, the cost was considerable, and Celia Franca was not alone in recognizing this. John Fraser had been asked to write a special article for *The New York Times*[247] when the company performed for the third time at the Metropolitan Opera House. Headlined "Nureyev Leave Canadian Ballet Alone," Fraser's article described the National Ballet of Canada as a pawn of the Sol Hurok empire, which had fallen into the trap of "leaping to prominence through someone else's greatness." Fraser ended by suggesting that Nureyev "pack up and move somewhere else."[248]

Celia's role had diminished to that of picking up and smoothing down in the wake of the capricious, explosive, unpredictable passage of Nureyev. She had gone from founder to fixer.

FIFTEEN

Dying Swan Song

O N JANUARY 11, 1974, the National Ballet announced in a media
release, "Celia Franca to Step Down as Artistic Director."
Board member Jock McLeod expressed the deep appreciation felt by
all Canadians for her contribution over the last twenty-three years
in creating and developing the nation's largest dance company and
in achieving an international reputation for the National Ballet.
He emphasized that she would remain actively involved in choreographing and coaching dancers.

That Celia should be stepping down surprised relatively few
inside or close to the company. Word that she wanted to leave
had been around for at least a year in the small, gossipy world of
ballet. What came as a surprise was the second paragraph of the
press release, announcing, "On July 1, 1974 Mr. David Haber will
assume responsibility as Artistic Director of the National Ballet."
While explaining that Haber and general manager Gerry Eldred

would be assuming tandem responsibility for the National Ballet's upcoming tours, the brief four-paragraph press release contained no reference to the striking fact that Haber, despite his unquestioned accomplishments and managerial experience, was, himself, not a trained ballet dancer.

To any informed observer, it was obvious that Celia had arranged things so as to be succeeded by someone whose limited grasp of the single most important aspect of the job, artistic

A moody publicity shot of Celia Franca with her anointed successor, David Haber. Courtesy of the National Ballet of Canada Archives

direction, would leave her if not the official director, then the National Ballet's offstage artistic mastermind, or, as someone unkindly but not inaccurately put it, the puppet master.

Perhaps the one person who really understood the sub-agenda was Jock McLeod, who later said, "I knew that Haber was a non-starter, but I also knew it was the only way to get Celia to step aside."

Just when Celia made up her mind to step down as artistic director cannot be pinned down. One key date was early July 1972, when the company was in Monte Carlo at the end of its first European tour. This was when Celia first discussed with Haber her thoughts about perhaps stepping down, and it was then she first broached to him the idea of his becoming co-artistic director. Haber agreed to take on the challenge. In fact, Haber was not her first choice. In a draft letter to Jock McLeod, she explained, "I wanted Jean Roberts, a first class theatrical [sic]. She was available. We lost her because Russell felt threatened. We now have David Haber who actually wants to enter our cesspool."

Undoubtedly, Celia had been thinking about leaving for some time. By now, she had been commuting back and forth from Ottawa for five years. The Palace Revolution of spring 1972 that resulted in the sudden departure of Wally Russell made clear the hostility of several board members towards her and left her angry and hurt. Her more than two decades as artistic director had been exhilarating, but they had also been brutally exhausting. She said years after her retirement, "My time with the National Ballet was one long fight. There wasn't anything that I achieved that I didn't fight for — nothing."[249]

Jock McLeod, whose professional life as a management consultant gave him a special perspective in understanding employee behaviour, had figured out Celia's intentions. He had taken note of the fact that, following the 1972 European tour and with the arrival of Nureyev, Celia had all but disappeared from the rehearsal studios. At this time, he happened to run into ballet mistress Joanne Nisbet[250] and was surprised to see how exhausted she looked. When he asked Nisbet why, she told him that she had been doubling up as Celia had stopped taking rehearsals. McLeod realized that after Franca had proved to de Valois and her English dance colleagues that she had created a world class ballet company, her burning commitment began to subside. She had also become more concerned about the state of her marriage.

McLeod's analysis is undoubtedly correct. Celia and the National Ballet's success in London validated her entire career. She also had the particular problem of having started in Canada at the very top and at the very young age of twenty-nine. She'd thus done everything the Canadian ballet world might have to offer, the greater part of it being her own creation, or in the case of the National Ballet School, a creation in union with Betty Oliphant. As well, by the National Ballet's association with Rudolf Nureyev, she had, no matter the difficulties, made the company internationally recognized. She had proved herself to all of the people she most wanted to impress. Thereafter, everything else could only be anticlimactic.

There is seldom an easy way down from the top of the ladder. Haber was the means Celia chose as the best way to be seen as moving out even while keeping a firm grasp on the top rung. Tall and lanky with a wide mouth from which would flash large white teeth — some dancers referred to him as "the tooth fairy" — Haber was a highly competent administrator and manager with a wealth of experience both in Canada and internationally. He'd been the National Ballet's stage manager near its beginning. Over the years he had performed a number of valuable services for Celia, such as arranging for the ballet to open Ottawa's new National Arts Centre in 1969 and stepping in at the last minute to salvage the European tour.

Given all the jealousies that are an inevitable part of the ballet world, the prospect that the transition from Franca to Haber would be smooth and easy was always slight. One problem was the way the changeover was made. Normal procedure would have been for the board, after having received Celia's resignation letter, to have set up a search committee to interview suitable candidates and select a successor. Nothing of the sort happened. Celia made a strong recommendation to Jock McLeod that Haber succeed her. The board rubber-stamped the deal and made it a *fait accompli*. In hindsight, Celia said that she took half the blame for the way her successor was appointed.

To make matters worse, Betty Oliphant, who had played an indispensable role in both the company and the school, had been kept in the dark about Haber's promotion until just before the announcement, at which time she was lying in a hospital bed recovering from a minor stroke. Hearing the news, she sobbed inconsolably. From the start Oliphant resented Haber's appointment as co-artistic director. In her autobiography she recounts a conversation in which she asked Celia why she had broken her promise not to make Haber artistic director. According to Oliphant, Celia's answer was, "You were a fool if you believed me."[251]

The other problem was that Celia's transition only went halfway. Although going, she wasn't really going. While McLeod had summoned enough courage to insist that Haber alone carry the title of artistic director, he and she for all practical purposes remained co-artistic directors. According to her pencilled notes, Celia prepared a disingenuous explanation for the odd new system. "Job of A.D. became too big for me to handle — hence Haber. He did so well I felt we could speed up my 'so-called retirement.'" She then outlined a long string of activities she would be undertaking in the succeeding months, everything from casting and rehearsing to overseeing the ballets for the Canadian Opera Company, to doing original choreography for *Faust* plus being available to tour.

At the time of Celia's announced retirement, *Chatelaine* magazine commissioned Don Rubin to write a profile tracing her career as founder of Canada's national ballet company. Published in March 1974 and titled *Celia Franca: Tartar in a Tutu*, it raised such questions as "Who is this dazzling enigma with an iron will, a sharp tongue and three husbands?" Rubin wrote, "After 23 years, not even intimate friends really know her, but admirers and foes agree Canadians owe her a great debt for building our boon dock ballet to international standards."

Rubin had gone to England to interview many people including her first husband, Leo Kersley. All of the information that Celia had carefully suppressed — including the fact that she was on her third marriage, that she came from a humble Jewish background, that there had been rumours about a possible lesbian relationship with Kay Ambrose, and that she was a very difficult woman — came into the open.

Celia was especially outraged that Rubin's article contained numerous quotes from Betty Oliphant, describing Celia as insensitive, intolerant of different opinions, and willing and able to "destroy" dancers emotionally.

Rubin, who has always claimed that he greatly admired Franca, ended the piece saying, "And it's only when she does step aside this summer that she may finally be able to look back and decide whether or not little Celia Franks from London really did make it in a world when by all logic and all odds, she never did belong." Effectively, he had unmasked her.[252]

Right up to the end of her career, Celia worked as hard as ever. During her last week as the National Ballet of Canada's artistic director, she attended a dinner reception for a group of Soviet dancers making their first performance in Toronto. The group was billed as "The Stars of Russian Ballet," which was something of a stretch. Among the Russian dancers were a pair from the Kirov Ballet: forty-one-year-old Irina Kolpakova, a lyrical dancer who happened also to be an ardent Communist, and a twenty-six-year-old man of exceptional talent named Mikhail Baryshnikov, whose main role on that trip was to partner aged ballerinas. Among balletomanes, he was ranked as the world's finest male ballet dancer, just as Nureyev was rated as the world's flashiest male dancer.

Four days after the dinner reception, an event in the ballet world took place that thrust Celia's imminent retirement out of the picture. On June 29, the last evening of the Kirov troupe's Toronto engagement, Baryshnikov dashed out the side door of the O'Keefe Centre, sprinted three blocks, and jumped into a waiting car.[253] A reliable team of people was in place to help him. Lawyer Jim Peterson, who later entered parliament and became the Minister of International Trade, was prepared to represent him in seeking asylum.

While initially kept in the dark, Celia was soon added to the team. Her diary for the days after the defection included mention of a 705 area code phone number for a cottage north of Toronto where Baryshnikov was lying low. Within a few days he felt confident enough to be seen in public, and needing to return to daily classes, he went to the St. Lawrence Hall studios. After doffing his striped dressing gown, he went through a series of dance exercises for the benefit of the media. David Haber, by now officially the artistic director, introduced Baryshnikov at the press conference, praising his talents as a dancer and declaring that the National Ballet hoped he would join the company.

Predictably, Baryshnikov's interest was not in Toronto but in New York City. Indeed, on July 27, less than a month later, he made his debut with the American Ballet Theatre, dancing in *Giselle* at the Lincoln Center. At the same time, Rudolf Nureyev and Karen Kain were performing in the National Ballet of Canada's *The Sleeping Beauty* at the Metropolitan Opera.

As a thank you to Canada and the National Ballet, Baryshnikov returned to Toronto to appear in a free open-air concert at Ontario Place. The ballet was *La Sylphide* and Celia was on hand to rehearse him and principal ballerinas Veronica Tennant and Nadia Potts. Looking somewhat shell-shocked, still with his poor Russian haircut and his face broken out from stress, Baryshnikov listened through a Russian translator to Celia's corrections. She sat on the raised platform in the studio, gently coaching him along as he struggled to master the Danish Bournonville style, and saying at the end of one rehearsal, "That was much better today, Misha." Despite a public transit strike, ten thousand people came out for the performance, which Baryshnikov did twice — once with Veronica Tennant and then again with Nadia Potts. His fee was two thousand dollars, which he promptly donated to the National Ballet School.

NBC dancer Sergiu Stefanshi, artistic director David Haber, and Mikhail Baryshnikov at Ontario Place in August 1974. Photograph by Franz Maier, courtesy of the National Ballet of Canada Archives

ON JULY 11, A real estate agent came to Celia's home on Glenrose Avenue to hammer in a For Sale sign. One of the greatest benefits of semi-retirement for Celia was that she no longer would have to endure the weekly commute to Ottawa to join her husband. She had been feeling guilty about her absence during Jay's deteriorating physical and mental health. In the early 1970s, he had an operation to remove a benign tumour from his leg. Far more worrying for a wind player, he'd had to have extensive dental surgery. Celia confided to her old friend, Bobbie Laidlaw, in a letter from California in February 1971, that she was hurrying home to Ottawa to be with Jay. "His big worry is that the new set-up [a dental bridge] will affect his clarinet playing. I have never known him to be so low and am quite worried."

Never outgoing by nature, Jay became progressively more taciturn, a condition worsened by his heavy drinking. Unwilling to disclose her concerns about Jay's mental health to anyone around her, Celia confided in letters to her South African cousin, Zelda, who replied in November 1972, "I'm really sorry to hear about Jay & I'm really sorry that I can't be with you now, to try and help you, to get him out of his depression." In her 1974 diary, Celia fretted, "Hope Jay's concerts went well in Toronto and last night in Windsor. I always long to see him and be with him even though he's seemingly in a permanent depression."

For a while the arrangement she had engineered with Haber seemed to be working, but Celia simply could not stop micromanaging. Haber, himself, remarked, "Celia wanted a certain amount of freedom but she didn't want to let go."[254] Her bossy interference extended to friendly board members. In briefing notes she prepared for Lyman Henderson in May 1975, she outlined several issues in which the board was dictating artistic policy to Haber. Hoping to put words into Henderson's mouth, she wrote, "[Miss Franca] had hoped that the Board, having worn out and discouraged one artistic director, to the point of her having to resign, would have learnt its lesson from that and would do its utmost to encourage the new artistic director, and give him greater support than was extended to the old one."

Although Franca and Haber worked in tandem, there were occasions of strain between them. When the National Ballet made its second European tour in the spring of 1975, Celia very properly went along for the trip. Initially, she immensely enjoyed herself, getting a lot of local media attention, including an interview on BBC Radio's popular show, *Women's Hour*. But since she was no longer official artistic director, things couldn't remain the same. On the National Ballet's opening night at the London Coliseum, Celia, dressed in a black-and-white evening gown, sat with the British ballet establishment, including Sir Frederick Ashton and Dame Ninette de Valois. Haber sat beside the royal guest, Princess Margaret. In his review in *The Globe and Mail*, John Fraser never mentioned Franca.

Celia had always been acutely aware of how difficult it would be to make a quasi- retirement work since it depended on Haber allowing her all the scope she wanted while he still performed as if he were the real artistic director. Even before the transition had taken place, she had written in her diary in March 1974:

> Well I would have thought that the worst was over, but the meeting Haber and I had with Jock this morning was too much. It appears that Betty has bent the ears back of many directors and persuaded them that Haber is unqualified to be artistic director. Independently some directors have stated that Jock steamrolled proceedings and got an acqui- escence from "intimidation." If it came to a vote Jock says we'd be finished. He suggested I make a positive statement and get out at the board meeting to be called the Monday before Boston. Then Haber should express his views of the future. Then Jock could let them bitch and get things out of their system. One thing is definite — if Haber is out so am I. Where Betty thinks she can get another Director, god knows!

That closing sentence was prophetic. As the year turned into 1975, Betty Oliphant made her opposition to Haber ever more clear, internally to the company and to the Board, and then publicly in the press, most particularly to *The Globe and Mail*.

First, she resigned her position as associate artistic director of the National Ballet claiming that Haber (and Franca) had failed to communicate future artistic plans to the rest of artistic staff. [255] In *The Globe and Mail*, Oliphant declared, "At a recent board meeting, the problems surfaced because I brought them up. I hated doing this since I feel artistic decisions should be made by the artistic staff, but the situation had reached, in my opinion, a critical point." She continued, "I think that ballet companies are basically very fragile and can rest on good reputations for only a year or two before dreadful things begin to happen. I've lived with the present situation as long as I could, always with the hope that things would work out. Now I see real problems and since I can't do anything to stop them, I can at least resign and state clearly why I am doing so."

On June 3, 1975, Jock McLeod, invited Haber to his University Avenue office. After some brief pleasantries, McLeod, ever the smooth management consultant, urged Haber to step down rather than face the humiliation of being let go. Immediately after the interview, Haber phoned Celia in Ottawa. "Are you sitting down? I've just been fired." Four days later Haber announced he would be leaving the company at the end of July, fixing the date so he could ensure that all went well for the company's upcoming three-week engagement at New York's Metropolitan Opera House.

In an interview with Rasky, Haber called McLeod a "cold fish" and said that he had been influenced by Betty Oliphant and perhaps by Gerry Eldred, the highly competent general manager. Indeed, Eldred might have wondered if he was even needed, since Haber had much the same skill sets in cultural management as him. Haber never doubted that Oliphant had played a major role in his downfall. He held no grudge against Celia, writing her a gracious note from New York:

> Please, please, dear Celia, look after yourself — & think of you and your future. And thank you for thinking of me

and giving me a very important opportunity. It didn't work out as we believed it should and would — but thanks for the chance. I'm truly sorry it didn't work and still believe the idea and principle were right — I keep telling myself I did not fail — that [*sic*] failed me by not having the foresight you and I shared.

> Please, darling, think of you
> Much, much love — always David

Haber remained badly bruised by this experience all his life. He started his own agency, Haber Artists Management, representing Karen Kain, Frank Augustyn, and Ann Ditchburn, among others, for a few years. After semi-retiring in the late 1970s, Haber took several freelance contracts, including one at Expo 86 in Vancouver. He died in Houston, Texas, in September 2008, where he had lived for many years with his partner, Dr. Didier Piot.

As a stopgap, the board asked Celia to temporarily step in again until the end of September in order to give them time to establish a proper search committee. Briefly, Celia flirted with the idea of coming back on a permanent basis, with the claim being made that all that had really happened was that she had taken a sabbatical. With some tact, word was passed to her that the end of September was really the end of her term as artistic director at the National Ballet of Canada. The board, aware of her ruse of trying to run the company from Ottawa with Haber as her mouthpiece, was more than ready to find a fresh artistic director.

In August, during the company's annual break, Celia and Jay vacationed at Killarney Lodge in Algonquin Park. Never much of a nature girl, the tranquility of the wilderness did nothing to revive Celia's spirits. In a long, rambling passage, scribbled in an exercise book, she came close to sounding utterly defeated:

> I suppose 54 years is long enough to live. What more can I get out of life? Certainly no affection from my husband, no

satisfaction from work, the confirmation that I have ruined
Haber's life by inviting him to join the National Ballet in the
first place. Today's *Toronto Star* announces the appointment
of Ted Barrows as O'Keefe general manager. Now what
will Haber do? All last week Jay and I would walk and I
would take his hand — we would walk hand in hand. He
never takes my hand. I'm very depressed tonight. It seems
to me there is nothing to live for. Jay appears not to need or
want me. I've tried to keep things cheerful and calm or whatever I thought he wanted. What a futile effort. The only time
he touches me is first thing in the morning in bed when he's
cold and then he cuddles in. Otherwise I cuddle in. What to
do? He said he was sorry I was in the dumps. When I told
him that he shows me no affection, he said he was sorry that
he was so uptight. Well.... had it out later. Tears on my part.
Quiet reassurance from Jay.

Apart from leaving the Sadler's Wells Ballet in 1946, this surely
was the lowest moment in Celia's life. She no longer had any
purpose. She was contrite at what she had done to Haber. And,
momentarily, she even dropped the pretense that her marriage to
Jay Morton was satisfying. She sounded suicidal.

Back at work with the company, the countdown to the end of
her active career at the National Ballet of Canada had begun. Late
in September she travelled with the company to Montreal where
it was performing Gerald Arpino's flashy *Kettentanz* and two Erik
Bruhn stagings, *Swan Lake* and *La Sylphide*. Bruhn, himself, was
there, along with guest artist Mikhail Baryshnikov. Baryshnikov
had been brought in to dance James in *La Sylphide* to entice the
Quebec audience, who maintained an antagonism to the English-
style ballet company.

During one evening performance, a most unfortunate event
occurred. The Montreal branch of the National Ballet Guild had
provided a dinner for the dancers including chicken that, as it

turned out, was tainted. It was mostly the younger, hungry, corps de ballet members who took advantage of this free meal. By the time of the evening performance, many of the dancers were violently ill. Veronica Tennant's then husband, Dr. John Wright, a gastroenterologist, hurried backstage and, realizing food poisoning was the cause, arranged for buckets to be placed in the wings. The dancers would glide onto the stage, come off, vomit, and then glide back on stage. Karen Kain, who did not get sick, recalls, "It was a bit of a nightmare. Sometimes the stage was empty and just the music was playing because people were throwing up."

With Bruhn rehearsing the dancers and retirement just days away, Celia sat in the background and set down her thoughts in her exercise book:

> Am experiencing mixed emotions. This is my last week with the company I've worked with for the past 24 years. I shouldn't be so ashamed of what surely must be a natural sense of loss and regret. On the other hand, it will be a relief to get out of petty politics. I dread the next days here. The sitting back and letting Bruhn and Baryshnikov "carry on" — too many cooks spoil the broth and agonizing though it is for me — it's better to shut up and watch things happen on the stage which one disapproves of. No time or energy for arguments.

She decided to slip out of the theatre during the Sunday matinee performance of *Kettentanz* to avoid any distressing emotions. Her last act in the post of artistic director was to go backstage during intermission to reprimand the lighting director for the lights being too dark in one particular scene. Then, taskmaster and perfectionist to the very end, Celia slipped out of Place des Arts, went back to her hotel, and, alone, took a train back to Ottawa.[256]

SIXTEEN

"Vinegared Perfume"

J UST OVER ONE YEAR after Celia's exit as artistic director, she was back on the O'Keefe Centre stage with the National Ballet. November 12, 1976, was the twenty-fifth anniversary of the founding of the company. Celia's initial reaction to general manager Gerry Eldred's invitation indicated she had no plans to be in Toronto in November. She added that, insofar as the actual anniversary celebrations were concerned, she wanted no mention made that she had been the company's founder. The invitation brought back all the pain and reminders of what she had lost: celebrity status, deference, power, and, not to be dismissed, financial independence. Eldred wrote back diplomatically, saying, "There will be a great gap if you are not with us to celebrate," and asked her to reconsider. Though still deeply resentful, Celia agreed to participate.

ALEXANDER GRANT, CHOSEN LARGELY for his similar background to Celia (he was a dancer and choreographer closely associated to de Valois and the British ballet style), had been appointed by the board as Celia's successor. Grant had decided to remount John Cranko's highly popular *Romeo and Juliet* and invited Celia Franca to return for the celebration to reprise her mime role as Lady Capulet.

Celia Franca and Yves Cousineau were invited by new artistic director Alexander Grant to reprise the roles of Lady Capulet and Tybalt in Cranko's *Romeo and Juliet* in the twenty-fifth anniversary performance. James Kudelka was Romeo. Courtesy of the National Ballet of Canada Archives

When Celia arrived in Toronto to begin rehearsals, Barbara Amiel, writing for *Maclean's* magazine, coaxed Franca to open up about her feelings. "I'm dancing Lady Capulet because otherwise the new regime would say I have sour grapes," Celia told Amiel. "But they can't hurt me anymore. After all, I don't rely on Lady Capulet to earn a living. My friends say, rise above it all. Well maybe by curtain time I will have done." Amiel's rejoinder in the article was the very shrewd "But, then, maybe not," followed by a

forecast that something shocking was going to happen — a predic-
tion that would prove remarkably accurate. She concluded: "The
bitterness of her 1975 exit from the National Ballet of Canada
clings to her like vinegared perfume. Rank and title were her
finishing accessories. Without them she moves uneasily and
ungraciously through the company's halls."²⁵⁷ Amiel captured
perfectly the poisonous atmosphere in St. Lawrence Hall where
Celia was humiliated to find the company had made no arrange-

Celia received a standing ovation while taking her curtain call at the twenty-
fifth anniversary production of *Romeo and Juliet*. Courtesy of the National Ballet of
Canada Archives

ments for a place where she could rest between costume fittings and rehearsals.

On Friday, November 12, twenty-five years to the day after her small company had made its first appearance at Eaton Auditorium, Celia Franca, costumed in her second-act white-and-gold Lady Capulet gown, received a standing ovation as she took her curtain call.[258] After the National Ballet's president, Paul Deacon, had read a message to the audience, Secretary of State John Roberts presented Celia with a framed scroll. These pleasantries completed, Celia was invited to address the audience.[259]

She started by making all the right comments about the importance of the occasion, about how richly deserved was the recognition of the company by both the Canadian people and the government, and about her own gratitude to have been presented with the scroll. At this point Celia switched to naming all the people who had played a vital role in the achievements of the National Ballet of Canada during her long tenure. Names tripped off Celia's tongue — one by one — with Celia pausing, every now and then, to add one more person who had made a special contribution. Then making a final deep curtsey, Celia left the stage.

Either by forgetfulness or, far more probably, by design, Celia had omitted from the long list the most obvious name of all: Betty Oliphant, the company's first ballet mistress, co-founder and director of the National Ballet School of Canada, and, from 1968 until 1975, associate artistic director of the company. In the audience, *Globe and Mail* editor Richard Doyle leaned over to John Fraser and commented, "Now I've seen the Great Bitch at work."

Oliphant, sitting between Yves Cousineau and Erik Bruhn, had moved toward the edge of her seat with each of Celia's acknowledgements. When Celia walked off the stage without having mentioned her name, she collapsed weeping and her two male companions had to hold her up between them as they moved her slowly towards the foyer.

Later, Oliphant told *Globe and Mail* reporter Lawrence O'Toole, "It was unbearable and I thought cruel. I was so ... sort of stunned. And I guess I had a few minutes of hysteria."

In fact, Oliphant was in a bad way psychologically through the 1970s, although she managed to keep up a public front most of that time. Her second marriage had failed, she had attempted suicide on more than one occasion, and, as she later admitted in her autobiography, she had been drinking too much. To add to her stress, she suffered back pain and had three operations within a one-year period.

Gerry Eldred, the general manager, recalls an earlier highly emotional incident near to the end of 1973, when the three of them were discussing contracts and promotions for the coming season in a New York restaurant. Celia named a dancer she thought should be promoted from the corps de ballet. Betty argued that the promotion was premature. When Celia insisted the advancement be made, Betty burst into tears, sobbing throughout the remainder of the meeting. Eldred, bemused at this behaviour, observed, "My sense was this was the way the two of them worked." Celia's recollection was a good deal harsher. First, she said that she didn't recall the incident at all, and then added that if Betty had indeed been crying it was probably because she didn't get her own way.

A few days after the anniversary event, *The Globe and Mail* ran a long story addressing the key question, "Did Franca Slight Oliphant?" The unconvincing explanation Celia gave to the newspaper for what she'd done was, "I was really winging it. I knew that I couldn't thank everybody and particularly wanted to give credit to the old dancers. That was the feeling behind my speech. After all, whatever work had been done, was done so the dancers could get on stage and give pleasure. To help publicize this twenty-fifth anniversary season I've been working really hard, giving interviews and the like. And I've mentioned Betty in the most glowing terms. I feel I've given her more than her due."

Much later, when Rasky brought up this incident in one of his interviews, Celia said she did not remember neglecting to mention Oliphant. Pausing for a few seconds, Celia added that she'd also failed to mention long-time musical director George Crum.

At that time and ever afterwards, ballet fans have been divided into two camps about the Oliphant name omission. General manager Gerry Eldred leans towards Celia, at least to the extent of saying diplomatically, "In my opinion it was an oversight." Monique Michaud, then the Canada Council's dance officer, believes Celia did it on purpose, adding, "I think it's a scar on her reputation. And an important one.... It said a lot about her character."

While the principle breaking point between Celia and Oliphant was over who deserved the credit as the founder of the National Ballet School, other factors caused their relationship to go toxic, to the extent that for several years the pair refused to talk to each other.

A certain social gap — difficult for non-British to detect — always existed between Celia Franca and Betty Oliphant. It was the gap, that widest and most impenetrable, of class. Oliphant came from a middle-upper-class Scottish family; her father, who had died when she was an infant, had been a successful lawyer. Feigning reticence to *The Globe and Mail*'s social reporter, Lotta Dempsey, Betty volunteered that the Oliphant lineage went back to a knight who had accompanied William the Conqueror, while on her mother's side, Betty's grandfather was at one time the British consul-general in China.

By contrast, Celia was the daughter of a Polish-Jewish immigrant tailor from London's East End. The class-conscious Marie Rambert had put Betty in her morning "quality" class while Celia was relegated to the afternoon class of "common" show dancers. Oliphant, in a discussion with Rasky about the twenty-fifth anniversary slight, recounted, "A board member came up to me and said, you know, you being here at this reception, that's class, but what happened on the stage tonight, that's not class."

Celia arrived in Canada with an intimidating, near-perfect, posh accent. No other Briton, though, would have been fooled by it, and certainly not in those class-ridden days. As Oliphant put it to Rasky, "If you come from England, you'd know Celia has a very phony English accent." When Rasky adroitly played this comment back to her, Celia reacted just as he must have hoped: "What a rude bitch. I never had a cockney accent." Rasky used this ploy twice. In her interview, Oliphant had referred to Celia's husband, Jay Morton, as an "anti-social alcoholic" — a not totally inaccurate observation. Celia's response when it was played back to her was that Betty was jealous because she, unlike Betty,[260] was enjoying a happy marriage — this boast being, sadly, an exaggeration.

Ironically, Oliphant was more of a scrapper while Celia tended not to air her dirty linen in public. Several dancers, including Ann Ditchburn and Karen Kain, were badly burned by Oliphant. Kain recalls,

> Betty was a devious, difficult woman. What I loved about Celia was she was honest and straightforward. And she was always that way with me and there was always something twisted with Betty that I never understood until she hurt me enough times or took my confidences and used them against me publicly or things like that where I finally realized that this was a dangerous woman who lacked integrity in the way she treated people. Not Celia, ever. She may have had her feelings hurt and I don't blame her, but she never lacked integrity in the way she treated me or spoke to me or dealt with me.

As well, Celia came to believe that Oliphant had been telling people she made a habit of suppressing the fact that she was Jewish. As she wrote in her 1974 diary,

According to Betty, I've always been ashamed of my Jewish background. I explained to M.A. [Mary Anne, her cat-sitter and housemate] that when I first came to Canada I experienced some anti-Semitism (dear Pearl [Whitehead], bless her heart). I had the choice of either returning to England, or, if I wanted to go through with the challenge of my new "job" keeping my mouth shut. I never denied being Jewish. Many of our Jewish directors knew most certainly.

Here, it was undoubtedly Betty who was closer to the truth. When Celia first arrived in Toronto, she had felt conflicted about her Jewish background. Back in England, many of her friends, such as Doris, Cyril, and Gerald Frankel, were Jewish. One of the things that first attracted Celia to her second husband, Bert Anderson, was that, as she described to Doris in a letter, "He's very ugly, has a kind interior, a heart of gold and lots of Jewish friends."

In Canada, though, she chose to downplay her Jewish heritage. In the mid-1970s Celia had been asked to agree to be featured in a proposed book, *The Jew in Canada*. She wrote back, "While my ancestors are Jewish I have not personally practiced the Jewish or any other religion. My husband parent's are not Jewish and we would both prefer that I not be mentioned in the book." According to Celia's first cousin, Esther Stern, Celia's parents, most especially her mother Gertie, were deeply pained at realizing their daughter had rejected her Jewish background.

Ironically, one of Celia's first public honours was the B'nai Brith Woman of the Year Award in 1958, followed by the Toronto Hadassah Award of Merit in 1967. After her death in 2008, Celia Franca was one of a highly selective group of Jewish women deemed to be trailblazers in the book *With Strength and Splendor: Jewish Women as Agents of Change*.[261]

Celia's public recognition was unquestionably another cause for Betty's animosity. From the beginning, Celia was a celebrity. She had charisma, she had a magnificent profile of the kind ballerinas are supposed to have, she spoke with great dramatic flair and gave "good quotes," she radiated confidence and poise. Oliphant, although tall, was easy to miss. She dressed in the garb of a Rosedale matron. So the public knew who Celia Franca was, while Betty Oliphant was known mainly to balletomanes and parents.

The David Haber affair widened the split beyond all repair. No doubt Betty had been deeply upset, wholly justifiably, that Celia had decided on Haber as her successor, and had sold him to the board without informing Betty, let alone consulting her. At that time, many insiders assumed this was because Oliphant had her eye on the top job herself. Then and later, Betty denied this vociferously, telling Rasky, "No, I never wanted to be. No, never, never, never, never, never did I want to be artistic director … People kept saying that that's what I wanted and that's what my schemes were all about." (It is striking that Oliphant mentioned "my schemes.") Oliphant's daughter, Carol Roach, confirmed that her mother never wanted to be artistic director, but added, "Whenever it was possible to talk badly about each other, they did."

While perhaps not wanting the job herself, Oliphant went to great lengths to ingratiate herself with certain board directors in order to directly manoeuvre Haber out and indirectly get rid of Franca. Franca, herself, remained convinced that Oliphant had engineered the Haber dismissal, telling *Globe and Mail* reporter Lawrence O'Toole, "She's [Oliphant] responsible for the Haber business. We had been the closest of friends but it does nothing to change my opinion of what she has done. She got her own way."

In fact, Betty's first choice for Celia's successor had been Erik Bruhn, who did take on the position in 1983. Originally very close to Celia from their days together at the Metropolitan Ballet in the late 1940s, as a result of which he later became associated with the National Ballet as both a dancer and choreographer, Bruhn came also to greatly admire Oliphant for her pedagogical talents. When he became the artistic director of the Royal Swedish Ballet in 1967, he invited Betty to reorganize that company's school.[262]

Oliphant would continue as the director of the National Ballet School until 1989. She then had the satisfaction of handing the reigns of the directorship over to her hand-picked successor, Mavis Staines. Originally a graduate from the National Ballet School, Staines joined the company in 1972 and went on to join the National Dutch Ballet in 1978. After an injury put an end to her performing career, she returned to take the Teacher Training Program at her alma mater.

This tale does not end well. Oliphant remained at the National Ballet School as an artistic adviser. In the meantime, Celia had phoned from Ottawa to say that she had heard that Staines was ruining the school. This led to Staines inviting her to visit the school and the two got on famously, with Celia describing her as "my best friend" and giving her the nickname "Mavallah."[263] Canada Council dance officer Monique Michaud observed, "It was very significant to us that when Mavis took over, Celia was in there like a dirty shirt."[264]

With Oliphant unable to refrain from interfering and criticizing her successor, and Celia befriending Staines, the almost predictable twist to the tortured tale came when Staines asked Oliphant to leave, and replaced her with Celia Franca.

Staines says that Celia "opened my eyes in directions I hadn't thought of before"[265] and that she'd felt the need to maintain continuity with the school's past. There's no doubt that Celia, with all her accumulated experience, provided important help to Staines. There's also little doubt that Celia (perhaps also Staines), was glad of the chance to show Oliphant that she was no longer needed or a part of the National Ballet School of Canada.

Occasions arose when these two old adversaries, Franca and Oliphant, had to appear together. At the twenty-fifth anniversary of the founding of the school in 1984, Oliphant was naturally the focal point. Lucy Potts, the school's vice-principal (and mother

Celia attended the 1984 celebrations for the twenty-fifth anniversary of the founding of the National Ballet School. Left to right: Vanessa Harwood, Erik Bruhn, Betty Oliphant, Monique Michaud, and Celia Franca. Courtesy of the National Ballet of Canada Archives

of ballerina Nadia Potts), had been a teacher at the school since the day it opened. During the performance, Lucy was strategically seated between Betty and Celia and noted that throughout the event they spoke not a word to one another. A photograph taken at reception that followed, however, shows a smiling Bruhn, Oliphant, and Franca amid the group, giving the impression that they were all the best of friends.

Understandably, after Oliphant's banishment from the school, her bitterness intensified. She declined an invitation to the fortieth anniversary gala of the school in 2000, which was to include a ribbon-cutting ceremony by Franca and Oliphant, because she objected to being described as a co-founder. Writing back to Staines, she protested that "Celia Franca's title as 'Director' was never more than a courtesy — and at that, only for a short time." She also wrote to the school's administrative director, Bob

Sirman, to complain about his comment that Franca had played a leadership role in the school's founding, calling it "simply untrue — whatever contemporary documents suggest."

It's surprising that only one year later, in 2001, Franca and Oliphant were on the stage together when a spectacular gala was held at Ottawa's National Arts Centre to mark Celia's eightieth birthday. Both behaved with complete propriety. Neither, though, ever apologized for or took back anything they had said about one another.

Oliphant did enter into psychotherapy to try and bring some peace and understanding into her tortured life. For her part, Celia dealt with unresolved feelings by suppressing them. It would have been far too threatening for Celia to take off her protective mask and confront her own devils. She used imperiousness and a clipped British accent to ward off intruders.

Personality conflicts aside, a potential for rivalry between these two strong women always existed. Its source was that between the two of them, they held two of the most important jobs in the comparatively small world of Canadian ballet. To magnify the probability for tensions, both had a pointe shoe, as it were, in the other's area of expertise. Betty had been first ballet mistress and later associate artistic director of the company. Celia had been co-founder of the school. Effectively, they were, forever, in each other's hair.

WHILE THE NATIONAL BALLET of Canada's twenty-fifth anniversary ended permanently Celia's professional and personal relationship with Oliphant, it served to revive another friendship. Dancer and choreographer Grant Strate had left the company in 1970 to become the first head of York University's Department of Dance. Towards the end of his time with the company, Strate had become disillusioned with Celia's unwavering attachment to the classical repertoire.[266]

Unable to attend the twenty-fifth anniversary performance, Strate wrote Celia a remarkable and moving letter:

> About six years have passed since we worked together and these have been years of my maturation (if one can really grow up after reaching 40). I feel very differently about my 20 years with the NBC now and I'm thinking less of what was *not* achieved and more of what was actually done. The record is staggering and there wouldn't even be a record if it had not been for your tenacious concern for building blocks. There were many times when I wished you would let it all go down the drain in favour of the creative process. You didn't and time proved you right.

She received another letter, as moving and even more personal. Its author was Jean Roberts, by that time director of English Theatre at Ottawa's National Arts Centre (although, unbeknownst to her, soon to be edged out of the post). Roberts wrote to Celia: "I must tell you that I *think* I have a touch of understanding of what it has cost you, although all the books and historians in the world will never be able to give us an accurate picture of what it has meant to you and what it has cost you."

Celia had, indeed, done what she had come to Canada to do. And she had paid a high personal price for her accomplishments. Now that her days of power and glory were behind her, that price was about to become higher.

SEVENTEEN

Not a Retiring Type

THE NATIONAL BALLET'S FORMER principal dancer, Veronica Tennant, has observed that a ballerina's life is choreographed for her. Strong discipline; the regimentation of classes, rehearsals, and performances; constant corrections, and, no less, self-corrections are the daily regime of all dancers. They fixate on their technique, their weight, their health and injuries, their stamina and resilience. Only the rarest of dancers become instant stars. Even more rarely — Margot Fonteyn is an uncommon exception — do dancers have a long professional career. Dancers could be called the mayflies of the arts.

After Celia gave up performing in 1959, she was freed of the tyranny of keeping her body in dancer's shape. She remained responsible, however, for keeping an entire ballet company in fighting shape, a task that took up each and every hour of her day. With retirement, Celia was abruptly set adrift. Overnight she went from being one of Canada's best-known personalities, frequently quoted in the media, a sought-after guest at all the best parties, and the possessor of real power, to being yesterday's woman.[267]

She wasn't that, of course. She still was, to huge numbers of Canadians, *the* Celia Franca, founder of the National Ballet of Canada; she possessed a great many admirers and supporters in high places; she was widely esteemed, respected, and more than a little feared. But she had lost her purpose in life. She no longer had a place to go each morning to spend exhaustingly long days. The company she had created, and that had been her life for twenty-four years, was continuing along without her, with others making the decisions that once had been hers alone. She was even living in a different city, Ottawa, with her husband Jay Morton.

In the mid-1970s Ottawa had a population of under half a million, mainly comprised of politicians and civil servants with a splash of exotic from diplomats. A high-tech industry was only just starting up in Canada's capital. Cultural life revolved around the National Arts Centre located at Confederation Square, with a concrete exterior looking somewhat like a block-long bunker; the more convivial inside featured four theatres, including one suitable for music, opera, and dance. During the early heydays of the NAC, the annual summer event Festival Canada presented lavish in-house operas that attracted some of the best international singers, and set and costume designers. Wealthy opera fans moored their yachts on the Rideau Canal directly alongside the NAC.

Jay and Celia Morton lived two blocks from Bank Street, where once the 1A bus had delivered the civil servants home in the evening, one could shoot a cannon down the street. The leafy-green area known as the Glebe was mainly home to middle-class families and Carleton University student renters. Small local businesses catered to this community, including a wooden-floored IGA, and the Mayfair — an independent single-screen movie theatre. Clemow Avenue — an anomaly in the neighbourhood with its large, grand homes — was at the northern boundary of the Glebe. A few minor embassies were scattered in the area. Fine dining was decidedly lacking, and food options were limited to such restaurants as the large Kentucky Fried Chicken at the corner of Clemow and Bank.

For the next twenty years in this quiet neighbourhood, Celia would be in charge of choreographing her own life. She had to create new roles for herself to play. The first part she assigned herself was that of happy housewife. Although this was the 1970s and feminism was challenging tradition, Celia, unconsciously, still held a pre-feminist view of a wife's duties. In Toronto she had hired the services of a housekeeper. Now, with only the help of a once-a-week cleaning lady, Celia was responsible for keeping the household running — Jay being able to escape to either National Arts Centre symphony rehearsals or to his office at the University of Ottawa. When home he would retreat to his upstairs studio, where he insisted on complete silence.

While she did do domestic chores, Celia in no way became domesticated. She told Rasky, "I don't believe I came to Canada to cook. I don't like washing the bathroom floor or the toilet, but I have to do it." She made daily meals for Jay, sending him out the door with a sandwich for lunch and serving a healthy dinner complete with a salad and fresh fruit promptly at 5:30. Because of Jay's diabetic condition, she had to adhere to a strict mealtime schedule.

They settled into a domestic routine of listening to the CBC news on either radio or television while they ate their evening meal. Wry amusement enabled Celia to get through the chores. One note she wrote to Jay went, "Darling, when you have a moment please fix washing machine. It's so 'off the mark' that it goes bang, bang & the spinner doesn't spin. Love Cele." She finished this note by drawing a big heart with kisses and wishing "Happy Easter & Passover."

Although only middle-aged, Celia continued to refuse to learn how to drive a car. She trundled her shopping cart to the local grocery store. She either took public transportation and taxis or relied on Jay and the goodwill of friends to squire her around. Lacking a driver's licence left Celia vulnerable, especially during Ottawa's bitterly cold winters.

As the spouse of one of the NAC's orchestra musicians, Celia faithfully and willingly attended all of Jay's performances in Ottawa. She became chummy with Mona Bernardi — wife of music director Mario Bernardi — and Vicki Prystawski — wife of concertmaster and master violinist Walter Prystawski. Through design or coincidence, they were the wives of the most powerful members of the National Arts Centre Orchestra. Celia faxed notes across the road to exchange gossip with Mona, describing people she didn't like as "disgusting" or "appalling." Mona said guests to the Morton's home would be startled by one of their cats appearing in odd places, such as on the top of the refrigerator. The Prystawskis were a sophisticated couple who had lived overseas for more than a decade, but Vicki treated Celia with deference, or perhaps felt protective. For many years, the Mortons joined the Prystawski family for festive occasions, such as Christmas dinner. Vicki, noticing that Celia carried her shoes in a plastic bag, made her a fabric bag befitting a person of her importance.[268] She agreed to become Celia's secretary, coming to Clemow Avenue on a part-time basis to help Celia deal with her correspondence and invitations.

The constant round of social occasions and attendance at NAC functions meant that Celia needed to update her wardrobe annually. While always stylishly attired and immaculately groomed, she had never been very interested in fashion. She considered her outfits costumes for the various roles she played in her life. While living in Toronto, she had found a dressmaker she liked — Collete Cox —and returned to her twice a year to pick up three or four items, mainly evening wear. Cox would put together a wardrobe of mix and match items, including cocktail suits with pants and an evening dress. She even provided the accessories, making it a no-brainer for Celia. She preferred a classic look and usually wore the diamond stud earrings given as a farewell thank-you gift when she had left the National Ballet. She continued to wear full theatrical makeup and her hair, which went from black to grey to white, was usually done up in a chignon.

A radical change in Celia's circumstances as the result of leaving the National Ballet was that, for the first time in her adult life, she had become financially dependent. During her last weekend as acting artistic director in September 1975, she noted in her diary, "I suspect Jay is worried about paying the bills for both of us now that I won't earn a regular salary from the National Ballet." In fact, as a full-time musician with the NAC orchestra and with additional income from both teaching privately and at the University of Ottawa, Jay made quite a comfortable living.

Celia had little savings. During her long years as artistic director, her salary had been miserably low. For years she received around seven thousand dollars, and even at the end her salary was only in the low twenty thousands — or somewhat over eighty-five thousand in today's terms. She had never been materialistic, with the exception of her black mink coat. It was only when board president Jock McLeod was discussing her resignation that he realized how anxious she was about her fiscal future. She had made almost no financial preparations. The National Ballet did provide her with a small annuity. At some point, the Canadian Old Age Pension and the National Ballet of Canada annuity would provide a little income, but since she was only fifty-three years old, that was still years away.

Soon after settling in Ottawa, she set about to find a new job. Celia knew that the director-general of Ottawa's National Arts Centre, Hamilton Southam, was preparing to step down. One of the search committee members for a replacement included her old friend and long-time National Ballet board member, Arthur

Gelber. She passed on word of her interest and on March 1, 1976, wrote to Gelber:[269]

> I again profess my interest in the position which will become vacant on Hamilton's retirement. Would you kindly bring this to the attention of the Search Committee and express my hope that the application will be kept confidential. My former assistant, David Walker, is sending bio material under separate cover for the committee's perusal. Very best wishes to you and Esther.

It is likely that someone discreetly indicated that it would not be worth her while to make a formal application and it's unclear if she was ever interviewed by the search committee. For one thing, the NAC was running up an ever-increasing deficit — this at a time when a global oil crisis was making the federal government jittery about the cultural centre's finances. And it was well-known that Celia's accomplishments at the National Ballet had never included any natural capacity or awareness for fiscal management.[270] To undermine her candidacy further, she was far from bilingual — an essential qualification in Trudeau's Ottawa.

Celia applied to the Canada Council for a Senior Arts Award to make it possible for her to write her memoirs. She may have been under the delusion that the book would make her money. More particularly, she wanted to make sure that her own version of her life and career were on record. Still fresh in her mind was Rubin's 1974 article *Celia Franca: Tartar in a Tutu*. At that time, she had written in her diary, "Dear Mr. Rubin — if I *do* get a book written, everyone of your lies will be avenged." Actually, she avoided nearly all personal details in what was basically a coffee-table book with photographs by Ken Bell. *The National Ballet of Canada: A Celebration* came out in 1978. To Celia's credit (or that of a judicious editor) she spoke well of Betty Oliphant in the chapter on the National Ballet School, ending it with, "Under Betty's skilled

Celia Franca with Earl Kraul and Grant Strate at the launch of her memoirs, published in 1978. Photograph by Robert Lansdale: University of Toronto Archives and Robert Lansdale

direction, the school has become one of the finest in the world, as its many lovely dancers gracing the stages of Canada and other countries have amply proved."

Amid the many congratulatory letters Celia received on the book's publication was one from her former husband, Bert Anderson, by then living in California. "Grant [Strate] and Earl [Kraul] sent me a copy of your wonderful book as a Christmas present, and, (sometimes with great waves of nostalgia sweeping over me), read it, and enjoyed your easy style and memories, and fine pictorial history of the ballet. (Even that picture of a ballet class with you directing and a funny guy sitting beside you)." By now, nearly three decades after their brief marriage, Anderson continued touchingly,

In retrospect, I understand and amaze at your fortitude, energy and determination to create a great Artistic

Institution. I wish I had had the insight and understanding to cope with it at the time. You were unique and dedicated, which I've never denied, but I guess I was too close, confused and insecure to grasp the magnitude of the situation to give you useful support. It's a little late, but I'm sorry for the hardships I must have unintentionally caused.

The photo Bert Anderson was referring to in his letter was taken during the early days of rehearsals at St. Lawrence Hall. Bert is the "funny guy" seated next to Celia. Photograph by Ken Bell, courtesy of the National Ballet of Canada Archives

A plum job that did come Celia's way was an appointment to the board of the Canada Council, where she served from 1982 to 1987. While prestigious, it paid only $225 a day for the few times it met each year. Initially, the council's two dance officers, Monique Michaud and Barbara Laskin, were concerned how Celia would perform because they knew she was a difficult person and assumed that she would have very much a classical ballet bias at a time when Canada's contemporary dance scene was growing and in need of seed money. Their misgivings proved unfounded. Instead, the two were impressed by Celia's demanding but fair-minded professionalism and by the fact that, as far as contemporary dance was concerned, "she was a fantastic support, an ally in everything." The National Arts Centre's dance producer, Cathy Levy, recalls a time when Celia attended a performance in which there was nudity. Turning to Levy, she sardonically observed, "Darling, there are parts of the body that you just can't choreograph."[271]

When Maureen Forrester stepped down as chairman of the Canada Council at the end of 1988, she wrote Celia a letter of praise. "You always kept your eye on the main thing — doing the best we can for artists and you always spoke with fairness and understanding ... last but not least, I've admired the way you kept your 'cool' even in the toughest Council discussions."

THE TIME IN HER retirement when Celia was happiest were those when she was in a dance studio, whether she was rehearsing professional dancers or teaching baby ballerinas. Through the late 1970s and 1980s, she went to New York several times to remount Antony Tudor ballets, such as *Pineapple Poll* or *Offenbach in the Underworld*, with the Joffrey Ballet. On one of these New York trips, Lorna Geddes[272] came along to teach the cancan dance, while Celia taught the major roles in *Offenbach*. Geddes remembers that they shared a hotel room and that Celia, no longer having to play her artistic director role, proved to be a lot of fun to be with.

Her ties to the National Ballet had by no means entirely ended. Whenever the company performed at Ottawa's National Arts Centre, she opened her Clemow Avenue home to the dancers for a reception. Each winter, she returned to Toronto to coach dancers in her 1964 version of the company's perennial moneymaker *The Nutcracker*. She continued to do this until 1995 when, by then age seventy-four, she handed the baton on to then artist-in-residence, James Kudelka. While Celia was fond of Kudelka, a product of the National Ballet School and the company's artistic director from 1996 to 2005, she was less fond of his new choreographies of classical ballets. When he replaced Erik Bruhn's version of *Swan Lake* in 1999, rethinking the material for a contemporary audience, Celia was perplexed. Karen Kain remembers attending a performance at the NAC and Celia turning to her wide-eyed, saying, "What's the story? Do you understand the story?"

A MAJOR BREAK IN routine for Celia came in 1978 when she went to China as one of only two non-Russian ballet experts invited to provide advice to Chinese dancers.[273] Accompanied by her friend and part-time secretary, Vicki Prystawski, the two women visited ballet schools in Canton, Shanghai, Hangzhou, and Peking. Celia brought along sample tutus, ballet pointe shoes, and a dancer's best friend, arnica — a homeopathic and highly effective pain-reliever for aching muscles. And to combat the cold in Hangzhou, she bought herself durable Chinese long johns.

At the tour's end, Celia was interviewed by *The Globe and Mail's* Peking correspondent John Fraser, whom she had known in Toronto when he had been the paper's dance critic. She spoke candidly:

> Obviously there's a lot of work to be done. But don't be fooled about what they can or can't do. They've had some excellent Russian training and it has been added to by very good and conscientious teachers. They are a lot better than they think they are and way, way better than we had assumed.... At the moment, though, they simply do not have a repertory capable of showing the range of their vocabulary in dance and their technical excellence.

Basically, Celia had outlined a job description for herself. Two years later, she returned to China for three months to produce at the Peking Ballet School the first full-length version of *Coppelia*

ever performed by Chinese ballet dancers. Celia threw her heart
and soul into the project. Calling her principal dancers "my
darlings," she rehearsed them for long hours. In her never-ceasing
desire to create excellence, she wanted the production to make
the Chinese dancers feel proud of themselves.[274] The premiere
took place on June 10, 1980. One Chinese custom she found discon-
certing was the practice of audience members walking in and out,
talking, and even spitting while the performance was going on.

Celia discovered that her Chinese ballet students had surprisingly good technical ability but needed to be challenged by new repertory. Courtesy of Library and
Archives Canada, e0084006972

For this project, Celia had set herself three goals: to wean
Chinese ballet teachers off a reliance on outmoded Soviet training
methods; to insist that Chinese dancers master traditional and
classical ballet technique; and to improve Chinese techniques
in lighting, costume design, and makeup. Interestingly, the first
two goals were exactly the same as those she had started out
with when she first arrived in Canada and insisted both that the
Volkoff-trained dancers drop the Russian bravura style and that
the dancers master classical ballet technique before experimenting
with contemporary choreography.

After her years of touring in war-torn Britain, coping with bed bugs and no hot water, Celia was well-equipped to handle the still primitive living conditions in China. At the Peking Hotel, Celia kept handy a special paperback book whose sole purpose was to "bop" the copious cockroaches. One night, opening a cupboard to get her Chinese vodka, she discovered cockroaches swarming all over the neck of the bottle.

On the plus side, Jay joined her for two months, he being — this really more a tribute to Celia than to him — the first North American woodwind specialist invited to teach in the country since the Cultural Revolution.

In 1979, between her two China visits, Celia cashed in on her status as the National Ballet of Canada's founding artistic director by serving as the star host of a package tour to Copenhagen for the Bournonville Centenary Festival, which commemorated the death of Danish choreographer August Bournonville by presenting all of his directly handed-down ballets during the course of a week.[275]

A couple of film projects in the mid 1980s brought a little glamour and fun back into Celia's life. Dancer Ann Ditchburn,[276] who had gone on to Hollywood after leaving the National Ballet, invited Celia to participate in an early version music video called *I Am a Hotel*, featuring Leonard Cohen singing five of his well-known songs. Celia travelled to Toronto in May 1983 to take on the role of an aging diva. Writing to Cyril Frankel, she described Cohen as a "sort of high class pop poet and song writer" who "sings his songs more or less throughout amidst masses of smoke." She added, "I play the elderly former actress arriving in the hotel foyer with white mink coat and too much luggage." The first scene of the film features Franca, looking very glamorous with her silvery hair swept up, making her grand entrance into the lobby of the King Edward Hotel. Later she appears as a lonely, wistful, but compelling and mysterious older woman. While Celia didn't hold out great hopes for the success of this low budget film, she was very proud that several of her previous dancers, including Ditchburn herself, appeared with her in the film.[277]

Somewhat reluctantly, Celia was in the spotlight again when Cyril Frankel agreed to direct a film on the National Ballet of Canada in 1984. "Cyril, I have certain reservations about the film, one being that I try to keep a 'low profile' these days. I'm not sure that the subject is good enough for you — and I'm not fishing for compliments," she wrote to him in early September 1983. "You say 'the film should be made now while the people who know the truth of the history are still around.' You'd be amazed at the different versions of the story which even now abound." Her worries were unwarranted. The documentary *Bold Steps*, produced by the Canadian independent film company Primedia, won a main prize at the Padua Film Festival.

WHEN FRANCA MOVED TO Ottawa, among the many dance schools were two on Rideau Street: Nesta Toumine's Classical Ballet School, and the Dance Centre run by Joyce Shietze and Judith Davies. The Dance Centre, which offered ballet, modern, and jazz dance, invited Franca to teach a few classes. In turn, Celia introduced the school to a young ballet dancer, Merrilee Hodgins, who had been with the Alberta Ballet and who had come to Ottawa to dance at the NAC's 1976 Summer Opera Festival in *The Queen of Spades*, for which Celia had been invited to choreograph the ballet scenes. Hodgins began to teach classes at the Dance Centre.

Shortly thereafter Judith Davies left the Dance Centre. In 1978, Shietze and Hodgins established the School of Dance. They invited Celia to become a third partner. Today Davies likens Franca to the cowbird known for laying its eggs in other birds' nests. She feels that Franca swooped down and, with her powerful personality, took over in order to create a school in accordance with her own standards.

For nearly three decades, the School of Dance was an integral

part of Celia's life, providing her with a place to teach ballet and
to funnel her boundless energy. A pre-professional ballet program
was soon established. In a January 1990 interview with the *Ottawa
Citizen*, Celia explained: "What happens there is [that] every four
years the seniors graduate and go on, and there's a new little batch.
I wait until the new little batch has some experience and then I
teach them some repertoire. I do what's necessary."[278]

Much the same process occurred as the result of an alliance
Celia struck up with Lawrence Gradus, an American-trained
dancer, who settled in Montreal after Expo 67 and established a
small company, Entre-Six. When his partner, Jacqueline Lemieux,
died in 1979, the company folded and Gradus brought his child
to Ottawa to start afresh. Together he and Celia formed a new
company, Theatre Ballet Canada, as an amalgamation of the
defunct Entre-Six and Toronto's Ballet Ys. Although Gradus's title
was that of artistic director at Theatre Ballet, no one doubted that
the energy and purposefulness was all Celia. As Gradus recalls,
"Her presence loomed large. A clearing of her throat during board
meetings would cause all heads to snap in her direction. A pregnant pause followed by pearls of wisdom, occasionally acid-tinged,
kept her audience glued to their chairs."[279] Eventually, Gradus simi-
larly was maneuvered out and replaced by Franca's choice, Frank
Augustyn, one of her own dancers from the National Ballet.[280]

Canada Council dance officer Monique Michaud, who witnessed all of these events, observed,

Celia's life, from the perspective of the dance community
always brought with her trouble. She did it here in Ottawa
and she did it with the school [National Ballet of Canada
School].... I would say Celia was never, ever satisfied, she
always needed to be the only one, the best one, the perfect
one, the one who did everything — she couldn't share anything with anybody either with the school or the company.
It's a bad fault.

Celia's habitual dissatisfaction generated a visceral hatred among those she cast aside. Its nature is captured aptly in the poem "The Dancing Queen" by Audrey Ogilvie.[281] Four lines provide a taste of its tone.

> The Black Queen had calculated
> The measurements of her stage.
> There was room for only one performer
> Dead centre.

BESIDES HER EXPERIENCE AND skills, Celia brought to these ventures the irreplaceable asset of her name and celebrity status. As was then rare in Ottawa, Celia fronted numerous fundraisers for both the School of Dance and Theatre Ballet Canada, these occasions adding glamour to Ottawa's bureaucratic greyness. Never the least bit hesitant to do "the ask," Franca, with her usual single-focus attitude, called in favours from whomever might be useful.

In particular she called on the dancers from the National Ballet. A 1984 gala, "Celia: A Celebration," began with dinners at the homes of socially prominent Ottawans. It was followed by a performance at the NAC with a star cast that included Veronica Tennant, Karen Kain, Frank Augustyn, Raymond Smith, and the Royal Winnipeg Ballet's prima ballerina, Evelyn Hart. The night was capped by a dance and dessert party held backstage. As a sign of the attention Celia still commanded, both Betty Oliphant and Ludmilla Chiraeff attended.[282]

Congratulatory telegrams were read out from such luminaries as Pierre Trudeau: "You have honoured us in Canada and all over the world by the inspiration you have given to the art of dance.... *Avec toute mon affection.*" From Tokyo, Nureyev, wrote, "Feet are here, heart is there. You have meant so much to so many, and none more than to me. Bless you for a lifetime of giving."

These fundraisers proliferated. In 1998, Franca again called on the good nature of Karen Kain, recently retired from the company, to perform free at Ottawa's National Gallery for a Celia Franca Scholarship Evening (specifically for the Ottawa School of Dance). Gently exerting pressure, Franca faxed Kain in October, saying, "We don't want to harass you unduly but it seems we need your help and influence."[283]

On Tuesday, June 26, 2001, an extravaganza of a different kind was held at the National Arts Centre. This was a celebration of Celia's eightieth birthday.[284] The main event was a performance by such ballet notables as National Ballet stars Rex Harrington and Ziao Nan Yu. In a clever turn of the tables, long-stem red roses were distributed to members of the audience. After viewing the performance from the royal box in Southam Hall in the company of Governor General Adrienne Clarkson, Celia moved out onto the rooftop terrace to join guests for white wine, chocolate covered strawberries, a huge chocolate birthday cake, and dancing. Pumped up by the excitement and attention, she had to be enticed by friends and relatives to leave the party around one a.m. Her first husband, Leo Kersley, flew from Britain to join her in the festivities. No one was certain how Celia felt about the surprise appearance from out of her long ago past of this tiny, impish man with bad teeth. "I couldn't tell if she was pleased to see him or not," says Celia's great-nephew, Jason Franks. "She insisted that he was 'tiring' but I didn't really believe her." After the death of his wife, Janet, Leo had begun to phone Celia. Initially annoyed at his insinuation back into her life, Celia eventually looked forward to his calls, during which the two exchanged gossip and reminisced about their long-ago dance experiences.

Other accolades continued to come her way. Already an Officer of the Order of Canada, she was given the country's highest honour in October 1985 when she, along with several others, including Pierre Trudeau, was elevated to Companion of the Order of Canada. Celia looked spectacular in a silver and blue gown with matching blue satin shoes, and later remembered Trudeau saying to her, "Shall we dance?"

Celia, standing, becomes a Companion of the Order of Canada on October 30, 1985. Courtesy of the National Ballet of Canada Archives

The Canadian Conference of the Arts Diplôme d'honneur followed, as did recognition by[285] the Canadian Dance Teachers Association — ironically, the same organization whose members had so mistrusted her when she first arrived in 1951. In 1994 she was the recipient of the Governor General's Performing Arts Award.[286] Celia herself thought it was about time she received this award, as two previous winners had been Ludmilla Chiriaeff (of Les Grands Ballets Canadiens) and Gweneth Lloyd (of the Royal Winnipeg Ballet). She also stretched her list of honorary degrees to nine.[287]

One honour eluded her, though. She was never made a Dame of the Order of the British Empire — a distinction that had been given to Ninette de Valois and Peggy van Praagh, who had gone out to Australia to create a national ballet company. In public Celia downplayed this omission, saying that she did not resent not being knighted, but that it would have added to the prestige of the National Ballet of Canada. In reality, not being able to put

"Dame" in front of her name offended her deeply. Sadler's Wells dancers who had performed during the war years, such as Robert Helpmann, Margot Fonteyn, Frederick Ashton, Beryl Grey, and Pamela May, had received OBEs. While Franca had received every Canadian honour, Britain failed to recognize her achievements. Yet again, she had been made to feel like an outsider.

AFTER CELIA'S DEPARTURE IN 1975, the National Ballet went through more difficult times, a circumstance about which her feelings were undoubtedly ambivalent. The next artistic director, Alexander Grant, had his contract terminated in June 1982. Once again Oliphant had been instrumental in the dismissal. Grant, in turn, was succeeded by Erik Bruhn. In 1985, Bruhn was looking for some time off from running the ballet. It is likely that he was feeling unwell; though no one knew it at the time, and though he had not yet received a diagnosis, Bruhn was becoming seriously ill. As Celia was to be in Toronto for *The Nutcracker*, he invited her to take his duties during December 1985 and January 1986. Celia's reply showed how successful she had been in gaining an emotional distance from her own creation. "When I left the National Ballet in 1975, I re-arranged my priorities — home and husband — since then have been and still are No 1 in my life. I am completely dependent on Jay for my livelihood so I must consider him and his well-being. I won't get the old-age pension for another 16 months or so! Jay doesn't like the idea of me being away from home for such a long period — so I would need to be free to travel home some weekends. Jay is willing to join me for a week in Toronto during December when he has a Xmas break from his teaching at the university."

Bruhn also asked her to take over the planning of the company's thirty-fifth anniversary in 1986. In his letter, he referred to "her" company. Celia replied in a long letter drafted on March 3, 1985. "First of all, Erik, the National Ballet is your company now.

When I refer in public to 'our company' I mean Canada's company, not mine or yours, when I refer to the direction of the company, it is yours and I couldn't be happier about that fact and hopefully I've made that clear to the world. I know from first-hand experience what a difficult job you have and want to help if you need me because I love you and the company."

This anniversary event was postponed by Bruhn's sudden death on April 1, 1986, only eighteen days after being diagnosed with lung cancer.

Bruhn had always had the upmost respect for Franca, whom he had known since the late 1940s when they appeared together with London's Metropolitan Ballet.[288] He recognized his and Celia's kindred spirit in the pursuit of perfection. An introspective man, he had once sent Celia his credo of life. In it he wrote, "Perfection maybe just an idea, or even a profound belief, and unfortunately still for a lot of people, a depressing disillusion, but if we fail to take this responsibility, we fail not only the ones who are to follow us; we have simply failed the life that was given us." Added to this typed message, he had written in longhand, "This is what I believe you have done for yourself and your company, may they and all of us keep trying to live up to it."[289] A year later, in February 1987, Celia did put together a thirty-fifth anniversary National Ballet program, inviting back all the retired dancers and remounting some of the company's earliest repertoire, including Kay Armstrong's *Étude,* first performed at the company's debut in November 1951. The New York ballet critic Anna Kisselgoff described the celebration as having "something touching about the democratic side of this community wingding."

EIGHTEEN

She Taught Canada to Dance

*F*OR MOST OF HER retirement years, Celia played with deception. The untruth was that she and her husband, Jay Morton, were a happily married couple.

Practically everyone who knew Celia, either before she retired or afterwards, agreed that she was deeply in love with Jay, that she took good care of him, and that she stood loyally by him through a number of difficult years. During her time as artistic director, Celia had leaned heavily on Jay for emotional support. In the *Chatelaine* article written at the time of Celia's retirement, she told Don Rubin, "Jay keeps me going. When I lose confidence, he's the one telling me to keep fighting. When I fight too much, he tells me to calm down." Yet their relationship utterly foundered and, at the end, Jay made it clear to Celia that he wished to have nothing to do with her.

It was shortly after Celia settled full-time in Ottawa that Jay created a crisis. Celia noted in her diary on Thursday, November 13, 1975, "J. threatens divorce." Having just become financially dependent on her husband, this was devastating. Her gut response must have been not so much anger, but panic at the prospect of another marriage coming apart, and of herself left alone and with very little money, not to mention the humiliation of being publicly spurned.

To add to her anguish, Celia at some point became aware of a close friendship Jay had developed with one of his former female students, who performed as a clarinetist with the NAC Orchestra. Whether or not the relationship was more than platonic, Celia believed this younger woman had usurped her place in Jay's life.

To discover what caused the final breach in their relationship is impossible. The easily detectable cause of their actual breakup was alcohol. Jay was drinking more and more, becoming, at times, a falling-down drunk. The result was a steady deterioration in his health.

Very few friends knew the true situation, and some of these friends turned a blind eye. Psychiatrist Benjamin Geneen and his wife, Pearl (Doris Margolis's cousin who had settled in Toronto in the mid 1950s), knew all three of Celia's husbands. Dr. Geneen said he felt Jay Morton was sick, both emotionally and physically, and that the couple had a codependence, with Jay needing Celia to look after him and Celia needing to have someone to look after. Pearl Geneen observed, "Celia married losers. She never found anyone to take care of her."[290]

While she, indeed, needed to be taken care of, Celia needed even more to be married. Seemingly unaffected by the women's movement of the sixties and seventies, Celia attached enormous importance to the institution of marriage. Perhaps she subconsciously wanted to please her mother by being a conventionally married woman. She managed to hang on to her blighted marriage for nearly two decades, and she worked hard keeping up the impression of being in a happy domestic situation. In an interview for the Life Styles section of the *Ottawa Citizen* in 1980, Celia volunteered her tips for giving a successful dinner party. "Fortunately," she said, "Jay makes a fabulous Gibson [a cocktail of gin and vermouth], so we have them for starters in the living room with canapés of smoked salmon or pate, or caviar if I'm feeling rich."

All her life Celia enjoyed the company and companionship of men. She felt incompletely attired without the accessory of a male escort. Yet there was something odd about her first two marriages. Leo Kersley was a rather attractive and louche character, but he clearly lacked the drive and ambition to keep up with her, and their marriage petered out before she left England. Her second marriage was even briefer. Bert Anderson, whom she married suddenly within six months of arriving in Toronto, was very probably homosexual (he never remarried) and, far too easily over-awed by her, came to function almost as a live-in man-servant. Afterwards, as an attractive single woman holding a high position, especially in the high-energy world of ballet, there was plenty of gossip about Celia. One such story was that she had an affair with Eddie Goodman. There were also those rumours — much more speculative ones — that she had a lesbian affair with Kay Ambrose, who quite certainly was captivated by Celia. It's entirely possible these supposed affairs and others may have been no more than stage-door gossip.

Jay Morton was quite different. Celia, having left school at the age of fourteen, regarded it a real accomplishment to be married to someone with a university degree, who had a comprehensive knowledge of music, and who later became a professor at the University of Ottawa. There were obvious tensions, or at least challenges, between them. She was strong, stubborn, and authoritarian. No matter how much she tried to stifle her inexhaustible energy, she couldn't have been easy to live with. She could be caustic, snippy, and overbearing.

While Jay was a cultured person, Celia had little to nothing in common with her in-laws, who, to make matters even more difficult, were teetotallers. She dreaded the obligatory family visits to Kansas, which usually occurred during her hard-earned and very brief summer vacations.[291] Jay's family made an effort to keep open the lines of communications with their exotic daughter-in-law, writing letters and, in 1964, driving to Salina, Kansas, to catch the performance of *Giselle* by the National Ballet of Canada at the Fine Arts Theatre.

There was also the fact that, for over five years before her retirement, Celia and Jay had lived apart — he in Ottawa with the NAC Orchestra and Celia in Toronto. Celia travelled to Ottawa nearly every weekend to be with her husband, but, inevitably, was ground down by this additional strain on top of the intensity of her job. An even more obvious complication was the fact that Celia was famous, a person all kinds of people wanted to be seen with, while Jay was an anonymous musician, though a first-rate one. Yet, a photo of Celia and Jay, taken sometime in the 1970s, shows the two of them looking relaxed and companionable, each holding one of their beloved cats in their arms. As Morton aged, he filled out, losing that thin, weedy look, and began sporting a full beard and more becoming glasses, giving him a certain presence.

Shortly before retiring, Celia found it more and more difficult to be away from Jay. During a flight to Los Angeles on April 2, 1974, she confided in her personal diary, "As usual it was agony tearing myself away from Jay."

Celia's retirement transformed the nature of their relationship. "My husband is eight years younger than I am, he keeps me," she said candidly to the *Ottawa Citizen* in 1990. She contributed unequally to the family income. In the summers, she followed along to various Ontario university towns, where Jay went to teach with the National Youth Orchestra, to look after him.

Celia certainly worked hard keeping up pretenses. Covering up for Jay's drinking became a full-time job. She began to discourage

Celia and Jay Morton at home in Ottawa with two of their beloved cats. Courtesy of Library and Archives Canada, e008439037

people from visiting their home and, on one occasion, when he fell in the driveway, she was mortified to require the help of a neighbour to get him into the house. A letter to Frank Rasky reveals a lot, albeit indirectly: Celia tells of the day Jay suffered a mild stroke at the university. Celia, waiting for a taxi to take her to the hospital, made him a smoked-meat sandwich because, as a diabetic, Jay had to eat at regular times. "Well, at least I had the amusement of his being x-rayed with the sandwich sitting on top of his substantial belly.... However he is left with very wobbly legs, constant exhaustion, weakness and low morale. He falls sometimes, sleeps until 1:30 and even later on his days off. As you can imagine I am on duty 24 hours a day." What she failed to say in this letter was that Jay was usually sleeping off the effects of alcohol.

In June 1994, no longer able to cope with the double demands of maintaining a house and looking after an alcoholic, Celia, along with Jay, moved into an apartment on Queen Elizabeth Drive, overlooking the Rideau Canal.[292] Jay's health and disposition continued to decline. Canada Council dance officer Barbara Laskin recalls visiting shortly after they moved in and being shocked at just how much Celia had to cope with. A close friend of Celia said that, on more than one occasion, she was forced to call 911 when Jay had passed out, only to be told by the ambulance attendants to put a pillow under his head and let him sleep it off. Not long after moving, Celia insisted that Jay go into a treatment centre for alcoholics. Writing to an English friend (Jenny Holt), Celia confided that Jay had been in an Alcoholics Anonymous retreat and that she had settled him into a flat. As soon as he was living in his own high-rise apartment in Vanier, Morton refused to have anything more to do with his wife of over thirty years.

Jay Morton died of esophageal cancer on August 31, 1997, the same night that Princess Diana died in a car crash in Paris. Celia had hurried to the hospital, but was unable to get there before Jay died. At his request he was cremated and his ashes scattered on the banks of the Rideau River at the bottom of McArthur Avenue, the last place he had lived. A celebration of his life was held in the salon of the National Arts Centre. One retired Canadian diplomat, a strong supporter of the NAC Orchestra, recalls that several of those who spoke were members of Morton's AA group. Also attending the service was Jay's long-time clarinetist female friend. Celia, on hearing that she would be there, stayed away.

The magnitude of the breach between Celia and Jay became fully plain after Morton's death. In his last will, drawn up only two months before his death, he left nothing to Celia, not even a small keepsake. He bequeathed the bulk of his estate, over half a million dollars, to members of his American family, to friends, to his goddaughter, to the University of Ottawa, to the National Arts Centre Orchestra Association Bursary Fund, and to the United Way. To his clarinetist female friend, he left thirty thousand dollars and all of his personal belongings. Celia did get her legal widow's share of his pensions, but nowhere in his will is the name Celia Franca Morton mentioned.

Celia never disowned Jay. Rather, she often spoke of him fondly. Interviewed by Julia Oliver of the *Ottawa Citizen* not long afterwards, Celia mentioned Jay's death several times. Asked whom she most admired, she replied, "My husband, James Morton — founding principal clarinet of the NAC Orchestra and later a professor of Wind Instruments at University of Ottawa. I think he was a very fine man. He was also a great musician and a great artist and he had a great appreciation of other people's art forms. I think he was just super." After a pause, she added, "He was the love of my life, although we had separated for the last two years." This candid and complex admission captured Celia's situation for much of her marriage. She had been dependent, emotionally as well as financially, on a man who no longer loved her. But she was still proud to have been married to him.

AND THEN CELIA'S LONELINESS was matched by the loneliness of someone else. For the first time in her life and close to its end, she found someone to take care of her. He was Bruce Corder, an Englishman born in the same year as Celia. During the war, Corder worked in theatre management in London and subsequently joined the Royal Opera House, Covent Garden, home of the Sadler's Wells Ballet. He accompanied the company on tours in Canada, liked what he saw, and when Toronto's O'Keefe Centre opened in 1960, he accepted their offer to become assistant general manager. Franca and Corder had known each other in passing through the years.

In 1969, Corder's wealth of experience in theatre management won him the post of the National Arts Centre's first director of operations. He remained with the NAC until his retirement in 1987, rising to acting director general. He took a leading role in the NAC's lavish summer opera festivals and eventually oversaw the establishment of the annual event as one of the pre-eminent opera festivals in North America. As an administrator, Corder

Bruce Corder (centre) was a cherished companion in Celia's later years, and the last love of her life. Courtesy NAC

was highly regarded for his professionalism and tough-mindedness.

In the mid 1990s, Corder's wife, Colleen, who had been in bad health for many years, died, leaving him a most eligible widower. Regulars at the National Arts Centre began noticing that Corder and Franca were frequently attending performances together.[293] The tall, courtly, impeccably dressed Corder and Celia, her Companion of Canada insignia pinned to her elegant evening gowns, with her white hair swept up in a chignon, made a singularly impressive entrance. They shared many common interests, the greatest being a love of symphonic music. Celia, unabashedly, confessed to Mavis Staines that, at the age of eighty, she was in love. Staines recalls, "They found complete pleasure in each other's company." People remember the two of them, a distinguished looking pair, holding hands as they walked down the street.

If a golden pair, they were also both well into their golden years. Bruce Corder died on March 25, 2004. Celia made a public statement, describing Corder with a poignant mixture of sadness and pride: "A gallant gentleman — lover of beauty: Gatineau hills in the fall; the music, dance, theatre and restaurant offerings at his beloved NAC; the National Gallery. A caring Boxing Day host at his home where the table setting was exquisite, with the silver dry mustard pot shined, and the wine glasses always filled. An avid reader, a devoted companion — in all, a love. He led a good life." Although the couple had never lived together, for several years Celia actually had someone who looked after her. And now, again, she was alone. She told Mavis Staines, "I've had enough."

CELIA HAD LONG BEEN a relatively heavy drinker. During the war, a good belt of whisky had been her standard way of coping, and later she relied on alcohol to alleviate stress and anxiety. Once in Toronto, she encountered the pervasively puritanical attitudes towards liquor, including deliberately ugly taverns with separate entrances for women and absurdly complicated rules for actually purchasing alcohol. In those days her drink of choice was Scotch.

When Celia was still dancing, she had to count the calories from alcohol. As artistic director she could be slightly more indulgent as she attended the incessant round of social and fund-raising events. Likely, there was a bit of *Days of Wine and Roses* syndrome, with Celia drinking companionably in the evening with her alcoholic husband Jay. Her drinks of preference became white wine and vodka. And for some time in retirement, she no doubt drank more of both than she admitted to herself. After Corder's death, all constraints were gone. Celia dulled her pains, both emotional and physical, with alcohol.

Loneliness, of course, was a principal factor. In 1985, Celia's father, Solly, died. Celia had made only one long flight to South Africa to visit him in Port Elizabeth in 1981; at the time, he was living in the home of his daughter-in-law Reva, who had remarried after her father's death. As always, Celia had managed to alert the media about her trip. The *Weekend Post* ran an article, "Renowned ballerina on short visit to PE," with a photograph of ninety-two-year-old Solomon with Celia leaning over his shoulder.

Although Celia had now lost all of her immediate kin, she still had a large extended family. For a time, Celia had written regularly to a favourite younger cousin, Zelda, a daughter of her uncle Alf, who had also gone to South Africa to work as a hairdresser. In their letters the two bantered back and forth, calling themselves "big Cus" and "Little Cus." Making plans to visit Celia in New York, Zelda enquired if she should bring a mink coat. "I can always borrow one in London," she wrote, "there are pretty rich Jews there, by the name of Morris and I think Rose has two or three."[294]

During the last years of her life, Celia became close to her great-nephew, Jason Franks, a son of David.[295] In 1995 David and Jason Franks went to Ottawa to visit Celia. As David Franks observed, "For some reason [Jason] and Celia took to each other immediately and they remained very close until her death. Perhaps they saw a rebellious streak in each other, although their interests are vastly different." Jason found a sympathetic listener who encouraged him in his aspirations to become a writer, once telling him, "Well, you've said it, now you have to do it." While Celia resisted ever learning to use a computer, she took delight in sending handwritten faxes to Jason to critique his writings.[296] When he was in Ottawa, she very much enjoyed going to local restaurants in the company of her tall, dark-haired, handsome great-nephew, who bears a strong resemblance to his grandfather — and Celia's brother — Vincent. Jason made frequent visits to his great-aunt in Ottawa. Celia faxed Karen Kain in October 1998 to report that her great-nephew was coming all the way from Australia for the National Gallery fundraiser event, ending with "I'm thrilled." When Jason was living temporarily in the United States in the early 2000s, he would visit her in Naples, Florida, when she fled there to escape part of the frigid Ottawa winters.

AS SHE AGED AND became frailer, Celia had the loyal support of a group of younger friends, among them Virginia and Stewart Goodings, whose mother, Betty, had performed with Celia when they were teenagers in *Spread It Abroad* in London in 1934.[297] While Celia was still living in the Queen Elizabeth apartment in Ottawa, these younger Goodings would do "the grocery and vodka runs" for her. Sometimes Stewart would take Celia out for dinner or to an art film. Once Jay was gone, Celia began to travel with Virginia, twice going on Caribbean cruises and once to the Dominican Republic, where she took delight in not being recognized and so able to relax without "her face on." Virginia, an ersatz daughter, also accompanied Celia to Naples, Florida, to help settle her into the luxurious condo she had rented with a view of the Gulf of Mexico.[298] Although mainly alone in Florida, Celia had the companionship of former National Ballet dancer Charles Kirby,[299] who lived nearby. He gladly became her chauffeur, taking her shopping and on outings.

When Virginia Goodings moved to London, Celia paid a two-week visit in the autumn of 2002 for a nostalgic last trip home. She made a pilgrimage up to Golders Green to take a look at her family home at 56 Golders Gardens, finding it much smaller than in her memories. She visited with such long-time friends as Cyril Frankel, and one evening went out for dinner *à deux* with ex-husband Leo.

While Celia had been in retirement in Ottawa, her company and school had been making headway. After forty-five years in St. Lawrence Hall, the National Ballet of Canada moved to the new Walter Carsen Centre, a four-storey headquarter at the foot of Spadina Avenue, specifically built to double the amount of space. It included five studios, a health wing, a shoe room, a wardrobe workshop and storage space, and bright modern offices. Celia returned to attend the opening ceremonies in mid-September 1996. The first floor reception area, the Celia Franca Atrium, featured a large metal silhouette of Franca's iconic long-necked profile. Celia did not speak at the opening, but was thrilled at receiving a commemorative token comprised of relics from St. Lawrence Hall, including a red brick and a sliver of the carpet.

Mavis Staines, Celia, and Robert Sirman at the official groundbreaking ceremony of "Project Grand Jeté at the National Ballet School on July 15, 2004. Ironically, Betty Oliphant had died three days earlier. Courtesy of Torstar

In November 2005 Celia returned to the National Ballet School to officially open an addition named the Celia Franca Centre. Dressed in a green pantsuit and accompanied by Mavis Staines, Celia ceremonially lit the fire in the central hall, reverting to her sinister role of Madge as she theatrically hammed it up for the cameras and the somewhat bemused students, many of whom had only a vague notion of her importance. Turning to the camera, Celia mugged, "The old witch at work. Did I do a good job?"

One mar to the day's ceremonial events was the complete omission of Betty Oliphant's name. While Mavis Staines insists the lapse was unintentional, Celia herself didn't appear to notice this oversight. Once again, Oliphant, who had contributed so much, had been ignored. Many people have commented on the irony that the dance school building is named after Celia Franca while the theatre is named after Betty Oliphant.

Shortly after the ceremony, Celia had a bad fall and sustained a compression fracture of the vertebrae. Thereafter, she was confined to a wheelchair. Accepting the inevitable, she was transferred from the hospital on December 16, 2005, to an elegant, assisted-living residence for seniors, Governor's Walk, on the edge of Ottawa's Rockcliffe neighbourhood, where she had a two-room suite. Thereafter, she almost never left the suite except to have her hair done and arranged to have all her meals in the suite, rarely leaving her bed. It was only then that Celia dropped her role and gave up her daily practice of "putting on her face" with her pencilled-in eyebrows and bright lipstick.

One reason for Celia's insistence of privacy was that shortness of breath from emphysema made it difficult and embarrassing for her to converse with visitors. After a life of constantly working to keep her body supple and strong, she refused to take any physiotherapy. Fed up with people imploring her to cooperate, she asked Mavis Staines to tell them to "fuck off, I'm not even flexing my ankle."

If Celia's body had failed her, her mind remained sharp. She filled her days doing crossword puzzles, talking on the phone, and watching TV or films. One of her greatest joys was listening to classical music, in particular the scores to the many ballets she had danced in or choreographed. She ate very little, but still enjoyed her vodka, which she always referred to as her "voddie."

To her dying days, Celia continued to attract the devotion of people around her. Now, it was the women care-workers at Governor's Walk. They pampered their famous ballerina resident, giving her pleasure by brushing out her long, white hair every evening. When they too tried to encourage her to get out of bed, she resisted, saying "I'm happy." While she was likely *not* happy, Celia had reached the stage of peaceful resignation.

Not all visitors were turned away. Regulars included Ottawa friends such as Vicki and Walter Prystawski, Merrilee Hodgins, and Toronto friends such as Mavis Staines, James Austin,[300] David and Joanna Scott, Veronica Tennant, and Karen Kain. With this group of trusted friends, she no longer felt the need to project her "Celia Franca persona."

Celia's favourite visitor remained her great-nephew Jason, who always lifted her spirits. He would stay with her, sleeping on a camp-cot in the living room and sharing meals in her bedroom. Once, her niece Jayne Goldin, nee Franks, came with Jason. Having not seen her aunt for many years, Jayne was touched to see an old woman lying in bed with her white hair loose on the pillow. "My first emotion was how she resembled my loved grandmother [Celia's mother] and I cried — feeling so strongly the connection to my father [Celia's brother Vincent] and my grandparents.... My nostalgia for my father's side of the family, long gone — came rushing back to me, and as I hugged her and cried some tears, she just kept saying, 'there, there dear.'"[301] This display of sentiment did not go over well with Celia, who had retained her belief in the stiff upper lip.

In her last year, Celia made two monumental efforts to appear in public. On June 26, 2006, she attended yet another fundraiser for the School of Dance. It was a celebration of her eighty-fifth birthday and her last visit to the National Arts Centre. By this time, donor fatigue was setting in for these birthday benefits. Celia, in considerable pain, balked at what must have seemed to her an embarrassing dog-and-pony show. Eventually, she was cajoled into going. With help from Virginia Goodings, she came to the evening in her wheelchair, at one point just managing to struggle upright to acknowledge the audience's applause. Virginia recalls, "She made a superhuman effort that night." A photo of Celia in her wheelchair encircled by Virginia Goodings, her masseuse Siri, and Merrilee Hodgins reveals Celia staring into the camera. She no longer had the energy to give her dramatic Celia Franca pose. The next day, however, back in bed, she gloried in the masses of bouquets that had been brought from the NAC to fill her rooms.

Celia Franca's final public appearance completed the circle of her life in Canada. Driven to Toronto by limousine[302] on October 3, 2006, she was the honoured guest for the world premiere of the documentary *Celia Franca: Tour de Force*, which celebrated Celia's life work in founding the National Ballet of Canada.[303] The gala was held at the refurbished Eaton Auditorium, now called the Carlu.

The fragile, gaunt, elderly woman sitting in a wheelchair contrasted painfully with the grainy images in the film of the twenty-nine-year-old ballerina. While in severe pain and battling exhaustion, Celia basked in the admiration and respect that poured down upon her from the sold-out audience.

The next morning, just before her limousine left for the drive back to Ottawa, Celia reached out to take the hands of Veronica Tennant and James Austin and told them, "This is the last time. You won't be asking me to do this again."

Four months later, on February 19, 2007, Celia Franca passed away quietly at the Ottawa Civic Hospital. In keeping with her wishes, no funeral was held, nor, as troubled some of her relatives, was shiva observed. Celia left the instructions:[304] "It is my strong desire and my direction that no form of funeral or

The last publicity photo taken of Celia Franca, with two of her prima ballerinas: Karen Kain and Veronica Tennant. Courtesy of Torstar

memorial service whatsoever shall be held following my death. I desire that my body be cremated and that my ashes shall be," followed by a blank space.[305] Celia, an atheist, told Virginia Goodings, "They can throw my ashes in the bin." A modest private reception was held at Ottawa's School of Dance on April 1, 2007.

Public tributes were abundant on both sides of the Atlantic. In Canada's Senate, Elizabeth Hubley, herself a former dance teacher, stood up to say that the finest tribute was contained in a single short sentence in the front-page obituary of the *Ottawa Citizen*. It declared, "She taught Canada to dance."

In her will, Celia gave part of her small estate to the National Ballet School Foundation and the National Ballet of Canada Endowment Foundation. Her personal belongings went to carefully thought out choices among her friends and family. Her great-nephew Jason received her treasured diamond stud earrings and Mavis Staines was left her signature black mink full-length coat.

To Canadians, Celia Franca left the National Ballet of Canada.

Epilogue

IN 1951, FRANCA STARTED the National Ballet of Canada with twenty-eight dancers plus herself. That year her charter company gave twenty-three performances with a repertoire of twelve short ballets to a total audience of 12,500, mainly at Toronto's Eaton Auditorium. Since neither the Canada Council for the Arts nor the Ontario Arts Council yet existed, the company relied on box office sales and private donations, which totalled slightly over eighty thousand dollars. The first year ended with a deficit of $24.18.

At her retirement in 1975, Franca left behind her a company of sixty-one dancers who, that year, gave a total of 124 performances in Canada, the United States, England, and the Netherlands. The budget was over two and a half million dollars. In 2007, the year of her death, the company had sixty-three dancers who gave eighty-six performances, almost all at Toronto's new, purpose-built, ballet-opera house, the Four Seasons Centre for the Performing Arts. Government grants that year totalled five million dollars while personal and corporate fundraising was close to seven million dollars.

November 2011 marks the sixtieth anniversary of the National Ballet of Canada. The company's artistic director, Karen Kain, has commissioned a world premiere of a new full-length production of *Romeo and Juliet* by the hottest ballet choreographer, Alexei Ratmansky, amidst other special dances. The company now has seventy dancers and an operating budget of twenty-seven million dollars. In 2013, after a hiatus of twenty-six years, the National Ballet of Canada will return to London, England.

Bibliography

Primary Sources

Library and Archives Canada (LAC-BAC) Celia Franca fonds MG 31, D 113. A finding aid (No 1343) was prepared by Anne Goddard in 1982. Final material was deposited after Franca's death in 2007.

Dance Collection Danse Frank Rasky Portfolio (not yet catalogued) contains seven linear feet of biographical research including more than two hundred hours of audio-recorded interviews.

National Ballet of Canada archives contains holdings which document its history from 1951 onwards and includes press clippings, programs, committee meeting minutes, photographs, costumes and films.

Royal Opera House Collections, Covent Garden, London, England. Sadler's Wells Ballet Clippings Books, 1946–1951, Celia Franca folders, Roger Woods photograph collection.

Secondary Sources

Ambrose, Kay. *Ballet Impromptu*. London: Golden Gallery Press (nd).
Ambrose, Kay (in collaboration with Celia Franca). *The Ballet Students Primer*. New York: Bonanza Books, 1953.

Amiel, Barbara. "The Iron Mistress." *Maclean's*, November 15, 1976.

Anderson, Carol. *Lunch with Lady Eaton*. Toronto: ECW, 2004.

Anderson, Zoë. *The Royal Ballet: 75 Years*. London: Faber and Faber, 2006.

Augustyn, Frank (with Barbara Sears). *Dancing from the Heart: A Memoir*. Toronto: McClelland & Stewart, 2000.

Ayre, John. "Berlin 1936: Canadian Dancers at Hitler's Olympics." *The Beaver*, February/March, 1996, Vol. 76, No 1.

Ayre, John. "Janet Baldwin: The Lady Dances." *Dance Collection Danse* No. 68, Fall 2009, pp 11–16.

Bland, Alexander. *The Royal Ballet: The First Fifty Years*. New York: Doubleday & Co., 1981.

Belkin-Epstein, Cheryl. *Norman Campbell*. The Canadian Broadcasting Corporation. The National Ballet of Canada, 2006.

Bowring, Amy. "Hopeful Innovations." The Canadian Ballet Festivals and the Professionalization of Dance in Canada. Unpublished manuscript.

Bregman, Neil. *Celia Franca: Tour de Force*. DVD. Directed by Veronica Tennant, Ottawa: Sound Venture International, 2006.

Buckner, Philip. *Canada and the End of the Empire*. Vancouver: UBC Press, 2005.

Capon, Naomi. *Dancers of Tomorrow: The Story of a Girl's Training at the Sadler's Wells School*. Leicester: Brockhampton Press Ltd., 1956.

Carpenter, Bernadette. *Spotlight News Letters: 1951–1956*. Toronto: Dance Collection Danse Presses, 1995.

Clark, Mary. *Dancers of Mercury: The Story of Ballet*. Rambert. A. & C. Black, 1962.

Cohen, Susan. "The National: How It Grew — and How It Didn't." *Maclean's*, November 15, 1976.

Cornell, Katherine. "The Ballet Problem: The Kirstein-Buckle Survey for the Canada Council." Odom, Selma Landen, and Warner, Mary Jane, ed., *Canadian Dance: Visions and Stories*. Toronto: Dance Collection Danse, 2004. Chapter pp. 225–238.

Crabb, Michael. "David Adams: His Dance Through Life." *Dance*

Collection Danse No. 66, Fall, 2008 12–18; No. 67, Spring 2009, 19–24; No. 68 Fall 2009 22–27.

Craine, Debra and Mackrell, Judith. *Oxford Dictionary of Dance.* Oxford: Oxford University Press, 2000.

Crisp, Clement. *Ballet Rambert: 50 Years and On.* Ilkley, England: Scolar Press, 1981.

Croce, Arlene. *Writing in the Dark, Dancing in the New Yorker.* New York: Farrar, Straus and Giroux, 2000.

Daneman, Meredith. *Margot Fonteyn.* London: Penguin, 2005.

Davidson, Gladys. *Ballet Biographies.* London: Werner Laurie, 1952.

De Valois, Ninette. *Step by Step: The Formation of an Establishment.* London: W. H. Allen, 1977.

Edmonstone, Wayne. *Nathan Cohen: The Making of a Critic.* Toronto: Lester and Orpen Ltd. 1977.

Fisher-Stitt, Norma Sue. *The Ballet Class: A History of Canada's National Ballet 1959–2009.* Toronto: Canada's National Ballet School, 2010.

Fonteyn, Margot. *Autobiography.* London: W. H. Allen, 1975.

Franca, Celia and Bell, Ken. *The National Ballet of Canada.* Toronto: University of Toronto Press, 1978.

Frost, Honor. *How a Ballet is Made.* London: Golden Galley Press Ltd, 1948.

Genné, Beth. "Creating a Canon, Creating the 'Classics in Twentieth Century British Ballet." *Dance Research: The Journal of the Society for Dance Research* Vol. 18, No. 2, 2000, 132–162.

Gilbert, Nathan & Zemans. Joyce ed. *Making Change: Fifty Years of the Laidlaw Foundation.* Toronto: ECW Press, 2001.

Goodman, Edwin. *The Life of the Party: The Memoirs of Eddie Goodman.* Toronto: Key Porter Books, 1988.

Gottlieb, Robert. *Reading Dance.* New York: Pantheon Books, 2008.

Gradus, Lawrence. *Wings on my Feet: A Dancer Remembers.* Artbookbindery.com, 2009.

Granatstein, J.L. "Culture and Scholarship: The First Ten Years of the Canada Council." *Canadian Historical Review.* LXV, 4, 1984, pp 441–474.

Gruen, John. *Erik Bruhn: Danseur Noble.* New York: Viking Press, 1979.

Guthrie, Tyrone. *A Life in the Theatre.* Toronto: McGraw-Hill Book Company, 1959.

Haskell, Arnold. *Ballet.* London: A Pelican Special, 1938.

Haskell, Arnold. *Miracle in the Gorbals.* Edinburgh: The Albyn Press, 1946.

Homans, Jennifer. *Apollo's Angels: A History of Ballet.* New York: Random House, 2010.

Horowitz, Joseph. *Artists in Exile: How Refugees from Twentieth-Century War and Revolution Transformed the American Performing Arts.* Harper Collins, 2008.

Horrall, Andrew. *Bringing Art to Life: A Biography of Alan Jarvis.* Montreal: McGill-Queen's University Press, 2009.

Howe-Beck, Linda. "Les Grands Ballets Canadiens at 50." *Dance Collection Danse,* No. 63, Spring 2007, 6–13.

Inglesby, Mona with Kay Hunter. *Ballet in the Blitz.* Suffolk, England: Groundnut Publishing, 2008.

Johnstone, Ken. "A Great Ballet Star." *Maclean's,* August 20, 1955, p 12, 14, 58, 60.

Jennings, Sarah. *Art and Politics: The History of the National Arts Centre.* Toronto: Dundurn Press, 2009.

Kain, Karen with Stephen Godfrey and Penelope Dobb. *Movement Never Lies: An Autobiography.* Toronto: McClelland & Stewart, 1994.

Kavanagh, Julie. *Nureyev: The Life.* New York: Pantheon Books, 2007.

Kelly, Brigitte. "Dancing for Joy: A Memoir: Part Three." *Dance Chronicle,* 1999, Vol. 2, No. 3, 359–418.

King, Paul. "The National Ballet Shakedown." *Toronto Life,* March 1969, 52–54.

Kogen, Lisa V. *With Strength and Splendor: Jewish Women as Agents of Change.* New York: Women's League for Conservative Judaism, 2008.

Kynaston, David. *A World to Build: Austerity Britain 1945–1948.* London: Bloomsbury, 2007.

Litt, Paul. *The Muses, the Masses and the Massey Commission.* Toronto:

University of Toronto Press, 1992.

Mackrell, Judith. *Bloomsbury Ballerina: Lydia Lopokova, Imperial Dancer and Mrs. John Maynard Keynes*. London: Weidenfeld & Nicholson, 2008.

Macpherson, Susan. *Encyclopedia of Dance in Canada*. Toronto: Dance Collection Danse, 2000.

McQueen, Rod. *The Eatons: The Rise and Fall of Canada's Royal Family*. Toronto: Stoddart, 1999.

Mitchell, Lillian. "Boris Volkoff: Dancer, Teacher, Choreographer." Ph.D dissertation, Texas Woman's University, 1982.

Neufeld, James. *Power to Rise: The Story of the National Ballet*. Toronto: University of Toronto Press, 1996.

Neufeld, James. *Passion to Dance: The National Ballet of Canada*. Toronto: Dundurn Press, 2011.

Neufeld, James. *Lois Marshall: A Biography*. Toronto: Dundurn Press, 2010.

Noble, Peter. *British Ballet*. London: Skelton Robinson, 1949.

Ogilvie, Audrey. *Enough White Lies to Ice a Cake*. Burlington, Vermont: Waterfront Books, 2007.

Oliphant, Betty. *Miss O: My life in Dance*. Winnipeg: Turnstone Press, 1996.

Palmer, Alexandra. *Couture & Commerce: The Transatlantic Fashion Trade in the 1950s*. Vancouver: UBC Press, 2001.

Parr, Joy. *Domestic Goods: The Material, the Moral and the Economic in the Post-War Years*. Toronto: University of Toronto, 1999.

Perlmutter, Donna. *Shadowplay: The Life of Antony Tudor*. New York: Viking, 1991.

Pitman, Walter G. *Louis Applebaum: A Passion for Culture*. Toronto: Dundurn Press, 2002.

Potts, Nadia. *Betty Oliphant: The Artistry of Teaching*. Toronto: Dance Collection Danse Press, 2007.

Rambert, Marie. *Quicksilver: An Autobiography*. London: Macmillan, 1983.

Reynolds, Nancy and Malcolm McCormick. *No Fixed Points: Dance in the Twentieth Century*. New Haven: Yale University Press, 2003.

Richler, Mordecai. "A Ballet Story of Hard Hats: And Balletomanes too." *The Canadian*, November 13, 1976, p12,14, 16, 19.

Robinson, Harlow. *The Last Impresario: The Life, Times, and Legacy of Sol Hurok*. New York: Viking Press, 1994.

Rubin, Don. "Celia Franca: Tartar in a Tutu." *Chatelaine*, March 1974, 37, 83–89.

Rutherford, Paul "The Persistence of Britain: The Culture Project in Postwar Canada." Philip Buckner, ed., *Canada and the End of the Empire*. Vancouver: University of British Columbia Press, 2004.

Sissons, Michael and Philip French. *Age of Austerity 1945–1951*. Oxford: Oxford University Press, 1986.

Smith, Cheryl. "'Stepping Out': Canada's Early Ballet Companies, 1939–1963." Ph.D Thesis, University of Toronto, 2000.

Smith, Allan "From Guthrie to Greenberg: Canadian High Culture and the End of Empire." Philip Buckner, ed., *Canada and the End of the Empire*. Vancouver: University of British Columbia Press, 2004.

Solway, Diane. *Nureyev: His Life*. London: Weidenfeld & Nicolson, 1998.

Strate, Grant. *Grant Strate: A Memoir*. Toronto: Dance Collection Danse, 2002.

Tennant, Veronica. *The Dancers' Story: The National Ballet of Canada*. DVD. Directed by Mark Adam. Ottawa: Sound Venture International, 2002.

Tippet, Marie. *Making Culture: English-Canadian Institutions and the Arts before the Massey Commission*. Toronto: University of Toronto Press, 1990.

Topaz, Muriel. *Undimmed Lustre: The Life of Antony Tudor*. London: The Scarecrow Press, 2002.

Vance, Jonathan F. *A History of Canadian Culture*. Don Mills: Oxford University Press, 2008.

Vaughan, David. *Frederick Ashton and His Ballets*. London: A&C Black Ltd., 1977.

Walker, Katherine and Robert Sorley. *Helpmann: A Rare Sense of Theatre*. Alton: Dance Books, 2009.

Walker, Hugh. *The O'Keefe Centre: Thirty Years of Theatre History.* Toronto: Key Porter, 1991.

Watson, Peter. *Nureyev: A Biography.* London: Hodder & Stoughton, 1994.

Whitaker, Herbert. *The Official History of the National Ballet of Canada.* Toronto: McClelland and Stewart, 1967.

Wilson, A. N. *London: A History.* New York: A Modern Library Chronicle Book, The Modern Library, 2004.

Woodcock, Sarah. *The Sadler's Wells Royal Ballet.* London: Sinclair-Stevenson, 1991.

Wyman, Max. *Dance Canada: An Illustrated History.* Vancouver: Douglas and McIntyre, 1989.

Acknowledgements

AT THE TIME OF Celia Franca's final retirement as artistic director of the National Ballet, her friend and colleague, the late Jean Roberts, then the director of English Theatre at Ottawa's National Art Centre, wrote to her saying that "all the books and historians in the world" would never be able to give an accurate account of what the company had meant to, and what it had cost, Celia Franca personally. While likely correct, my attempt to make Celia's life story as truthful as possible has been helped enormously by the help and generosity of a great many people.

The skeletal framework of a biography is made up of collected facts. Franca donated a vast amount of material to Library and Archives Canada in Ottawa where I was helped by Archivist Jennifer Devine, and Special Collections Photo Researcher Jean Matheson. Adrienne Nevile, Archives Coordinator of the National Ballet of Canada, answered my emails with grace and promptness, providing information and photographs. Co-founder and Director Miriam Adams, and Director of Research Amy Bowring of Dance Collection Danse in Toronto cleared off space in their tiny archives facility to allow me to read through all of Frank Rasky's written material and listen to his taped interviews. Their *Encyclopedia of Theatre Dance in Canada* and their website (www.dcd.ca) answered many of my questions.

After the facts have been collected, it's time to start adding flesh and blood to bring the subject alive. The flesh and blood for this biography mainly comes from interviews with people who knew Celia Franca in all the facets of her life.

Franca's acquaintances in Canada may be surprised to learn that she had a network of relatives spread all over the world. From Australia, I emailed with her nephew, David, the son of her brother Vincent, who had emigrated from South Africa, and also with his son, and Celia's great-nephew, Jason Franks. Celia's niece, Jayne, now known by the name Sheyna Goldin, emailed and sent me early family photographs from her home in Brooklyn, N.Y. Two of Celia's cousins were generous with their thoughts and information. One is Esther Stern, the daughter of Solomon Franks's sister Annie now living in Bournemouth, England. The other is Asher Tarmon, residing in Israel, who not only provided me with information about Celia's youngest days in East End London, but read the entire manuscript and carried out careful copyediting. Both of these cousins, now in their early nineties, still have vivid memories of their cousin Celia Franks and remember that her childhood focus was always ballet.

Celia is survived by her first husband Leo Kersley, still spritely, who I met in England twice: once in Harlow, Essex, where he had started a ballet school, and a second time at London's Peacock Theatre, where he was attending a ballet in which some of his former students were performing.

By complete fluke I made contact with the film producer, Cyril Frankel, once one of Celia's closest London friends. I had been

told that he had died, but decided to try the existing London telephone number anyway and found myself speaking directly to Mr.
Frankel, living on Harley St. The first time I visited him, he said
that he had been wondering what to do with the cache of letters
that Celia had written to him during the war and later in Canada.
He entrusted them to me and asked that I deposit them with the
rest of her papers in the National Archives after I had finished with
them.

Ballet dancers are a hardy breed. There are several surviving
charter members who joined the company in 1951. I interviewed
Myrna Aaron, André Dufresne, Colleen Kenney, Brian Macdonald,
Marilyn Rollo, and Grant Strate along with others who joined
shortly afterwards, including Yves Cousineau, Lorne Geddes,
and Jocelyn Terrell Allen. Dancers who I spoke to that joined the
National Ballet later on include Miriam Adams (nee Weinstein),
Vicky Bertram, Anne Ditchburn, Karen Kain, Nadia Potts, Mavis
Staines, Veronica Tennant, and Martine van Hamel. Among
the people who helped Celia create the National Ballet, I inter-
viewed General Managers Walter Homburger and Gerald Eldred
along with Deborah Guild daughter of the late General Manager,
Carmen Guild, who loaned me a set of taped interviews her father
had conducted with Celia in 1999. Other National Ballet personnel
I spoke to includes publicists Joe Lewis and Mary Joliffe, Ballet
Master David Scott, Ballet Mistress Joanne Nesbitt, long-time
Rehearsal Pianist and good friend Mary McDonald, and Celia's
dresser and wardrobe person, the late Cynthia MacLennan.

I spoke to three of the board presidents who dealt with Celia
throughout her tenure: Antony (Tony) Griffin, Lyman Henderson,
and Ian (Jock) Mcleod.

Although a couple of Franca's Ottawa friends were uncoopera-
tive, several others such as her long-time neighbour and fellow
orchestra wife, Mona Bernardi; Stewart and Virginia Goodings;
the children of Betty Goodings; and Carol Roach, daughter of
Betty Oliphant, gave me insights into Celia's personal life.

A major bonus was the extensive cache of taped interviews conducted in the late 1980s and early 1990s by the late Frank Rasky. He spoke to numerous people closely associated with Celia in England, such as Dame Ninette de Valois and Celia's aunt Lena. In Canada he interviewed most of the major characters, including David Haber, Eddie Goodman, and Bert Anderson. Many of these people have subsequently died, but the tapes provide an irreplaceable trove of information. My thanks to Brenda Rasky for contributing her late husband's materials to Dance Collection Danse.

Several people have read drafts of my book to catch inaccuracies or to add more information to my story. Jane Pritchard, dance curator at London's Victoria and Albert Museum, read the chapters dealing with Celia's dance career in England. Scholar and dancer Annabel Rutherford; dancer and filmmaker Veronica Tennant; professor and author of *Rise to Power: The Story of the National Ballet of Canada* and the 2011 updated version *Passion to Dance,* James Neufeld; and DCD Director of Research Amy Bowring took the time from their own busy lives to read the book.

Thanks to my agent, John Pearce, of Westwood Creative Artists, and the team at Cormorant Books, including publisher Marc Côté, editorial director Barry Jowett, and designers Tannice Goddard and Angel Guerra.

My gratitude goes to the current National Ballet wardrobe supervisor, Marjory Fielding, my neighbour who has spent many an early morning dog-walk with me bombarding her with questions.

The greatest thank you of all goes to my mentor and beloved husband, Richard Gwyn, who likely knows almost as much about Celia Franca as he does about Sir John A. Macdonald.

If I have left anyone out, I certainly was not employing Celia's calculated exclusion style. Any errors are mine alone.

Toronto, November 2011

Notes

ONE

Information on Franca's earliest years came from her surviving relatives, including cousins Asher Tarmon, in Israel; and Esther Stern, in England; along with her nephew David Franks, in Australia; and niece Jayne (Sheyna) Goldin nee Franks, in the United States. Frank Rasky interviewed Celia's aunt Lena in England. Alf Morris wrote his memoirs.

1   To make things more complicated, the brother Herschel changed his name to Harris while the Feigenbaum eldest son, Sam, changed his to Jackson.

2   When Celia collaborated with Kay Ambrose to write *The Ballet Student's Primer* in 1953, she emphasized the danger of girls younger than ten years of age and with less than two years training rising en pointe.

3   Although a small section of Camden High Street still has the tall,

red-bricked Victorian buildings that house a variety of commercial establishments, number 85 has been torn down and replaced with a Paddy Power Betting Shop.

4 Wilson, London, 119.

5 Alf had married in 1927 and had three children — Kenneth, Sydney and Zelda. He divorced, and the children were brought up by Rose Costelle, his partner for forty-two years.

6 Guild tape interview.

7 Judith Espinosa (1876–1949) was a sister of Edouard Espinosa, one of the founders of the Royal Academy of Dance (RAD). (Brought together by Philip Richardson, former editor of *Dancing Times*, the other founding members were Adeline Genée, Tamara Karsavina, Lucia Cormani and Phyllis Bedells.) The goal of the group was the improvement of ballet teaching in England.

8 Celia and Margery Tymms had danced a duet titled "The Old Year Out and the New Year In" at the March 19, 1929 Guildhall Dramatic and Dancing Recital as pupils of Madame Soutten.

9 Visual artists Mark Gertler and David Bomberg were also recipients of grants from the Jewish Education Aid Society.

10 1970s feminist film and dance studies came up with the notion of "the male gaze" or voyeuristic leering, which treats women as sexual objects to be viewed.

11 The names of the chorus girls were not listed in the program. Another young dancer, Betty Shepard Goodings, was hired amidst the veterans. She later came to Canada and renewed her friendship with Celia. When Betty Shepard Goodings was dying, Celia phoned frequently and sent weekly letters to cheer her friend up.

TWO ⟶

Leo Kersley provided information about Celia's years with the Ballet Rambert. During a visit to Saffron Waldon, Essex, I bought a cache of British dance history books in a second-hand bookstore. I discovered that they came from the estate of British principal dancer Michael Somes, Margot Fonteyn's primary dance partner from 1950–1961. Franca would have known him. Among the books I found useful were *Arnold Haskell's Ballet* (1938), *Vic-Wells: A Ballet Progress* (1942), and *Ballet Biographies* (1952). Just as choreography is passed down from generation to generation, I felt a connection knowing that I was holding books read by Somes.

12 Perlmutter, 244.

13 Inglesby, 5.

14 Rasky interview.

15 *Celia Franca: Tour de Force* documentary.

16 *Canadian Home Journal*, Jan. 1953.

17 Years later in Canada, Franca would remount *Dark Elegies* for her own company. But she soon recognized that almost two decades after its premiere in London, Canadian audiences were not yet ready for Tudor's disturbing psychological themes. "I think it was a little too much too soon," she said in an interview with the *Toronto Star.* "It was hard enough for the dancers to do in 1955, let alone the audience to accept it."

18 Years later, after de Mille had choreographed for many of Broadway's greatest musicals, such as *Oklahoma*, she came to Manitoba to work with the Royal Winnipeg Ballet. Its artistic director, Arnold Spohr, forged a professional relationship with de Mille, who choreographed an original work, *The Rehearsal,* in 1964 and remounted other of her works with the company.

19 Solomon Franks, before his death, sent Celia a tape recording of a variety of events he remembered. The visit to the casino in Monte Carlo was one of them. "What you did — you cheeky little thing you — you went around the corner, you put on a pair of very dark spectacles, you put a handkerchief over your head and you walked in as if you were one of the gamblers."

20 Clark, 111. She erred in using Celia's stage name, Franca, because she was still billed as Franks in 1937.

21 Among the vast number of roles Franca undertook during those seminal Ballet Rambert years were: "Nymph in *L'Après-midi d'un*

Faune, Bluebird Pas de Deux in *Aurora's Wedding*, Goulue in *Bar aux Folies-Bergère*, Sport Girl in *Boxing*, First Guest in *Cinderella*, Danse de Tendresse in *Croquis de Mercure*, Night in *Descent of Hebe*, Polka in *Façade*, Lady-Friend and Wife in *Les Masques*, Marguerite in *Mephisto Valse*, Bride in *Mermaid*, Chief Guest in *La Muse S'Amuse*, Lonely Lady in *Our Lady 's Juggler*, Minerva in *Pas des Deésses*, Mortal born under Neptune in *The Planets*, Mazurka and Prelude in *Les Sylphides*, Pas de Trois in *Lac des Cynes*, Pavane in *Capriol Suite*. (From biographical index in Peter Noble. *The British Ballet*.)

22   Crisp, 53.

23   As was the case with his friend, the much-better-known Frederic Ashton, choreographer Walter Gore needed work on London's commercial stage to earn a living wage. Today Gore is little known. At the time, the Scottish-born Gore was one of the best known male dancers in Britain and was just beginning to receive recognition as an outstanding choreographer for both ballet and West End musicals.

THREE ᎧᎤ

The detail in this chapter derives principally from personal letters written by Celia Franca to Doris Margolis and Cyril Frankel. The Frankel letters were given to me by Cyril himself, but it is a mystery how the Margolis letters were returned to Franca and subsequently deposited in Franca's papers at the National Archives of Canada (Box 20–12). Franca also saved newspaper clippings from her years dancing with Ballet Rambert and the Sadler's Wells. The dance archives at London's Royal Opera House, Covent Garden and London's Theatre Museum provided additional information, as did Rasky's interview with Dame Ninette de Valois.

24   It played at the New Theatre from February 22 to March 11 and then transferred to the Saville Theatre for another run from March 21 to May 6. On Wednesdays and Saturdays, Celia had to perform in matinee and evening performances.

25 Leo Kersley interview in Theatre Archive Project. www.bl.uk/projects/theatrearchives/Kersley.

26 John Regain had been a member of the Markova/Dolin Company and had received training from Cecchetti and Nicolai Legat.

27 Celia had professionally presented her first piece of choreography, *Good Humoured Ladies* to Beethoven's Minuet in G on Jan 7, 1938 in Eastbourne with small group of Rambert dancers (according to Leo Kersley via Jane Pritchard).

28 *Celia Franca: Tour de Force* documentary.

29 Frank Rasky interview with Dame Ninette de Valois.

30 Rasky interview.

31 An article in the magazine *Illustrated* (December 8, 1945) titled "Economics of Ballet."

32 Part of an exhibition — *Dancing Through the War: The Royal Ballet 1939–1946* — mounted in 2007 at Whitehall's Cabinet War Rooms.

33 Rasky interview.

34 Anderson, 74.

35 Doris Margolis suffered from a hair loss disease (alopecia) and eventually was forced to wear a wig, adding to her shyness.

36 Daneman, 110.

37 Ibid.

38 Anderson, 69.

39 She published *Classical Dances and Costumes of India* in 1950.

40 *Ballet Impromptu: Variations on a Theme* (n.d) Golden Gallery Press, London.

41 Leo went on to have a happy and long marriage with Janet Sinclair, a young gallery girl, who became a respected writer on dance. Together they wrote *A Dictionary of Ballet Terms* and created the Harrow Ballet School in Essex.

42 *Celia Franca: Tour de Force* transcript.

43 In 1946, Arnold Haskell published a book, *The Helpmann-Bliss Ballet: Miracle in the Gorbals*, which contained illustrations, facsimiles of Helpmann's notes, and the score by Arthur Bliss, which includes several photos of Celia as the prostitute. Naxos has a

DVD of Sir Arthur Bliss's *Miracle in the Gorbals* recorded by the Queensland Symphony Orchestra, Australia in 1995.

44 When de Valois revived *The Rake's Progress* in autumn 1942, Celia, along with Palma Nye, were cast as ladies of the town.

45 The Sadler's Wells had by now moved to the larger Prince's Theatre (now The Shaftesbury Theatre).

46 Walker (Helpmann part 2, 234).

47 LAC MG31-D113 (20–12).

48 Rasky, Tape 21.

49 A second review in the *Dancing Times* in August found Franca less satisfying. "Celia Franca as the Spider faithfully portrays the baleful characteristics of this inhuman monster, but one longs for the flash of fire this dancer so often gives us in such roles as the Queen in *Hamlet*."

50 Celia interview with Carman Guild.

51 Fonteyn, p 92–93.

52 Lieutenant Cyril Frankel managed leave to see Celia dance in Hanover as well as in Paris during her first ENSA tour.

53 At that time, Keynes was also in the midst of helping to establish the World Bank and the International Monetary Fund. Keynes also drafted the constitution for the Arts Council of Great Britain.

FOUR ⌒

Much of the information in this chapter comes from material in the Celia Franca fonds at Library and Archives Canada. One lucky find in Box 21, which contains Franca's notes for her memoirs, was a small maroon notebook in which she had jotted down many of the details involved in creating *Khadra*. Reading those notes in Franca's distinctive tiny handwriting gave me insight into her thought processes. She calculated that 180 war-ration coupons would be required for forty yards of white stockinette, and that she needed people to contribute their coupons. A 1948 limited edition book by Honor Frost, *How a Ballet is Made*, included an illustration of the stage backdrop with its vivid pinks, reds, golds, and greens invoking a Persian art style, along with coloured costume illustrations, which gave me a sense of how the ballet would have appeared to an audience.

54 *Adam Zero*, with its life-cycle theme, from birth to death and with symbols linked to current postwar affairs, premiered on April 10 starring Helpmann and Brae, but was a disappointment and quickly disappeared from the company's repertoire. However, Brae received a rave review from Arnold Haskell in the first *Ballet Annual* (1947). "Given an opportunity that no dancer has had since Verchinina in *Les Presages* in 1933, she [Brae] seized it to make a true personal triumph, both on the crowded stage, no easy task, and alone with Helpmann in the beautiful dance of death that terminates his existence."

55 Homans, 425.

56 *Dancing Times*, August 1942.

57 Frank Rasky interview with ninety-one year old Dame Ninette de Valois in 1989, Tape 44.

58 Rasky interview.

59 Leo Kersley, Dance and Dancers, August 1985. p 34–35.

60 Frost, 23.

61 LAC Box 21 Pre-Canada file.

62 The first person onstage was a sage who slipped out between the curtains and settled himself down in a chair. This was the twenty-one-year-old Alexander Grant, who would come to Canada to replace Celia Franca as the artistic director of the National Ballet from 1976 to 1983.

63 Khadra was danced by Sheila O'Reilly while another fifteen-year-old, Anne Heaton, danced the role of the Beloved, partnered with Leo Kersley. The *Evening Standard* (May 28, 1946) commented: "Fifteen-year-old Anne Heaton showed a lovely line and a gift for repose as the snow-white maiden and Leo Kersely, her lover, danced with his accustomed virility and a newly added elegance and tact. Sheila O'Reilly, also 15, and the company's coming comedienne, added to Khadra's wonder some of her own high spirit."

64 Celia's comments were in the documentary, *Tour de Force: Celia Franca*.

65 Honor Frost returned to her first love, archaelogy. In 1948 she published a beautifully illustrated book, *How A Ballet Is Made*, devoted to the creation of *Khadra*.

66 David Walker danced under the name of David Kerval from 1955 to 1958 with the National Ballet of Canada and then become Celia's indispensable assistant.

67 In a lecture to the Ballet Circle on April 24, 1949, Celia described David Adam's first performance in *Dances of Galanta*. "His interpretation was somewhat immature and, like most dancers, he attacked his role like a battering ram and gave everything he had with terrific strength and sincerity all the way through, but later on he developed the gentle art of contrast and was able to put more light and shade into his performance."

68 November 26, 1947.

69 *Dancing Times*, Christmas, 1949. *Pleasuredome* was choreographed by Rosella Hightower, music by John Lanchbery and décor by Leonard Rosoman.

70 June 1948 and November 1949, which was just before the disbandment of the company.

71 This book was for an educational series titled "Women at Work." Franca used Svetlana Beriosova as her subject to describe in detail the daily life of a ballerina. Interestingly Svetlana Beriosova, the daughter of Lithuanian ballet master Nicholas Beriozoff, made her dance debut at the age of fifteen in a production of *The Nutcracker* in Nesta Toumine's Ottawa Ballet Company in March, 1947 staged at the Capitol Theatre, Ottawa.

72 Daneman, 177.

73 She played Phrynette, the coquettish laundry maid in the nineteenth-century three-act French mime play, *L'Enfant Prodique*, which opened on September 18. The Kensington News reported, "Phrynette is a captivating minx, and Celia Franca brings freshness and spontaneity to the part."

FIVE ✑

Information about Boris Volkoff and his school came from the Janet Baldwin Collection held by the Toronto Public Reference Library; the works cited from this collection are articles by John Ayre and a Ph.D. dissertation on Volkoff by Lilian Mitchell. Additionally, Amy Bowring's work-in-progress, *Hopeful Innovations: The Canadian Ballet Festivals and the Professionalization of Dance in Canada*, provided history on the early development of ballet companies in Canada. Cheryl Smith's Ph.D. thesis, *Stepping Out*, provided some of the information on the "Three Ladies." The Aileen Woods correspondence file at Toronto's National Ballet of Canada archives gave details concerning the start-up of the company. For example, an expense report for Celia's 1950 trip showed that Celia's airfare had been paid for by the T. Eaton Company, and she had received a per diem for taxis, tips, and theatre tickets.

74 In fact, Volkoff's frequently repeated claim was untrue. In researching an article for *The Beaver* Magazine (Feb/March, 1996), "Berlin 1936: Canadian Dancers and the Olympics," John Ayre spoke to one of the dancers who attended. Jim Pape explained, "We understood it was non-competitive, but I think it was Laban [Rudolf von Laban, chief organizer of the dance festival] who told us that if we looked at different groups, he would feel we would place about fifth. It was an informal thing."

75 Catherine Janet Baldwin's parents were William Willcocks Baldwin, a lawyer only three generations removed from Robert Baldwin, while her mother, Kathleen Gordon, was from a wealthy family member of the accountancy firm Clarkson Gordon. Janet grew up in her grandparents' St. George Street home and vacationed annually in Bermuda. Timothy Findley, in his memoir *Inside Memory*, recalled as a young boy being impressed by Janet's beautiful hair "... wore it long with a braid coiled either at the back of her head or wound over her ears — and her eyes — wide spread and blue (pale like ice) these were the trademarks of her appearance."

76 Bolm had moved to San Francisco in 1933 to become the director of the San Francisco Ballet School and ballet master for the company, a position he held until 1938.

77 Rutherford, 196.

78 Ayes, 9.

79 Whittaker, 16.

80 Neufeld, 11.

81 Rasky interview, June 1989, Tape 44.

82 Amy Bowring, manuscript in progress on the Canadian Ballet Festivals.

83 *Dancing Gazette*, 1951: 48–49.

84 Interview by Lillian Mitchell with Janet Baldwin. Mitchell, 320.

85 Parr, 44.

SIX ⌒

During her first six months in Canada, Celia wrote frequently to Margolis and Frankel. These letters provided irreplaceable personal insight into Celia's life. Her small appointment books from the 1950s (Library and Archives Canada, Boxes 11 and 12) were mainly helpful in establishing her whereabouts, but also gave insightful clues as to how she lived. For example, her frequent dentist appointments in 1951 puzzled me until I realized that she probably had little access to dentists during the war years in Britain. As well, the warm, strong voice of Bert Anderson in the Rasky interview helped me to understand why Celia had been attracted to him. Jonathan Vance's 2009 book, *A History of Canadian Culture*, provided context to the obstacles Franca faced in 1951 before the formation of the Canada Council. Andrew Horrall's 2009 book, *Bringing Art to Life: A Biography of Alan Jarvis*, followed a parallel story of Celia's, dealing with the visual arts in postwar Canada.

86 This sketch was left in Celia's will to her good friend, Mona Bernardi.

87 Lloyd received her teacher accreditation for both the Imperial Society of Teachers of Dancing (Classical, not Ballet Cecchetti

Method) and the Royal Academy of Dancing. She acted as an examiner in Canada for both organizations.

88   Myrna Aaron interview with author, June 11, 2011.

89   The Canadian Dance Teachers Association had been created at the second Canadian Ballet Festival in 1949 with Mildred Wickson as the first president.

90   Enrico Cecchetti, an Italian, established a method of teaching ballet, and after being a character dancer and ballet master of Diaghilev's Ballets Russes from 1909 to 1918, taught dance in London England with students including Marie Rambert and Ninette de Valois. In London, the Cecchetti Society was formed and in 1924 it was incorporated into the Imperial Society of Teachers of Dancing. Oliphant studied under Margaret Saul.

91   Rasky interview with Betty Oliphant, July, 1989.

92   Rasky interview.

93   In November 1953, Celia was a candidate for the Intermediate Level. Her examiner, Margaret Saul, from England's Imperial Society of Dance Inc., Cecchetti Society Branch, passed her, praising her pointe work and knowledge of general theory with the exception of a few minor details.

94   This production provided a sneak preview of some of the new dancers, including David Adams (who had been performing in August at the Grandstand Show at the Canadian National Exhibition with his wife Lois Smith).

95   At the beginning, wardrobe was housed in another part of St. Lawrence Hall, while the scenery "workshop" was part of the floor space of an aircraft hangar at Toronto Island Airport. The administrative office was in another building on Temperance Street.

96   Rasky, Tape 27.

97   Robert Ito, a Japanese-Canadian who had been interned with his family during the war, after leaving the National Ballet of Canada in 1958, went on to fame and fortune in Hollywood as an actor in such popular TV series as *Quincy M.E.*

98 Oliphant, 99.

99 Charter members: Myrna Aaron, David Adams, Irene Apiné, Natalie Butko, Connie Campbell, Diane Childerhose, Judie Colpman, André Dufresne, Maria (Oldyna) Dynowska, Walter Foster, Celia Franca, Jury Gotshalks, Joyce Hill, Fergus Hunter, Robert Ito, Lilian Jarvis, Vera Keiss, Colleen Kenney, Earl Kraul, Angela Leigh, Brian Macdonald, Howard Meadows, Marilyn Rollo, Katherine Stewart, Lois Smith, Grant Strate, Mary Toochina, Elena Trieste, Olivia Wyatt.

100 Brian Macdonald, André Dufresne, Grant Strate, Earl Kraul, Robert Ito, and Hy Meadows.

101 Neufeld, 32.

102 This scene setter by Mordecai Richler appeared in *The Canadian* magazine on November 13, 1976, in an article about the twenty-fifth anniversary of the founding of the National Ballet of Canada. The article also appeared in the 1976 souvenir program of the National Ballet of Canada.

103 Goodman, 276.

104 Franca had first seen Armstrong's *Étude* at the 1950 Canadian Ballet Festival and singled her out for praise in the article she wrote in the *Royal Academy of Dancing Gazette* (February 1951). "Miss Armstrong's intellectual approach to her work is comparable to that of Antony Tudor ... Her ballet *Étude*, is purely classical and delightful to watch."

105 *Dance in Canada*, 1987.

SEVEN ✑

Charter dancers, including Myrna Aaron, André Dufresne, Colleen Kenney, Brian Macdonald, Marilyn Rollo, and Grant Strate, shared with me their remembrances of their first years with the company. Others involved with the company from the 1950s whom I interviewed include dancers Jocelyn Terrell Allen, Yves Cousineau, and Lorna Geddes; general manager Walter Homburger; administrative staffer, the late Charlotte Norcop; rehearsal pianist Mary McDonald;

wardrobe department staffer, the late Cynthia MacLennan (who also worked as Franca's dresser on tour); and board president Antony Griffin (1954–1957).

106 Walter Homburger went on to be pianist Glenn Gould's manager and in 1961 the general manager of the Toronto Symphony Orchestra, a position he held until 1987.

107 James denied a rumour that he had mismanaged or over-spent by $5,000, telling an interviewer years later that he never had access to more than a $45 petty cash limit and had to produce receipts to get another $45. James went on to become a stockbroker. He died in Toronto on December 25, 1998.

108 The redhead Celia Sutton, known as "the other Celia," who worked in the beauty department at Eaton's (and the then-girl-friend of the manager of Eaton Auditorium, Paul Johnson) made room for Franca in her flat for a short time after she had given up her overly expensive furnished apartment. Franca resorted to drawing a line through the address and phone number of her posh cream-coloured stationary and writing in 27A Breadalbane Street, a more humble address near to Eaton's College department store. Celia Sutton, a proficient seamstress, became the company's first wardrobe mistress.

Like Stewart James, Celia Sutton soon disappeared from sight. Both she and James were amateurs who had done the very best they could to help Celia, while on a steep learning curve. Although both were well meaning, Celia simply didn't have the time to coach them along and so they were expendable. In their places came the professionals, Walter Homburger, the general manager, and Kay Ambrose, the costume designer.

109 Bell/Franca 206.

110 Rasky interview.

111 George Crum (1926–2007) was the National Ballet of Canada's musical director from 1951 to 1984. He was named musical director emeritus in 1984 and continued to arrange for dance pieces following his retirement.

112 Rasky interview, March 1990.

113 Interview with Cynthia MacLennan at her Stratford, Ontario home on May 16, 2009. MacLennan died on September 24, 2009.

114 April 24, 1951.

115 Doris Margolis moved to California and became the housekeeper for Gower and Marge Champion, a successful Hollywood dance team. Gower became one of Broadway's most successful director/choreographers producing such blockbusters as *Bye Bye Birdie*, *Carnival*, and *Hello Dolly*. Doris also took care of the couple's two sons. In a letter Doris wrote to Celia in March 1964, she was looking for a more independent life away from the Gowers. And while alone, she concluded her letter telling Celia that she still loved living in California.

116 Mary Toochina had a miserable time with the company constantly being reprimanded for her weight fluctuations. On the other hand, David Adam who had a rather stocky build, was not criticized by Celia and Betty.

117 Bell/Franca, 24.

118 Mitchell, 319.

119 Kenney interview with author, April 9, 2009.

120 As well as still performing character mime roles, Geddes was Pointe Shoe Manager and Assistant Ballet Mistress of the company.

121 Geddes interview with author April 8, 2009.

122 Celia, in her memoirs, gave a more embellished rendition of the story writing that Aaron was dancing in the *Polovtsian* dances, and after tripping on stage "she crawled on her hands and knees off to the wings." The author's version comes from Aaron herself.

123 Rasky interview.

124 Robert Laidlaw was a wealthy businessman who established the Laidlaw Foundation in 1949 to benefit charitable, educational, conservation, and cultural organizations in Ontario.

125 Lucy Waverman (nee Geneen), has become one of Canada's

best known cookbook writers. Celia attended Lucy's wedding in 1966 and gave the couple a very generous cheque. Once Celia moved full-time to Ottawa, the Geneen family rarely saw Celia. Although she visited Ben, accompanied by Bruce Corder, when Ben was very ill, Celia failed to send a note when Pearl Geneen died in 2004. However, when she saw Lucy at the Carlu Theatre in November 2006, she apologized for her oversight and told Lucy that she had really liked Pearl.

EIGHT ❧

James Neufeld's book *Power to Rise: The Story of the National Ballet of Canada*, with its 1951–1991 "Appendix of Performance Records," has been my constant reference; particularly Appendix D: "Dancers of the National Ballet of Canada," and Appendix E: "Members of the Board." Franca's own book, *The National Ballet of Canada*, and Herbert Whittaker's *The Official History of the National Ballet of Canada*, also provided information for this period. Additionally, Cheryl Smith's Ph.D. thesis, "Stepping Out: Canada's Early Ballet Companies, 1939–1963," and Cheryl Belkin-Epstein's paper "Norman Campbell, the Canadian Broadcasting Corporation and the National Ballet of Canada," provided an overview of the National Ballet of Canada's participation in televised ballet.

126 Not all Canadian artists were so hide-bound. Three years later, a group calling themselves the Painters Eleven held an exhibition of abstract art in Toronto.

127 The National Ballet was one of the first companies to perform this ever-popular pastiche of stories about flirtations amid *parisiennes* in an 1870s French café. Kay Ambrose designed all of the colourful costumes.

128 Celia invited a few Canadian choreographers such, as Montrealer Elizabeth Leese, and Kay Armstrong from British Columbia, to mount short works on the company. She completely ignored Boris Volkoff who had created original Canadian-themed ballets such as *Mon-Ka-Ta* (1936), based on a Canadian aboriginal legend.

Gweneth Lloyd declined to mount a work on the National Ballet company when invited to do so in 1952.

129 Bell/Franca, 85.

130 In the summer of 1952, Celia Franca agreed to choreograph for the Grandstand stage at the Toronto exhibition grounds, a version of *Midsummer's Night Dream* which included David Adams and Lois Smith in lead roles, and Franca herself as Queen of the Night.

131 Mounting Antony Tudor's *Dark of Moon* and *Gala Performance*, and Act Two of *Swan Lake,* cost $30,000; the addition of $20,000 in rehearsal wages created the $50,000 deficit.

132 *Toronto Star,* Thursday, January 28, 1954, pg. 6.

133 Transcript of outs from *Celia Franca: Tour de Force.*

134 Franca letter to Cyril Frankel.

135 *Maclean's,* August 20, 1955.

136 Goodman, 274.

137 *Maclean's,* August 20, 1955.

138 Yves Cousineau interview with author, March 9, 2009.

139 *Mayfair,* Feb. 1956, Alex Barris.

140 Rasky interview.

141 One wonders if Bettina Byers' kindness altered Celia's first impression of her. In a letter to Doris on April 15, 1951 she wrote of Byers, "In my opinion, she's a bit of a bitch and considers herself too good to come into close contact with the Teachers' Association. She doesn't know me very well or what I am doing. She stopped some of her pupils coming to my class." In fact, Byers had been influential in founding the Canadian Dance Teachers' Association. A very competent dance teacher who studied in England with Phyllis Bedells, Byers returned to Canada to further the work of the Royal Academy of Dance. She taught some of the National Ballet of Canada charter members such as Myrna Aaron, Judie Colpman, and Oldyna Dynowska.

142 Over his forty-seven-year career with CBC-TV, Campbell produced and directed sixteen full-length ballets by the National Ballet of Canada along with numerous variety shows and specials featuring

dancers from the company. He won two Emmys: one in 1968 for *Cinderella* and another in 1972 for *The Sleeping Beauty*. He also received the Prix Rene Barthelemy in 1966 for *Romeo and Juliet*. All three of these award-winning productions starred Veronica Tennant who, after an illustrious career as a prima ballerina, has gone on herself to become an award-winning filmmaker.

143 *Coppelia* and *Winter Night*, Dec. 19, 1957; *The Nutcracker*, Dec. 23, 1958; *Pineapple Poll*, Dec. 22, 1959; *Swan Lake*, Dec. 18, 1961; *The Looking Glass People*, a documentary, Dec. 10, 1962 along with *Giselle*, Dec. 17, 1962. After 1962, the Christmas shows, while featuring some ballet, became light-hearted variety shows with other guests such as the comedians John Wayne and Frank Shuster.

144 Epstein, 138.

145 Bell/Franca 139.

146 Strate, 54.

147 *Toronto Telegram*, November 19, 1958.

NINE ⌒

Betty Oliphant's youngest daughter, Carol Roach, talked to me about the National Ballet School and Betty's relationship with Franca. I interviewed the late Lucy Potts, who had been with the National Ballet School as its French teacher from the day the school opened its doors in September 1959 until her retirement. One of the first students of the National Ballet School, Carmen von Richthofen, corresponded with me via email.

148 Rasky interview.

149 A dance donated by Walter Gore, which Celia and Grant Strate had learned during a "repertoire hunting" trip to London in 1957.

150 Strate, 56.

151 Queen Elizabeth had attended the official ceremonies of the opening of the St. Lawrence Seaway on June 26 along with US President Dwight Eisenhower.

152 *Toronto Telegram*, June 3.

153 The original Sadler's Wells Ballet School (now the Royal Ballet School) had been located in an old mansion in Barons Court. In 1955, the school moved to White Lodge, Richmond Park, a former royal residence and hunting lodge and has a residence for out-of-town and foreign ballet students. In January 2003, the Royal Ballet Upper School moved to a newly constructed studio complex in Floral Street, adjacent to the Royal Opera House in Covent Garden. A bridge, known as the Bridge of Aspiration, built between the school and Opera House, links the school with the theatre and Royal Ballet Company's own studios.

154 Celia Franca papers LAC MG31-DII3 (61–38).

155 Ballet staff consisted of Betty Oliphant, Celia Franca, Juliette Fischer, Lucille McClure and Nancy Schwenker. The academic personnel were hastily hired in early September during one single day of interviewing. Anna Hayworth, academic director, also taught English and Latin; Mary McLean, history, geography and art; Lucy Potts, French; and Diana Dignam, elementary grade.

156 She shared with two American students: Sarah Thomas from Buffalo and Diane Dobson from California.

157 *New York Times* dance critic Alastair Macaulay in a November 2010 review singled out two female dancers in *The Nutcracker* saying they "seem to have been sampling half the sweet realm." When attacked for his attitude, he responded, "Dancers — even when sheathed in tights, tunics, tutus — open their bodies up in the geometric shapes and academic movements that ballet has codified, and so they make their bodies subject to the most intense scrutiny. If you want to make your appearance irrelevant to criticism, do not choose ballet as a career." (*National Post*, Dec. 14, 2010.)

158 Ambrose had been working on a manuscript entitled *The Canadian Book* and had completed several draft chapters, as well as many pencil sketches, such as humorous drawings of cowboys. She appears to have left the work in Canada, as it was donated

as part of the Celia Franca collection to Library and Archives Canada.

159 Rubin, *Chatelaine* magazine, March 1974, p. 86.

160 Bert Anderson formally divorced Celia in Canada in 1962.

161 It's unclear if this quickie divorce was legal. If Franca did not go to Mexico herself, then the one-day residency stipulation had not been fulfilled. An article in *Time* magazine (Dec. 27, 1963) "Domestic Relations: The Perils of Mexican Divorce" did not reach a conclusion, stating that while some American lawyers held the opinion that Mexican divorces were worthless, others believed that if correctly handled, a Mexican divorce was perfectly valid. Bert Anderson divorced Celia through the Canadian legal system in 1962.

162 Author interview with Cyril Frankel at his Harley Street, London, apartment, April 18, 2008. It appears that the pair had talked about marriage several times. In one of Celia's wartime letters to Cyril, she acknowledges that he had withdrawn his marriage proposal. This may have been caused by her affair with "Mortie." Celia wrote, "One thing was not quite clear in your letter. You didn't say whether or not you are still in love with me. I realized, of course that the proposal of marriage was withdrawn, but you should ask yourself — 'Do I still love her?' and when you have decided I hope you will tell me."

TEN ✐

The Buckle and Kirstein reports are in the Library and Archives Canada Council fonds R854-0-7-E in the operational records RG63 Volume 1348. Richard Buckle's letter to Franca is in MG31-D-113, 20–2. Cheryl Smith's "The Infamous Ballet Survey" and Kate Cornell's "The Ballet Problem: The Kirstein-Buckle Ballet Survey for the Canada Council" explore issues addressed in the Third Annual Report of the Canada Council for 1958–1959, which provides a financial report on the three companies. It is interesting to note that the province of Quebec gave financial support to Les Grands Ballets Canadiens, while Ontario and Manitoba had not yet created arts councils.

163 Briefs concerning ballet were submitted by the Ballet Appreciation Club of Ottawa, the Banff School of Fine Arts, and the Canadian Ballet Festival Association.

164 The Arts Council of Great Britain was created during the Second World War and its first chairman was John Maynard Keynes. The United States created the National Endowment for the Arts (NEA) later in 1965, which the Republicans periodically attempted to abolish.

165 These self-made multi-millionaires were Isaak Walton Killam, the richest Canadian of his day, and Sir James Dunn, a millionaire before the age of forty.

166 This unusual temporary venue of the prime minister's office in the centre block of the Parliament Buildings was due to the fact that parliament had been dissolved and an election was about to begin.

167 Antony Griffin interview with author, October 17, 2007. Griffin was a board member 1953–1961 and 1969–1971 and president of the board from 1954–1957.

168 Canada Council Records, minutes April 30–May 1, 1957.

169 Material taken from J.L. Granatstein's *Culture and Scholarship: The First Ten Years of the Canada Council. Canadian Historical Review*, LXV, 4, 1984.

170 Kenneth Le Mesurier Carter, who reported back to the Council in January, 1959, had undertaken the fullest exploration of the financial state of the arts ever made in Canada at that time.

171 These were Melissa Hayden, born in Toronto and trained with Boris Volkoff; Patricia Wilde, born in Ottawa and danced with the Metropolitan Ballet in 1949–1950 along with Celia; and Robert Lindgren, born in Victoria, B.C. and trained with June Roper.

172 Kirstein, Lincoln. *What Ballet is About: An America Glossary, Dance Perspectives*, 1959.

173 Kavanagh, 150.

174 Neufeld, 243.

175 Address to University of Michigan, March 1963.

176 Kay Ambrose befriended a young man, originally training to become an opera singer, who in the mid 1960s became a European pop star. David Garrick's (a stage name) first costumes were made by none other than Kay Ambrose. Garrick says on his official website, "Kay came up with the basic idea for my 'look' and made all the stage gear. The 18th century 'dandy' image. I loved it and what's more it looked good on T.V."

ELEVEN ⟋

National Ballet people active during this period whom I interviewed include dancers Miriam Adams, nee Weinstein (joined 1963), Vicky Bertram (joined 1963), Nadia Potts (joined 1964), and Veronica Tennant (joined 1964). This also includes ballet master and mistress respectively David Scott and Joanne Nisbet. A helpful book was Hugh Walker's *The O'Keefe Centre Years*.

177 This lack of new repertoire was particularly bad timing for the National Ballet with the Canada Council Ballet Survey about to begin.

178 Leila Zorina also appeared with the London Festival Ballet in the early 1960s.

179 Since both Franca and Oliphant discouraged their dancers from taking classes from other teachers, she likely did not know that Adams and Smith during the company's early years had also been taking evening classes with Boris Volkoff.

180 Taken from chapter "Ballet in America Comes of Age." *No Fixed Point*, Reynolds and McCormick, 302.

181 NBOC. Grant Strate to John Paterson.

182 Headed by Louis Applebaum, amidst the elite members were Zubin Mehta, conductor of the Montreal Symphony Orchestra; Herman Geiger-Torel, director of the Canadian Opera Company; Wallace Russell, who will soon enter the Celia Franca story; and Ludmilla Cheriaeff, artistic director of Les Grands Ballets Canadiens.

183 Later, the stage and rehearsal room at the O'Keefe Centre was

rebuilt to the specifications of the production director, Dieter Penzhorn. Around 1992, the company began to lay down a portable spring floor, a specially constructed wooden floor that is dancer friendly.

184 The first cast included Celia's close friends, Walter Gore and Alicia Markova.

185 Don Gillies, a Canadian who had danced the Sadler's Wells Theatre Ballet, based *The Remarkable Rocket* on an Oscar Wilde short story. The sets and costumes were by Jack Nichols, a Canadian war artist. It appears that Celia had met Nichols in England since she noted in her diary lunching with him within weeks of her arrival in Toronto in 1951. Nichols' costumes were destroyed in the St. Lawrence fire in 1973. The National Archives of Canada holds the sketches for the costumes.

186 Carman Guild interview with Celia Franca, August 11, 1999.

187 John Cranko had become the Stuttgart Ballet's artistic director in 1961.

188 In January 1965, eighteen-year-old National Ballet School graduate Veronica Tennant, who had entered the company as a principal, stepped into the role of Juliet. Lois Smith, then over forty years old, was disappointed never to be given the Juliet role.

189 *Celia Franca: Tour de Force.*

190 Neufeld, 92.

191 Cousineau and Bowes had seen a performance in Stuttgart in March 1970 with guest artist, Margot Fonteyn in the lead.

192 The issue was finally resolved in 1975 with an addendum to the original contract in which the National Ballet was given the license to perform Romeo and Juliet throughout the world (with discretion) for the fee of $5000 for these rights in perpetuity and an additional $1000 for each and every performance at New York's Metropolitan Opera House. Sadly, Cranko himself had died by this time. Flying back to Germany on June 26, 1973, after a successful season in New York, Cranko, then forty-five, choked to death as the result of an allergic reaction to a prescription

medication. The National Ballet of Canada acquired two more of Cranko's full-length ballets after his death: Onegin in 1983/84 and *The Taming of the Shrew* 1992 plus *Concerto for Flute and Harp* 1990/91.

193 From 1969 to 1973 the National Ballet's *The Nutcracker* was a regular at the nation's capital, the National Arts Centre. Once the other Canadian ballet companies created their own *The Nutcracker*, however, the NAC began to alternate the various productions.

194 After Paul Hellyer left the federal government, he was a board member of the National Ballet of Canada from 1970 to 1975. Although recognizing Franca's autocratic manner, he told the author that he had great sympathy for her "grand vision for a grand company."

195 August Bournonville, the most influential Danish choreographer of the nineteenth century, had choreographed *La Sylphide*, which defines the Danish ballet style which "is marked by the buoyancy of its technique, the warmth of its characterizations, the brilliance of its allegro and the grace of its presentation." (*Oxford Dictionary of Dance*.)

196 Gruen, 144.

197 Gruen, 119.

198 On January 6, Bruhn returned to the role of James partnered with Lois Smith. The audience refused to leave to theatre giving the couple twenty-three curtain calls.

199 The Royal Winnipeg Ballet commissioned Brian Macdonald to create *Rose Latullippe*, based on the French-Canadian legend of a devout, young girl possessed by the devil.

200 With music by Godfrey Ridout, sets and costumes by Lawrence Schafer, the ballet was first performed in Montreal in late October 1967 and then saved for a Toronto premiere in April 1968. On both occasions, the dance bombed.

201 Martine van Hamel left the National Ballet in 1970 to go to New York as a soloist with the Joffrey Ballet. After taking a demotion to the corps de ballet with the American Ballet Theatre in 1971,

she was promoted to a principal in 1973 and enjoyed a career as one of the leading classical ballerinas in America.

202 *Toronto Telegram* reviewer Ralph Hicklen was no kinder to it than Barnes was to *Cinderella*. His April 30, 1968, review stated, "When I saw it in the dying days of Expo last year, I thought *La Prima Ballerina* a disaster. I was wrong: It is much worse than that. If it had any value at all, it is as an object lesson in all the things a ballet must not be."

TWELVE ᲛᲣ

I spoke to Ann Ditchburn, who joined the National Ballet in 1968, and Karen Kain, who followed one year later. Grant Strate discusses this period in his book *Grant Strate: A Memoir*.

203 Rose's inability to meet deadlines added another ten thousand dollars to these costs.

204 To add to Celia's stress level, Asher Tarmon, her second cousin, who had stoically attended Celia's childhood dance recitals, had brought his family, then living in Detroit, to Toronto. Unable to cope with a family of five in her Glenrose home, she booked them into the King Edward Hotel. Tarmon, now in his early nineties recalls, "It was one of the happiest occasions I can ever remember — the hotel suite, the enormous bunch of welcoming flowers, the visits to Celia's house and meeting her five gorgeous cats, the tour of Toronto, the restaurant meals, the talk about our mutual family — and above all, the ballet performances themselves." (Correspondence with author.) It appears that Celia felt badly about not being able to accommodate her relatives. Her mother wrote on April 18, "It's a pity that Asher & family are going to Toronto just when you are so busy. You did the right thing to book them into a hotel."

205 Interview with Carol Roach, April 22, 2009.

206 Nathan Cohen had a driving ambition to become a professional cultural critic. Arriving in Toronto in the late 1940s, he published his own quarterly journal called *The Critic* which survived from

1950–1953. After a short stint at the *Toronto Telegram*, Cohen moved over to the *Toronto Star*. As demanding of himself, he read widely on dance. The author bought a copy of a 1946 book, *Soviet Ballet*, and discovered it had belonged to Cohen.

207 After the Bolshoi Ballet visited Toronto in 1963, Kay Ambrose, then living in London, England, wrote to Celia, "I'm sure Cohen gave them rave reviews, the poor pathological lump."

208 Interview with William Littler, January 22, 2009.

209 Rasky interview.

210 Celia and her parents were joined by the eighteen-year-old Veronica Tennant, who was visiting English relatives while recuperating from a back injury, which had delayed her entry into the National Ballet Company, in attending an evening performance of *The Sleeping Beauty* in London. Tennant has the fond memory of Solly Franks saying to her at the end of the evening, "Take care of my daughter for me, will you?"

211 Spain and Gordon, both with shoulder-length hair, had dropped out of the National Ballet School, chaffing at its old-fashioned regulations such as short hair, a school uniform, and other rules such as no gum chewing. They had told Oliphant that they were wasting their time at the school and had gone off to study their academic subjects independently. Ditchburn did graduate from NBS.

212 *Toronto Star*, Nathan Cohen, November 16, 1968.

213 Mrs. St. Clair-Balfour, Dr. James Fleck, and Mr. Lyman Henderson.

214 Rasky, tape 8.

THIRTEEN ❧

I spoke to Lyman Henderson, board president from 1969–1971, who also gave me a copy of chapter eighteen of his memoirs, which deals with his years on the board of the National Ballet of Canada. I also interviewed the Honourable Paul Hellyer, who was a National Ballet board member from 1970–1975. During the writing of this book, several other books exploring Canada's twentieth century cultural history were published. Sarah Jennings' 2009 book, *Art and Politics: The History of the National Art Centre* (NAC), goes beyond the building of Ottawa's NAC to examine the history of Canada's arts from the 1960s to today. The clever illustration that accompanied Marci McDonald's *Toronto Star* article was by the renowned illustrator Huntley Brown.

215 Information from Sarah Jennings, interview with Celia Franca in 2003.

216 This comical tale comes from Sarah Jennings book, *Arts and Politics: The History of the National Arts Centre.*

217 Rubin, *Chatelaine*, March 1974.

218 Transcript, *Celia Franca: Tour de Force.*

219 Vincent and Reva had made one trip to Canada in the early 1960s to visit Celia and Jay Morton. The four of them went to Niagara Falls.

220 Vincent's family experienced more tragedy in 1974 when one of Celia's nephews, Michael, a university student, committed suicide. Celia did not go to South Africa that time.

221 Rubin, *Chatelaine*, March 1974.

222 Other National Ballet of Canada persons quit as well: David Conrad, director of development; Janis Neilson rehearsal pianist; and three members of the executive board: H. Peter Holland, campaign chair of the fundraising drive; Leighton McCarthy; and Mrs. Bernard Protter. Janis Neilson returned to the company in the early 2000s and is the principal pianist as well as a major contributor to the Celia Franca Society.

223 The gala was to raise funds for the British Royal Academy of Dance and the Ceccheti branch of the Imperial Society of Teachers of Dancing.

224 One major disappointment on the following evening was the absence of Erik Bruhn in *La Sylphide*. He had been forced off stage by recurring illness, but brought the Royal Danish Ballet's Niels Kehlet to London and rehearsed him with Veronica Tennant.

225 She also agreed to engage Niels Kehlet, of the Royal Danish Ballet to appear in *La Sylphide* in London and Paris and Georges Piletta, of the Paris Opera Ballet, repeated his role in Petit's *Kraanerg* in London, Brussels, and Glasgow.

226 Canada's diplomatic service gave star treatment to the National Ballet of Canada. The Canadian High Commission sponsored the backstage champagne reception at London's Coliseum Theatre May 17th, Canada's Ambassador to Paris hosted a reception at his residence, as did the Canadian Ambassador to Germany at the Stuttgart Opera House. Celia, in her memoirs, recalled that in Monte Carlo "the company was stiffly entertained to dinner by Prince Rainier and Princess Grace."

227 In the 1970s, the Soviet Union was still reluctant to invite foreign ballet companies to visit Moscow and (then) Leningrad. Besides exposing their ballet dancers to the new trends and thus whetting their appetites for new repertoire, which in turn encouraged defections, the Soviets didn't want their audiences to compare Western ballet with the moribund Russian repertoire of old classics and social realism. However, the Russian companies, with tight security for the dancers, did perform in the West (mainly through Hurok Concerts Inc.) to gain hard currency.

FOURTEEN

There are numerous biographies on the dancer Rudolf Nureyev. I found Julie Kavanagh's *Nureyev: The Life* and Diane Solway's *Nureyev: His Life* to be especially helpful. Potts, and Veronica Tennant spoke to me about their experiences with Nureyev. Celia spoke to Frank Rasky, in an interview, about her difficulties with the Russian superstar.

228 The deficit had been whittled down by fifty-six percent after the first leg of the 1972 tour.

229 *Celia Franca: Tour de Force.*

230 Ranked as one of the leading ballet designers of the latter part of the twentieth century, the Greek-born Georgiadis created costumes for four of Royal Ballet's Kenneth MacMillan's full-length ballets,

along with Cranko's *Daphnis and Chloe* and Nureyev's *Swan Lake* (Vienna, 1964) and *The Sleeping Beauty* (Milan, 1966 and National Ballet of Canada, 1972).

231 Rasky interview.

232 Nureyev used the Marius Petipa version of *The Sleeping Beauty*, which had been in repertoire of the Kirov Ballet since 1890. He adapted the ballet to add more solos for his own role as Prince Florimund.

233 Kavanagh, 443.

234 All of Celia's quotes concerning working with Nureyev come from Rasky transcripts (Tape 40).

235 Natalie Makarova was present at the ballet's premiere at Ottawa's National Arts Centre. She wanted to dance the role for Norman Campbell's televised production of *The Sleeping Beauty*. Tennant danced the role.

236 Author interview with Karen Kain December 1, 2009.

237 *The Globe and Mail*, September 4, 1972.

238 William Littler, *Toronto Star*. September 2, 1972.

239 Unfortunately, Nureyev never got Limon's intentions and there was no second chance since Limon died that December. With his dramatic dark face paint, one critic said that Nureyev's desperate, rolling eyes and flared nostrils reminded him of a close-up from the Russian film *Ivan the Terrible*.

240 Karen Kain interview with author, December, 1, 2009.

241 Episode taken from Diane Solway's book *Nureyev: His Life*. p. 385.

242 *New York Times*, May 9, 1973.

243 On March 5, 1974, Sol Hurok, on his way to a meeting with David Rockefeller to discuss another project, "Nureyev and Friends," collapsed and died. He was eighty-six years old. Hurok Concerts Inc. did not survive long after his death. The National Ballet of Canada, with Nureyev, had been booked into the Met for the 1974–75 season before his death.

244 All Kain quotes from author interview, December, 1, 2009, at the Walter Carsen Centre.

245 Neufeld, 144.

246 While spelling it incorrectly, Celia was using an actual ballet term, *cucu,* which describes tight-fitting underwear worn by dancers. This fascinating fact comes from Katherine Barber's book *Six Words You Never Knew had Something to Do with Pigs,* in which she explains that the word *tutu* was nineteenth century baby talk for the word *cucu,* "a derivative of *cul,* a rather coarse word for backside."

247 *New York Times,* July 27, 1975.

248 The company and board were not happy with Fraser's comments writing letters to the *New York Times* to disassociate themselves from his remarks. Shortly after writing the article, Fraser switched beats to drama.

249 *Celia Franca: Tour de Force.*

FIFTEEN

Board President Ian (Jock) McLeod (1972–1975) briefed me on the issue of the hiring and firing of David Haber. I interviewed John Fraser, then dance critic with *The Globe and Mail,* about his experience with the Baryshnikov defection and also consulted his article, "Defection" (pp. 253–260) in Robert Gotlieb's anthology, *Reading Dance.* Box 70 in Library and Archives Canada contains Franca's 1974 diary, though *diary* is, perhaps, too ambitious a word, as she had used a three-ring notebook to jot a few entries usually on air flights. She harangued about Air Canada and delayed flights, and recorded her in-flight drinks of choice: screwdrivers and Bloody Marys. If she did not have the notebook, she scribbled on yellow lined paper and stuffed it into the diary. As with most journal writers, it was mainly a forum to vent her frustrations. She did record that, after the opening evening at the National Art Centre on March 7, followed by a reception with Governor General Jules Leger, she went home to Clemow Avenue and, to unwind, had a couple of Scotches and washed the kitchen floor.

250 Joanne Nisbet and David Scott confirmed that after 1972, Celia

stopped giving classes and was away for longer periods of time in Ottawa.

251 Oliphant, p. 116.

252 Franca always had been enraged at her lack of control over what had been written about her. Earlier in 1967 when Herbert Whittaker, a dance critic for *The Globe and Mail,* had written *The Official History of the National Ballet of Canada,* Celia had demanded complete editorial control.

253 *Globe and Mail* dance critic John Fraser was another of the players in the Baryshnikov defection, having received word from New York that plans had been finalized. His task was to contact the Russian dancer and give him a phone number. Fraser provides a hilarious account of this episode, explaining that after inveigling himself into the reception at the O'Keefe Centre, and sidling up to Baryshnikov, he discovered that the phone number in the crumbled piece of paper hidden in his hand was unreadable and he, a journalist, without a pen. Somehow the message was passed on.

254 Neufeld, 160.

255 One particular issue was Franca and Haber's decision to present Fokine's 1937 one-act ballet *Le Coq d'Or* with Celia's old friend, Nicholas Beriozoff from Metropolitan Ballet days (who had been Fokine's rehearsal assistant at the Ballet Russe de Monte Carlo), as the répétiteur. In briefing notes to Lyman Henderson, Celia wrote, "While critics will almost certainly ask why we bother to re-create a 'museum piece' one must realize that if major ballet companies do not preserve the classics, who will? Nothing wrong with being a museum — if there were, then why are there so many in the world?" The board refused to authorize the funds to mount *Le Coq d-Or,* but in a compromise agreed to pay for Beriozoff to come to Toronto to teach the dance which was videotaped as a form of notation for future consideration.

256 She actually had little time to reflect at this point as she went directly to New York, where she had been in the midst of setting Tudor's *Offenbach in the Underworld* on the Joffrey Ballet.

257 Whether Franca boycotted the event or was not invited, she did not appear to attend the weekend (November 15 and 16) international conference "Visions: Ballet and Its Future," organized by Betty Oliphant and colleagues. Participants included Dame Ninette de Valois and Sir Frederick Ashton.

SIXTEEN

I consulted Betty Oliphant's autobiography, *Miss O: My Life in Dance*, for her account of her relationship with Franca. Mary Ann West, now the artistic operations manager at the National Ballet School, spoke to me about being Oliphant's assistant and Franca's boarder at the same time. West said that she felt somewhat uncomfortable as her loyalties were divided. Although she was accustomed to calling Oliphant by her first name, Celia was always "Miss Franca." Two Canada Council dancer officers, Monique Michaud and Barbara Laskin, whom I interviewed together, discussed the Oliphant/Franca schism. Norma-Sue Fisher-Stitt's 2010 *History of the National Ballet School* contains quotes from an interview she did with Franca in 2001.

258 At the thirtieth anniversary on November 12, 1981, Grant presented Bournonville's Napoli with a stellar cast. The widow complete with black veil who appeared in one of the walk-on background parts was none other than Celia Franca.

259 Franca repeated her rather paranoid feelings in another twenty-fifth anniversary article, written by Mordecai Richler, in which she wondered why she should go back to Toronto to dance "in front of all my enemies." Richler noted that Celia had miraculously founded and brought her ballet company to international stature, and, as is inevitable, by her very success, made herself redundant.

260 Betty's second marriage to Reginald Mawyer had been as unhappy as her first one.

261 Celia was one of only two Canadian women included; the other being Dora Wasserman, who created a Yiddish Theatre in Montreal.

262 Since little in the tangled affairs of Franca and Oliphant is ever straightforward, during the company's visit to London in 1972, Bruhn, living in Nureyev's London home, invited the pair over after an evening performance. During the long evening, Bruhn exposed his frailties, drinking heavily, smoking incessantly, and rambling on about his worries, insecurities, and physical ailments. At least this is what happened if Celia was right in her later comment, "At that time, Betty saw that he was too neurotic."

263 Later, Staines took Celia with her on a three-week tour of Australia to visit ballet schools.

264 Author interview with Canada Council dance officers Monique Michaud and Barbara Laskin in Ottawa, December 2007.

265 *Celia Franca: Tour de Force.*

266 Oliphant's treatment of Strate certainly was a factor in his decision to seek a new direction. He tells in his memoir of meeting Oliphant in the halls of the St. Lawrence Centre, where she informed him that he was no longer the company's resident choreographer. "I countered by saying, as gracefully as I could, that under the circumstances I thought it was the right thing. Betty told me that it did not matter what I thought because she had already decided." p. 119.

SEVENTEEN ⌒

I interviewed Judith Davis by telephone and contacted Joyce Shietze by email. Merrilee Hodgins declined to be interviewed. I spoke to Celia's friends Mona Bernardi and Vicki Prystawski, who were very protective of Celia's privacy. I also corresponded via email with Celia's great-nephew Jason Franks.

267 This author remembers being in a small Ottawa grocery store shortly after Celia's final resignation, and seeing her pushing a cart down the aisles, shopping for her husband's dinner. Somehow it didn't seem right for Celia Franca, with her "face on" and hair swept up into its usual chignon, to be doing something so dull and ordinary.

268 Episode related to Frank Rasky by Celia Franca (Tape 7).

269 If she had received the position, Jay Morton would have been back in the uncomfortable position of having his wife as his boss.

270 Southam's replacement was Donald MacSween, a Montreal lawyer, who had been the director of the National Theatre School. He was bilingual.

271 Deirde Kelly, *The Globe and Mail*, March 3, 2007.

272 Geddes joined the National Ballet in 1959 and now is the company's pointe shoe manager and assistant ballet mistress.

273 The other was Beryl Grey, who had been with the Sadler's Wells with Celia during the war years. In effect, Ninette de Valois was continuing with her mission of introducing the "English Style" of ballet technique to foreign countries.

274 Rasky, Tape 42.

275 Franca, Karen Kain, and Frank Augustyn were celebrity guests of a Caribbean ballet cruise in January 1999.

276 Ditchburn flitted in and out of the National Ballet Company and had some success as a choreographer, creating *Mad Shadows* during Alexander Grant's first year as replacement to Celia Franca as artistic director. In Hollywood she appeared in several films, including the 1978 *Slow Dancing in the Big City*.

277 In fact, the video won the Golden Rose international television award at Montreux, Switzerland. The dancers were Robert Desrossiers, Ann Ditchburn, and Claudia Moore.

278 *Ottawa Citizen*, January 18, 1990 (H3).

279 Gradus, 153.

280 Augustyn changed the name to Ottawa Ballet. After he resigned in 1994, the company suspended operations.

281 Audrey Ogilvie, poet and author, has uncannily captured the animosity Celia created with her take-overs in Ottawa. This stanza is one of a much longer poem which includes such phrases as "She dipped her face into Five Roses flour before each outing" and "With the Centre for Arts in her silk-lined pocket, She was certain she'd never be found out."

282 Ironically, after Chiriaeff and Franca, two *grandes dames* of Canadian ballet, retired, they became friends. Celia, in a letter to Frank Rasky in September 1992, told of going for a day to visit Chiriaeff who had become seriously ill. (She died in 1996.)

283 After Kain's participation, Franca faxed her a thank-you note saying, "it's not surprising that everyone loves you. Your generosity is evident through your dancing and through you as a human being."

284 These fundraisers in the guise of a birthday celebration for Celia Franca continued. On June 25, 2005, "The Love of Dance" at the NAC marked the occasion of both Celia's eighty-fourth birthday and the twenty-sixth anniversary of the School of Dance.

285 This award is presented to a person who has provided a sustained contribution to the cultural life of Canada. Erik Bruhn received it in 1974, Ludmilla Chiriaeff in 1975, and Betty Oliphant in 1982.

286 Franca also received the Molson Prize and the Order of Ontario.

287 Honorary degrees included LL.D: Windsor, 1959; Mount Allison, 1966; University of Toronto, 1974; Dalhousie, 1976; York University, 1976 (served for a time as a Board member of York University); Trent University, 1977; McGill University, 1986; and D.C.L. Bishop's University, 1967 and D.Litt Guelph University, 1976.

288 Franca and Bruhn performed a pas de deux in Frank Staff's ballet *The Lovers' Gallery* during their time with the Metropolitan Ballet.

289 Celia saved this letter dated January 1973. It is among her papers at Library and Archives Canada. MG31-D113, Vol 20, 20.6.

EIGHTEEN ⌒

James Neufeld alerted me to the diary entry in which Franca recorded, "J. threatens divorce." I discovered the despondent note concerning "nothing for her to live for" in another of those ruled notebooks scattered throughout the Franca fonds (Library and Archives Canada 21–13). I acquired James Morton's will, revised in June 1997, in which he ignored Franca and left all of his personal belongings, along with thirty thousand dollars, to Joy Skrapek. I spoke via phone with Strapek, Morton's student and fellow clarinetist, who explained that since most of Morton's personal belongings related to his music career, Morton was confident that she would know how to disperse them. Morton's obituary, written by Jacob Siskind in *the Ottawa Citizen* on September 6, 1997, made no mention of Celia Franca.

I was in contact, both by telephone and email, with Stewart and Virginia Goodings. I conducted a lengthy telephone interview with Mavis Staines, the current artistic director of the National Ballet School, and James Austen, who had started with the National Ballet just as Franca retired, but remained a steadfast friend.

290 Rasky interview with Dr. Ben and Pearl Geneen.

291 She wrote to Cyril Frankel reporting that she and Jay would be going to El Dorado, Kansas, in August 1983 "to visit mother-in-law who is 75 and about to move to a retirement home." And in another letter to Frankel, written July 14, 1992, she reported that Jay's mother had died on July 1 while they were in Guelph, Ontario, where Jay was teaching again for the National Youth Orchestra.

292 Shortly after moving in, Celia wrote to the author saying, "Our apartment looks over the canal — fabulous view. Unfortunately the summer is over — too chilly to sit on the balcony."

293 Celia had been given a lifetime pass to the NAC at row zz, seat 56 of the orchestra.

294 She was flippantly referring to her father Alf and his mistress, Rose. Family albums have several photos of the two "cuzs" in affectionate poses.

295 With the political unrest in South Africa, her nephew David had taken his family to Australia while her niece, Jayne, had moved to the United States. Her third nephew Michael had committed suicide while a university student in 1974. She had once met Jason as a tiny boy when she visited South Africa in 1981.

296 Jason Franks is a software engineer, and also writes comics and

graphic novels in the horror genre. His blog says that he paints, draws, plays the guitar, loves coffee and Guinness, and never sleeps. He wrote to the author, "Now that I'm finally experiencing a bit of success, I only wish that Celia was here to see it."

297 Betty (Shepard) Goodings had moved to Canada in 1953 to join her war-bride sister, Joan, in Port Arthur. Already trained in the RAD syllabus, Betty took summer courses with Betty Oliphant and Celia Franca to qualify to teach the Cecchetti style. Virginia also took classes at the summer school.

298 Celia, always anxious about money, was assured by her accountant that she was able to afford such a luxurious treat for herself.

299 Kirby had a long career with the National Ballet of Canada from 1965 to 1991.

300 Austen worked for the National Ballet of Canada for thirty-three years, beginning just before Franca's retirement as supervisor of wigs and footwear and ending with his own retirement in 2007 from his post as artistic administrator.

301 Jayne's attempts to honour Celia's Jewish heritage didn't always meet with her aunt's approval. Jayne relates that she requested a rabbi in Ottawa to go and light a menorah for Celia on Chanukah. However when Jayne put up a mezuzah in Celia's room at Governor's Walk, after she left Celia requested that it be taken down.

302 She would not have been able to bear the pain of travelling by air but could travel lying down in the limousine. She stayed overnight at the Four Seasons Hotel in a special room for the disabled with a hospital-style bed.

303 It was also tied into the launching of the Celia Franca Society to encourage individuals to include the National Ballet in their will or estate plans.

304 In an earlier will from 1986, when James Morton was her sole executor.

305 The author has never been able to discover what was done with Celia Franca's ashes. Her executor, Victoria Prystawski, and her

friend Merrilee Hodgins, did not cooperate with the author in the writing of this biography.

Index